Costs & Funding following the Civil Justice Reforms: Questions & Answers

Costs & Funding following the Civil Justice Reforms: Questions & Answers

SWEET & MAXWELL

Practical Law

Published in 2015 by Thomson Reuters (Professional) UK
Limited
trading as Sweet & Maxwell,
Friars House, 160 Blackfriars Road, London, SE1 8EZ
(Registered in England & Wales, Company No 1679046.
Registered Office and address for service:
2nd floor, 1 Mark Square, Leonard Street, London EC2A 4EG

ISBN 978-0-41405-006-8

The material in this publication is of the nature of opinion and general comment only. It is not tailored to any particular factual situation and is not a substitute for reading the Civil Procedure Rules and Practice Directions. No responsibility can be accepted by the Publisher or the Authors for action taken or inaction as a result of the information contained in this publication. It is not offered as legal advice on any specific issue or matter and should not be taken as such. Readers should take specific advice when dealing with specific situations.

Contributors

Peter Hurst, General Editor. Peter was the Senior Costs Judge of England & Wales, at the Royal Courts of Justice, from 1992 to 2014. During a judicial career which has spanned thirty years, he was also Judicial Taxing Officer of the House of Lords from 2002 to 2009 and of the United Kingdom Supreme Court from 2009 to 2014 and also of the Judicial Committee of the Privy Council from 2002 to 2014. He sat not only as a costs judge in the SCCO but also as a recorder in civil and criminal matters, including costs appeals from District Judges. He sat as an assessor with High Court Judges dealing with numerous costs appeals. He was invited to sit with the Court of Appeal as an assessor when that Court was dealing with difficult or complex costs appeals. He joined 39 Essex Street Chambers as a door tenant in December 2014.

He is the author of *Civil Costs* (Sweet & Maxwell Litigation Library), now in its fifth edition, and *Criminal Costs* (OUP). He was, until retirement, a member of the Senior Editorial Board of *Civil Procedure* (the *White Book*, Sweet & Maxwell) as well as being an editor contributing the commentary on all the costs rules and practice directions. He is now an advisory editor of the *White Book*.

Simon Middleton was appointed a District Judge in 2004 and a Regional Costs Judge at the inception of the scheme in 2005. He has sat in both the Midlands and the Western regions. Before his appointment he was a solicitor with Higher Court (Civil Advocacy) qualification.

Simon was a member of the Judicial College tutor team for six years. In that capacity he was a member of the team charged with delivering education on the April 2013 reforms. He is currently one of the Course Directors appointed for civil education. In that role he is responsible for, amongst other things, the current training on case and costs management.

Simon has written and lectured extensively on the subject of costs and case and costs management.

Roger Mallalieu is a barrister at 4 New Square specialising in matters relating to costs, litigation funding and civil procedure. He routinely ranks as one of the leading juniors in the field of costs law of all types and has appeared in a considerable number of the leading cases in the area. He is regularly instructed on important test issues and appears regularly in the Court of Appeal and other higher courts on such matters.

Publisher's Note

Costs & Funding following the Civil Justice Reforms: Questions & Answers is a unique book. Produced in conjunction with **Practical Law™,** it tackles common practitioner questions on the effects of the 2013 Jackson reforms on costs and funding. The authors answer questions on topics ranging from funding of litigation, case and costs management and proportionality to settlement offers, QOCS and summary assessment.

Subscribers to the *White Book Service* 2015 are offered this book gratis as part of their subscription. It is up to date generally to February 19, 2015, with the exception of Chapter 5 on Part 36 and settlement offers, which is up to date to April 6, 2015, and takes into account the changes made to Part 36 by the Civil Procedure (Amendment No.8) Rules 2014 (SI 3299/2014) and the 78th CPR Update.

This book would not have been possible without the time, help and expertise of Peter Hurst, Simon Middleton and Roger Mallalieu. The publisher wishes to thank them for the impressive speed with which they wrote, updated and edited the book. This project was the result of collaboration between the Dispute Resolution team at Practical Law and the author team; it would not have got off the ground without either of them.

We welcome any feedback – please email *whitebook@sweetandmaxwell.co.uk*

Contents

		Page
1	**Introduction** *Peter Hurst*	1
2	**Funding Litigation** *Roger Mallalieu*	5
3	**Proportionality** *Simon Middleton*	27
4	**Case and Costs Management** *Simon Middleton*	41
5	**Part 36 Settlement Offers and Costs Consequences** *Peter Hurst*	83
6	**Qualified one-way costs shifting** *Roger Mallalieu*	109
7	**Fixed Costs, Indemnity Costs, Litigants in Person** *Peter Hurst*	123
8	**The Court's Power in relation to Wasted Costs and Misconduct, Non-Party Costs** *Peter Hurst*	137
9	**Assessments of Costs and Payments on Account of Costs** *Simon Middleton*	149
10	**The Effect of the Jackson Civil Justice Reforms on Solicitor-Client Costs** *Roger Mallalieu*	171

List of Questions

Page

Chapter 1   **Introduction**

Chapter 2   **Funding litigation**
  Q1. Is it possible to assign pre LASPO Conditional Fee Agreement
    and to retain between the parties recoverability of success fees?   19
  Q2. What is the effect on recoverability of the success fee of
    assigning a pre-April 2013 CFA post-April 2013?   20
  Q3. Is it possible to vary a pre-April 2013 CFA and still recover the
    success fee?   20
  Q4. My client instructed me prior to April 1, 2013, but I was not able
    to offer a CFA until later. Is it possible to backdate the CFA to the
    date of first instruction?   21
  Q5. My client entered into a CFA prior to April 1, 2013, but has now
    died. I wish to offer the personal representatives a CFA to continue
    the claim. Will I be able to recover the success fee?   21
  Q6. Is a pre-April 2013 ATE policy premium still recoverable if the
    policy holder changes solicitors post-April 2013? Should the policy
    be 'assigned' to the new firm?   22
  Q7. If a staged premium ATE policy was incepted prior to April 1,
    2013, but the further staged premiums are only incurred after that
    date, will the further premiums be recoverable?   22
  Q8. Is there a long stop date whereby a party who has entered into
    a pre-April 2013 funding arrangement in relation to a claim must
    issue proceedings?   22
  Q9. Is a notice of funding required for a Damages Based
    Agreement?   23
  Q10. How should the success fee be calculated in a post-April 2013
    CFA?   23
  Q11. If the solicitor has entered into a pre-April 2013 CFA, but
    counsel's CFA with the solicitor postdates April 2013, is counsel's
    success fee recoverable between the parties?   23
  Q12. I wish to enter into a CFA with my client whereby in addition
    to the success fee being capped as required by s.58 of the Courts
    & Legal Services Act 1990 and the CFA Order 2013, the total costs
    payable under the agreement will also be capped as a percentage
    of the damage. I have been told that this means my agreement is
    a contingency fee agreement, or DBA, and must comply with the
    DBA Regulations 2013. Is this correct?   24

Q13. What is the effect on the success fee where a CFA relating to a group claim was entered into before April 1, 2013, but some of the claimants were added after that date?   24

Chapter 3   **Proportionality**
   Q1. Is there any distinction between proportionality and reasonableness in reality?   31
   Q2. Is there not a risk that similar claims will have different outcomes because of the determination by separate case managing judges of what is proportionate in a particular case?   31
   Q3. Is proportionality a 'fixed sum' throughout the life of a claim?   31
   Q4. If there is no 'good reason' to depart from the budget on assessment how does the court apply the proportionality 'cross check' under CPR 44.3(2) at the end of the assessment?   33
   Q5. How do the transitional provisions relate to proportionality at assessment?   33
   Q6. Does the court look at the sums reasonably claimed or the sums recovered when determining 'the sums in issue in the proceedings' under CPR 44.3(5)(a)?   34
   Q7. Why is only the conduct of the paying party included in the definition?   35
   Q8. If the effect of CPR 44.3(2) is that the sum to be allowed on an assessment is that which is proportionate, why does the court trouble first with undertaking an assessment of what is reasonably incurred and reasonable in amount?   36
   Q9. Is proportionality to be applied in all cases, or, as some wish to suggest, is it really for the small to medium value claims, where disproportionate costs are more likely?   37
   Q10. What relevance, if any, does proportionality have in cases where an order for costs is made on the indemnity basis?   38
   Q11. Is the effect of proportionality that in a case about money, the costs cannot exceed the sums in dispute?   39

Chapter 4   **Case and Costs Management**
   Q1. How prescriptive is the wording of CPR 3.12(1) and (1A)? In particular can the court costs manage cases that fall within the definition of those outside the scheme and when may the court exclude cases from the regime under CPR 3.12(1)(c)?   58
   Q2. Should a party file its Form H on the basis of the way in which it thinks the claim should progress, e.g. if it thinks a split trial is appropriate should the budget be completed on that basis?   60
   Q3. If a defendant brings an additional claim against a party other than the claimant, does the defendant need to produce two budgets—one for the defence of the claim and one for the pursuit of the additional claim—or will one total budget suffice?   61

Q4. Does the court give the directions first and subsequently costs manage? 61

Q5. Should the court set hourly rates as part of the budgeting exercise? 62

Q6. How can the court set the budget without assessing prospectively the work that is required and the appropriate hourly rate(s) at which that work should be done? 63

Q7. If the court is budgeting only be reference to a global sum and not taking account of the respective hourly rates, surely this means that a party who has agreed a lower hourly rate retainer will be able to do more work than one with a higher hourly rate? If so this appears unfair. 63

Q8. If the court does set the hourly rate in the budget what happens if, at assessment, the assessing court sets a different hourly rate for the non budgeted work? 64

Q9. Is the budget 'without prejudice' to any subsequent assessment? 64

Q10. What, if anything, can the court do when the parties agree budgets or phases of the budgets in sums that the court thinks are disproportionate? 64

Q11. Can the parties agree to vary their budgets from that recorded by the court in a costs management order, where there has been no 'significant development' in the litigation, but both are unhappy with the amount budgeted by the court? 65

Q12. What effect will a 'costs sanction' for unreasonable conduct, as suggested by the Court of Appeal in *Denton v T H White*, have on a costs budget? 66

Q13. What guidance is there on what may constitute 'good reason' under CPR 3.18 to enable a departure from a budget at assessment? 66

Q14. Will the introduction of 'J-Codes' lead to Form H being completed to include all costs—including those of a solicitor/client nature? 67

Q15. Does the statement of truth on the budget prevent a solicitor recovering more than the budget from the client? 67

Q16. What if a client still wants the legal representatives to incur costs that the court has not allowed within the budget? 68

Q17. Can the budgeted sum exceed the sum due from that party to the solicitor under the contractual retainer, and, if so, is this a permitted breach of the indemnity principle? 68

Q18. How important is the breakdown between disbursements and solicitors' fees in an approved/agreed budget? 69

Q19. Does the introduction of costs management mean that the court is rarely likely to dispense with a case/costs management conference and deal with directions and budgets as a paper exercise? 69

Q20. How detailed should be the assumptions upon which the budget is based? 70

Q21. The guidance for completion of Form H is brief and it is not always clear where certain items of work should be included. Is there any sanction for inserting items in what the court may regard as the wrong phase of the budget?   70

Q22. Does costs management apply to the disposal stage of a claim after the entry of a default judgment for damages to be decided by the court?   71

Q23. What should parties do when the notice of provisional allocation under CPR 26.3 is to the multi track, but one or more parties believe that the appropriate allocation is to the fast track?   71

Q24. What sort of applications fall within the provisions of CPR 3 PD E 7.9? How does this link with the provision for contingencies in the budget?   72

Q25. Do the costs allocated to contingencies count when determining whether or not a budget exceeds £25,000 and, in consequence, in determining whether only page 1 of the Form H needs to be completed?   72

Q26. If there has been a significant front loading of the costs so that by the time of the costs management hearing the costs already spent exceed what the court regards as the proportionate expenditure on the claim, can the court set a budget going forward of nil?   73

Q27. Does the fact that a party has a contractual right to indemnity costs against the other party mean costs management is not applicable or pointless because the claimant has a contractual right to claim costs under *Gomba Holdings (UK) Ltd v Minories Finance Ltd (No.2)*?   73

Q28. Does the emphasis on proportionality impact on the situation where a claim falls within fast track financial limits, but the number of witnesses is such that the time needed for trial exceeds one day?   74

Q29. What is the position if a Part 7 claim commences as a fast track claim, but subsequently it becomes apparent that the claim is undervalued and needs to be re-tracked to the multi track, but it is not within one of the costs management exceptions in CPR 3.12(1)?   75

Q30. Is it better for a party to over-estimate costs in the budget filed and exchanged, on the basis that it is then likely to see a higher budget set and less likely to need to go back to the court asking for the budget to be varied under CPR 3 PD E 7.6? Conversely, if a party recognises that it is likely to be the paying party is underestimation better, trying to persuade the court to reduce the budgets of all parties to that level to limit the potential liability for costs or limit the work that can be undertaken, making the outcome of the claim less certain as a result?   76

Q31. To which sum do the percentages in CPR 3 PD E 7.2 apply—the total sum in the Form H after the budget has been set or just those parts of the Form H that the court has budgeted? 76

Q32. Is a further Form H required with a pre-trial checklist ("PTCL") as CPR 29 imposes no such requirement and yet the wording of the PTCL requires one? 77

Q33. Can the court costs manage detailed assessment proceedings? 78

Q34. Does the decision of the Court of Appeal in *Denton v T H White* mean that relief from sanction will be granted provided that there is no prejudice to any other party that cannot be compensated by a costs order and that a trial date can still be met? 79

Q35. What is the position in respect of CPR 3.13 where a directions questionnaire ("DQ") is not filed within the time specified in the notice of provisional allocation under CPR 26.3(1), but is filed accompanied by a Form H within the further time provided by the court under CPR 26.3(7A)? Is CPR 3.8(4) of any relevance in this situation? 79

Q36. Will cost capping be ordered more rarely? 80

Chapter 5   **Part 36 Settlement Offers and Costs Consequences**

Q1. Where there has been a trial of preliminary issues, what is the position with regard to Part 36 offers which may have been made? 98

Q2. Are costs recoverable if a claimant's Part 36 offer is accepted in circumstances where the claimant's costs budget has not been filed on time? 100

Q3. What is the position where a Part 36 offer is withdrawn at the same time as the claimant purports to accept it? 100

Q4. Are defendants who refuse Part 36 offers which are successful always going to be penalised in costs or does the Court have a discretion? 101

Q5. Is the following case still good law—*Hammersmatch Properties (Welwyn) Ltd v Saint Gobain Ceramics and Plastics Ltd*? Is Eder J's costs decision in *Sugar Hut etc. v AJ Insurance* reintroducing Carver by the back door? 102

Q6. How important is mediation and refusal to mediate in relation to Part 36? 102

Q7. Do you agree that it may be difficult to decide who has obtained the more advantageous result in a detailed assessment? Also, does the amendment to r.36.14(3) (now r.36.17(4)) in April 2013, to enhance claimants' recovery by 10 per cent apply in detailed assessments? 104

Q8. If a defendant makes a Part 36 offer which does not take into account its counterclaim and the offer is then accepted, what happens to the counterclaim? 105

Q9. What is the requirement for open offers in detailed assessment proceedings meant to achieve and how they will co-exist with Part 36 offers?   105

Q10. How are Calderbank offers treated in relation to costs?   106

Q11. How does the cap on damages in the IPEC apply where there is also a claim for costs?   106

Q12. When the question of costs is being decided is it possible for a party to refer to without prejudice correspondence in order to establish that the other party did not respond to Part 36 offers?   107

Chapter 6   **Qualified One-Way Costs Shifting**

Q1. How will QOCS apply where a claim compromises both a personal injury and a non personal injury element?   118

Q2. Will QOCS be extended to other areas in due course?   118

Q3. Do parties still have to costs budget where QOCS applies and, if so, is the agreeing of budgets in such cases likely to be more difficult?   118

Q4. Is QOCS excluded where the claimant has Before the Event Insurance?   119

Q5. Does QOCS apply to costs incurred prior to April 1, 2013?   119

Q6. Is QOCS excluded where the claimant has entered into a pre-commencement funding arrangement, even if the claimant then is advised to not pursue the claim by the initially instructed solicitor but later does so under a post April 2013 funding arrangement with a different firm?   119

Q7. The claimant has incurred costs unnecessarily in an unmeritous claim. They have now served a notice of discontinuance and, as QOCS applies, they are not liable for the defendant's costs (unless an exception applies). In the above circumstances, is it possible for the defendant to apply for a wasted costs order even though a notice of discontinuance has been filed by the claimant?   120

Q8. I need to discontinue proceedings against a number of defendants in an action. Obviously, when I file a notice of discontinuance, there will be a deemed order for costs against the claimant. According to your maintained guidance "Discontinuance: an overview" the court may vary such an order only in some circumstances. However, my understandings of QOCS (from CPR 44.14, 44.15 and 44.16) is that an order for costs may only be enforced if the claim has been struck out (no court permission needed) or if it is fundamentally dishonest (court permission needed). We do not have sufficient time to obtain written consent from each and every defendant in a consent order but in any event consider that we would be QOCS protected even by serving a Notice of Discontinuance.   121

Chapter 7 **Fixed Costs, Indemnity Costs, Non-Party Costs, Litigants in Person**

Q1. It is unfortunate that there will not be fixed costs across the entire fast track as Jackson recommended [yet] but merely some more fixed costs for certain lower value claims. 131

Q2. What guidance can be given about retainer arrangements to emphasise the importance of the advice to a client about these and ensuring that retainer arrangements are still clear and enforceable where a legal representative is asked to represent a client in litigation which will inevitably involve the application of fixed costs? 132

Q3. Is the indemnity basis applicable in cases where there is an abuse of process or where a party has been guilty of unreasonable conduct? 133

Q4. What is the position of litigation funders in relation to orders for costs, particularly orders for costs on the indemnity basis? 133

Q5. The rules suggest that costs management does not affect indemnity costs. However there is now a confusion about this since Coulson J's decision in *Elvanite Full Circle Ltd v Amec Earth and Environmental UK Ltd* suggests otherwise. 134

Q6. What is the position of a solicitor or barrister acting on his or her own behalf? 135

Q7. If a litigant in person instructs a barrister under the Direct Access scheme can the litigant recover any costs? 136

Q8. In proceedings in the Intellectual Property Enterprise Court where costs are awarded against a party for unreasonable behaviour does the stage costs cap in Part 45 apply? 136

Chapter 8 **The Court's Powers in relation to Wasted Costs and Misconduct**

Q1. To what extent can advocates be held liable for loss or damages resulting from their conduct or advice? 143

Q2. Can you give some examples of situations in which non-party costs orders may be made? 144

Q3. Is it possible to obtain a non-party costs order where the successful party already has an order in its favour? 145

Q4. How "controlling" does a non-party have to be to be the subject of a non-party costs order? 145

Q5. What is the position where the successful party needs to obtain more information before applying for a non-party costs order? Does the court have power to order disclosure? 146

Q6. What is the potential liability of solicitors who fund litigation for their clients by acting without ATE or funding disbursements? 146

Chapter 9 **Assessments of Costs and Payments on Account of Costs**

Q1. What is the position when form N260 is either served/filed late or not at all? 155

Q2. Does the introduction of the breakdown of time spent on documents on the Form N260 mean that the court will deal with challenges to this on an item by item basis or will the court make one overall assessment of time spent on documents?   157

Q3. How does the proportionality cross check at CPR 44.3(2) work in the summary assessment process that is already one undertaken with a broad brush?   157

Q4. How can the court use the costs budgets at assessment of the costs of the claim when neither the N260 nor the bill is divided into the same phases as the Form H to enable easy comparison?   158

Q5. Albeit in a family context, does not the case of *SB v MB (Costs)* suggest that summary assessment is confined to fast track trials and other hearings lasting a day or less?   160

Q6. Does qualified one-way costs shifting ("QOCS") apply to the detailed assessment procedure?   160

Q7. Is there any sanction if a paying party fails to make an open offer under CPR 47 PD 8.3?   161

Q8. Does the £75,000 limit for provisional assessment include or exclude VAT?   162

Q9. There seems to be a feeling that a paying party who does not serve Replies to the Points of Dispute is at a disadvantage at a provisional assessment. Should receiving parties serve Replies in this situation as a matter of course?   162

Q10. Does the costs cap include or exclude success fees (where the transitional provisions still permit recovery of success fees between the parties)?   162

Q11. Does the costs cap include the additional amount under CPR 36.14(3)(d) (from April 6, 2015 CPR 36.17(4)(d)) as applied by CPR 47.20?   163

Q12. How does the £1,500 cap operate in respect of cases that are dealt with under the provisional assessment provisions, but where there are interim applications, e.g. to set aside a default costs certificate, for an interim costs certificate or for relief from sanction?   163

Q13. Is the amount of the bill or the sum in which it is assessed in a provisional assessment likely to inform how much of the capped fee is awarded, e.g. does a bill of £70,000 justify an award of a higher proportion of the £1,500 than a bill of £20,000?   164

Q14. Can the court make more than one award of costs for the provisional assessment and, if so, is the total amount apportioned between the parties limited to £1,500 or may there be separate awards to each party, each with a cap of £1,500?   164

Q15. Does the £1,500 cap on costs under CPR 47.14 include costs incurred in 'Costs Only Proceedings' under CPR 46.14?   165

Q16. How does the court deal with the proportionality cross check

after a provisional assessment where the assessed bill is returned to
the parties to do the arithmetic? 166

Q17. What happens in respect of the costs where at an oral hearing
a party does not achieve an adjustment in its favour of 20 per cent
or more, but the adjustment made does make a CPR 47.20 offer
relevant? 167

Q18. Is there any rule of thumb as to what proportion of the
costs claimed the court will order as a reasonable sum by way of
payment on account? 169

Chapter 10   **The Effect of the Jackson Civil Justice Reforms
on Solicitor-Client Costs**
   Q1. Have the 'Jackson' reforms changed the basis on which I, as a
solicitor, can charge my client? 185
   Q2. Can you advise the client of the full range of funding options
but then say but we as a firm do not offer X, or Y or only offer X or
Y on this basis? 185
   Q3. My case is subject to costs management. Am I required to seek
my client's approval to the budget and does the budget, if agreed
or approved, limit the costs I can charge my client? 186
   Q4. Do the revised rules on Part 36 apply in a solicitor-client
assessment? 186
   Q5. Can I charge/recover for preparing the solicitor/client estimate? 187

Table of Cases

ABCI (formerly Arab Business Consortium International Finance & Investment Co)
v Banque Franco-Tunisienne (Costs) [2002] EWHC 567 (Comm)..............................7–14
Abraham v Thompson [1997] 4 All E.R. 362; [1997] C.L.C. 1370; (1997) 94(37)
L.S.G. 41; (1997) 141 S.J.L.B. 217 8–13
AF v BG [2009] EWCA Civ 757; [2010] 2 Costs L.R. 164...5–05
Agassi v Robinson (Inspector of Taxes) [2005] EWCA Civ 1507; [2006] 1 W.L.R.
2126; [2006] 1 All E.R. 900; [2006] S.T.C. 580, CA; [2006] 2 Costs L.R. 283; [2006]
B.T.C. 3; [2005] S.T.I. 1994; (2005) 155 N.L.J. 1885; (2006) 150 S.J.L.B. 28; [2005]
N.P.C. 140 7–18
Aiden Shipping Co Ltd v Interbulk Ltd (The Vimeira) (No.2) [1986] A.C. 965; [1986]
2 W.L.R. 1051; [1986] 2 Lloyd's Rep. 117; (1986) 130 S.J. 429 8–07
Allen v Colman Coyle LLP [2007] EWHC 90075 (Costs) 10–23
Altomart v Salford Estates (No.2) Ltd [2014] EWCA Civ 1408; [2015] C.P. Rep. 8;
[2014] 6 Costs L.R. 1013..5–33, 9–23
Americhem Europe Ltd v Rakem Ltd [2014] EWHC 1881 (TCC); 155 Con. L.R. 80;
[2014] 4 Costs L.R. 682...4–16, 4–44
Angel Airlines v Dean & Dean [2008] EWHC 1513 (QB); [2009] 2 Costs L.R. 159......10–08
Arthur JS Hall & Co v Simons [2002] 1 A.C. 615; [2000] 3 W.L.R. 543; [2000] 3 All
E.R. 673; [2000] B.L.R. 407; [2000] E.C.C. 487; [2000] 2 F.L.R. 545; [2000] 2 F.C.R.
673; [2001] P.N.L.R. 6; [2000] Fam. Law 806; [2000] E.G. 99 (C.S.); (2000) 97(32)
L.S.G. 38; (2000) 150 N.L.J. 1147; (2000) 144 S.J.L.B. 238; [2000] N.P.C. 87 8–02
Arundel Chiropractic Centre Pty Ltd v Deputy Commissioner of Taxation [2001]
179 A.L.R. 406 8–08
Bahai v Rashidian [1985] 1 W.L.R. 1337; [1985] 3 All E.R. 385; (1985) 82 L.S.G. 2162;
(1985) 135 N.L.J. 1033; (1985) 129 S.J. 777 8–07
Bank of Ireland v Philip Pank Partnership [2014] EWHC 284 (TCC); [2014] 2 Costs
L.R. 301 ....4–16, 4–44
Barrister (Wasted Costs Order) (No.1 of 1999), Re [1993] Q.B. 293; [1992] 3 W.L.R.
662; [1992] 3 All E.R. 429; (1992) 95 Cr. App. R. 288; (1992) 142 N.L.J. 636; (1992)
136 S.J.L.B. 147 8–02
Bartkauskaute v Bartkauskiene [2013] EWCA Civ 1805; [2014] 1 W.L.R. 3567; [2014]
C.P. Rep. 25; [2014] 4 Costs L.O. 551 9–31
Beasley v Alexander [2012] EWHC 2715 (QB); [2013] 1 W.L.R. 762; [2012] 6 Costs
L.R. 1137; [2013] R.T.R. 7 5–10
Bent v Highways and Utilities Construction & Allianz Insurance [2011] EWCA Civ
1539; [2012] 2 Costs L.O. 127 5–14
Blackmore v Cummins [2009] EWCA Civ 1276; [2012] 2 Costs L.O. 127 9–13
Blankley v Central Manchester Children's University Hospital NHS Trust [2015]
EWCA Civ 18..2–09
Brendon v Spiro [1938] K.B. 176; [1937] 2 All E.R. 496 8–07
Brighton & Hove Bus v Brooks [2011] EWHC 2504...6–10
Bristol and West Building Society v Evans Bullock & Co, unreported, February 5,
1996 CA 5–07
Brown v Bennett [2002] 1 W.L.R. 713; [2002] 2 All E.R. 273; [2002] Lloyd's Rep. P.N.
155; [2002] P.N.L.R. 17; (2002) 99(2) L.S.G. 27; (2001) 151 N.L.J. 1733; (2001) 145
S.J.L.B. 267 8–03

Buckland v Watts [1970] 1 Q.B. 27; [1969] 3 W.L.R. 92; [1969] 2 All E.R. 985; (1969)
    113 S.J. 384 7–08
Butt v Nizami [2006] EWHC 159 (QB); [2006] 1 W.L.R. 3307; [2006] 2 All E.R. 140;
    [2006] 3 Costs L.R. 483; [2006] R.T.R. 25; (2006) 103(9) L.S.G. 30; (2006) 156
    N.L.J. 272 10–16
Byrne v South Sefton HA [2001] EWCA Civ 1904; [2002] 1 W.L.R. 775; (2002) 99(1)
    L.S.G. 19; (2001) 145 S.J.L.B. 268 8–03
C v D [2011] EWCA Civ 646; [2012] 1 W.L.R. 1962; [2012] 1 All E.R. 302; [2011] C.P.
    Rep. 38; 136 Con. L.R. 109; [2011] 5 Costs L.R. 773; [2011] 2 E.G.L.R. 95; [2011]
    23 E.G. 86 (C.S.); (2011) 161 N.L.J. 780 ....5–06, 5–22
Caliendo v Mischon De Reya LLP [2014] EWHC 3414 (Ch); [2014] 6 Costs L.O. 935 ...2–07
Carillion J M Ltd v PHI Group Ltd [2012] EWCA Civ 588; [2012] C.P. Rep. 37; [2012]
    B.L.R. 329; [2012] T.C.L.R. 5; 142 Con. L.R. 96; [2012] 4 Costs L.O. 523; [2012]
    C.I.L.L. 3180 ....5–06, 5–14
Chantrey Vellacott v The Convergence Group plc [2007] EWHC 1774 (Ch) 5–15
CIP Properties (AIPT) Ltd v Galliford Try Infrastructure Ltd [2014] EWHC 3546
    (TCC); 156 Con. L.R. 202; [2014] 6 Costs L.R. 1026 ....3–04, 4–23, 4–26
Commissioners of Customs and Excise v Ross [1990] 2 All E.R. 65; [1990] S.T.C. 353...7–09
Courtwell Properties Ltd v Greencore PF (UK) Ltd [2014] EWHC 184 (TCC); [2014]
    2 Costs L.O. 289; [2014] C.I.L.L. 3481. ....3–17, 4–21
Coventry v Lawrence (No.2) [2014] UKSC 46; [2015] A.C. 106; [2014] 3 W.L.R. 555;
    [2014] 4 All E.R. 517; [2014] P.T.S.R. 1014; [2014] 5 Costs L.O. 759; [2014] H.L.R.
    42; [2014] 2 P. & C.R. 19..2–12
Coward v Phaestos Ltd [2014] EWCA Civ 1256; [2015] C.P. Rep. 2; [2014] 6 Costs
    L.O. 843 5–34
Crosbie v Munroe [2003] EWCA Civ 350; [2003] 1 W.L.R. 2033; [2003] 2 All E.R.
    856; [2003] C.P. Rep. 43; [2003] 3 Costs L.R. 377; [2003] R.T.R. 33; (2003) 100(20)
    L.S.G. 27; (2003) 147 S.J.L.B. 356 .... 4–56, 9–31, 9–32
Crouch v Kings Healthcare NHS Trust [2004] EWCA Civ 1332; [2005] 1 W.L.R. 2015;
    [2005] 1 All E.R. 207; [2005] C.P. Rep. 10; [2005] 2 Costs L.R. 200; [2005] P.I.Q.R.
    Q4; [2005] Lloyd's Rep. Med. 50; (2005) 83 B.M.L.R. 47; (2004) 101(44) L.S.G. 29;
    (2004) 154 N.L.J. 1616; (2004) 148 S.J.L.B. 1245 5–01
Cumper v Pothecary [1941] 2 KB 58; [1941] 2 All E.R. 516 5–26
Currie & Co v Law Society [1977] Q.B. 990; [1976] 3 W.L.R. 785; [1976] 3 All E.R.
    832; (1976) 120 S.J. 819..8–01
Customs and Excise Commissioners v Anchor Foods [1999] 1 W.L.R. 1139; [1999] 3
    All E.R. 268; [2000] C.P. Rep. 19; (1999) 96(12) L.S.G. 34; (1999) 143 S.J.L.B. 96......8–03
Daniels v Commissioner of Police of the Metropolis [2005] EWCA Civ 1312; [2006]
    CP Rep.9; (2005) 102(44) L.S.G. 30 5–29
David Truex (A Firm) v Kitchin [2007] EWCA Civ 618; [2007] 4 Costs L.R. 587;
    [2007] 2 F.L.R. 1203; [2007] P.N.L.R. 33; [2007] Fam. Law 903; (2007) 157 N.L.J.
    1011; (2007) 151 S.J.L.B. 926; [2007] N.P.C. 87 10–19
Davies v Jones [2009] EWCA Civ 1164; [2010] 2 All E.R. (Comm) 755; [2010] 1 P. &
    C.R. 22; [2010] 1 E.G.L.R. 67; [2010] 5 E.G. 114; [2009] 46 E.G. 142 (C.S.); [2009]
    N.P.C. 126 2–09
Davy-Chiesman v Davy-Chiesman [1984] Fam. 48; [1984] 2 W.L.R. 291; [1984] 1 All
    E.R. 321; (1984) 81 L.S.G. 44; (1983) 127 S.J. 805 8–01
Day v Day (Costs) [2006] EWCA Civ 415; [2006] CP Rep 35; (2006) 103(13) L.S.G. 235–21
Denton v T H White Ltd [2014] EWCA Civ 906; [2014] 1 WLR 3926; [2014] C.P.
    Rep. 40; [2014] B.L.R. 547; 154 Con. L.R. 1; [2014] 4 Costs L.R. 752; [2014] C.I.L.L.
    3568; (2014) 164(7614) N.L.J. 17... 2–07, 3–13, 3–17, 4–04, 4–20, 4–35, 4–57, 5–25, 9–16
Deutsche Bank AG v Sebastian Holdings Inc [2014] EWHC 2073 (Comm); [2014] 4
    Costs LR 711 8–11

D Pride & Partners v Institute for Animal Health [2009] EWHC 1617 (QB); [2009] 5
Costs LR 803 5–14

Drew v Whitbread [2010] EWCA Civ 53; [2010] 1 W.L.R. 1725; [2010] C.P. Rep. 22;
[2010] 2 Costs L.R. 213; [2010] P.I.Q.R. P11; (2010) 107(8) L.S.G. 23; (2010) 160
N.L.J. 270 3–11

Dufoo v Tolaini; sub nom. Quiet Moments Ltd, Re [2014] EWCA Civ 1536; [2014] 6
Costs L.R. 1106 5–13

Dunfermline Building Society v Ghana Commercial Finance Ltd [2014] EWHC
3397 (QB)..8–12

Dymocks Franchise Systems (NSW) Pty Ltd v Todd [2004] UKPC 39; [2004] 1 W.L.R.
2807; [2005] 4 All E.R. 195; [2005] 1 Costs L.R. 52; (2004) 154 N.L.J. 1325; (2004)
148 S.J.L.B. 971 8–08

Edwards v Edwards [1958] P. 235; [1958] 2 W.L.R. 956; [1958] 2 All E.R. 179; (1958)
102 S.J. 402 8–01

Elsevier Ltd v Munro [2014] EWHC 2728 (QB); [2014] 5 Costs L.O. 797 5–27

Elvanite Full Circle Ltd v AMEC Earth & Environment [2013] EWHC 1643 (TCC);
[2013] 4 All E.R. 765; [2013] B.L.R. 473; [2013] T.C.L.R. 7; [2013] 4 Costs L.R. 612;
[2013] C.I.L.L. 3385 .... 3–17, 4–20, 7–16, 9–39

Evans v Royal Wolverhampton Hospitals NHS Foundation Trust [2014] EWHC 3185
(QB); [2014] 6 Costs L.O. 899...5–26

Excalibur Ventures LLC v Texas Keystone Inc (Defendants and Costs Claimants)
and Psari Holdings Ltd (Costs Defendants) [2014] EWHC 3436 (Comm); [2014] 6
Costs L.O. 975 ....7–15, 8–08

Excelsior Commercial & Industrial Holdings Ltd v Salisbury Hammer Aspden &
Johnson [2002] EWCA Civ 879; [2002] C.P. Rep. 67; [2002] C.P.L.R. 693........7–07, 7–14

Experience Hendrix LLC v Times Newspapers Ltd [2008] EWHC 458 (Ch) 5–10

Feltham v Bouskell (Costs) [2013] EWHC 3086 (Ch); [2014] 1 Costs L.O. 29 .....5–12, 5–27

Fitzpatrick Contractors Ltd v Tyco Fire & Integrated Solutions (UK) Ltd [2009]
EWHC 274 (TCC); [2009] B.L.R. 144; 123 Con. L.R. 69; [2010] 2 Costs L.R. 115;
[2009] C.I.L.L. 2700..5–23

Flatman v Germany [2013] EWCA Civ 278; [2013] 1 W.L.R. 2676; [2013] 4 All E.R.
349; [2013] C.P. Rep. 31; (2013) 163(7556) N.L.J. 16; (2013) 157(15) S.J.L.B. 31.......8–14

Flex Associates Ltd, Re [2009] EWHC 3690 (Ch)..7–14

Fox v Foundation Piling Ltd [2011] EWCA Civ 790; [2011] C.P. Rep. 41; [2011] 6
Costs L.R. 961 4–13

Franks v Sinclair (Costs) [2006] EWHC 3656 (Ch); [2007] W.T.L.R. 785 7–07

Fred Perry (Holdings) Ltd v Brands Plaza Trading Ltd [2012] EWCA Civ 224; [2012]
6 Costs L.R. 1007; [2012] F.S.R. 28 4–03

Garrett v Halton BC: sub nom. Myatt v National Coal Board [2006] EWCA Civ 1017;
[2007] 1 W.L.R. 554; [2007] 1 All E.R. 147; [2006] 5 Costs L.R. 798; (2006) 103(31)
L.S.G. 26; (2006) 150 S.J.L.B. 1190...8–14

Garritt-Critchley v Ronnan [2014] EWHC 1774 5–29

Gleeson v J Wippel & Co Ltd [1977] 1 W.L.R. 510; [1977] 3 All E.R. 54; [1977] F.S.R.
301; (1977) 121 S.J. 157..8–07

Globe Equities Ltd v Globe Legal Services Ltd [2000] C.P.L.R. 233; [1999] B.L.R. 232 ...8–07

Gomba Holdings (UK) Ltd v Minories Finance Ltd (No.2) [1993] Ch 171; [1992] 3
W.L.R. 723; [1992] 4 All E.R. 588; [1992] B.C.C. 877; (1992) 136 S.J.L.B. 54; [1992]
N.P.C. 12 4–50

Gosling v Hailo & Screwfix Direct, unreported, April 29, 2014 CC (Cambridge)..........6–11

Gray v Going Places Leisure Travel Ltd [2005] EWCA Civ 189; [2005] C.P. Rep. 21;
[2005] 3 Costs L.R. 405; [2005] P.N.L.R. 26 8–02

Group M UK Ltd v Cabinet Office [2014] EWHC 3863 (TCC); [2014] 6 Costs L.R.
1090 9–16

Gupta v Comer [1991] 1 Q.B. 629; [1991] 2 W.L.R. 494; [1991] 1 All E.R. 289; (1990) 140 N.L.J. 1606 8–01
Hall & Barker, Re (1878) 9 Ch. D. 538 10–06
Hallam Estates Ltd v Baker [2014] EWCA Civ 661; [2014] C.P. Rep. 38; [2014] 4 Costs L.R. 660; (2014) 164(7608) N.L.J. 19 ....4–24, 4–25
Halsey v Milton Keynes General NHS Trust [2004] EWCA Civ 576; [2004] 1 W.L.R. 3002; [2004] 4 All E.R. 920; [2004] C.P. Rep. 34; [2004] 3 Costs L.R. 393; (2005) 81 B.M.L.R. 108; (2004) 101(22) L.S.G. 31; (2004) 154 N.L.J. 769; (2004) 148 S.J.L.B. 629. 5–29
Hammersmatch Properties (Welwyn) Ltd v Saint-Cobain Ceramics & Plastics Ltd [2013] EWHC 2227 (TCC); [2013] B.L.R. 554; 149 Con. L.R. 147; [2013] 5 Costs L.R. 758; [2013] 3 E.G.L.R. 123; (2013) 163(7571) N.L.J. 20 ....5–13, 5–14, 5–28
Hatton v Connew [2013] EWCA Civ 1560 4–12
Hatton v Kendrick [2002] EWCA Civ 1783; [2003] C.P. Rep. 32 7–17
Hawksford Trustees Jersey Ltd v Stella Global UK Ltd [2012] EWCA Civ 987; [2012] 1 WLR 3581; [2012] C.P. Rep. 41; [2012] 5 Costs L.R. 886; [2013] Lloyd's Rep. I.R. 337 6–06
Hegglin v Person(s) Unknown, Google Inc. [2014] EWHC 3793 (QB); [2015] 1 Costs L.O. 65 ....4–52, 4–59
Henry v News Group Newspapers Ltd [2013] EWCA Civ 19; [2013] 2 All E.R. 840; [2013] C.P. Rep. 20; [2013] 2 Costs L.R. 334; (2013) 163 N.L.J. 140; (2013) 157(5) S.J.L.B. 31 ....4–20, 4–36
Heron v TNT UK Ltd [2013] EWCA Civ 469; [2014] 1 W.L.R. 1277; [2013] 3 All E.R. 479; [2013] 4 Costs L.R. 551; [2013] P.N.L.R. 21 8–14
Holden & Co v Crown Prosecution Service [1990] 2 Q.B. 261 8–01
Hollington v F Hewthorn & Co Ltd [1943] K.B. 587; [1943] 2 All E.R. 35 8–07
Howell v Lees-Millais [2011] EWCA Civ 786; [2011] 4 Costs L.O. 456; [2011] W.T.L.R. 1795 5–22
Jenkins v Young Brothers Transport Ltd [2006] EWHC 151 (QB); [2006] 1 W.L.R. 3189; [2006] 2 All E.R. 798; [2006] 3 Costs L.R. 495 ....2–09, 2–19
Jolly v Harsco Infrastructure Services Ltd [2012] EWHC 3086 (QB); [2013] 1 Costs L.R. 115 5–11
Joseph v Boyd & Hutchinson [2003] EWHC 413 (Ch); [2003] 3 Costs L.R. 358; (2003) 100(19) L.S.G. 29 7–17
Joyce v West Bus Coach Services Ltd [2012] EWHC 404 (QB); [2012] 3 Costs L.R. 540 5–08
Kellie v Wheatley & Lloyd Architects Ltd [2014] EWHC 2886 (TCC); [2014] B.L.R. 644; [2014] 5 Costs L.R. 854 4–20
Kelly v Black Horse Ltd [2013] EWHC B17 (Costs) 2–11
Kilby v Gawith [2008] EWCA Civ 812; [2009] 1 W.L.R. 853; [2008] C.P. Rep. 33; [2008] 6 Costs L.R. 959; [2009] R.T.R. 2; (2008) 105(22) L.S.G. 25; (2008) 152(21) S.J.L.B. 28 10–16
Kilroy v Kilroy [1997] P.N.L.R. 66 8–03
Kingsley v Orban [2014] EWHC 2991 (Ch); [2014] B.P.I.R. 1468 9–15
Kunaka v Barclays Bank Plc [2010] EWCA Civ 1035; [2011] 2 Costs L.R. 179 5–23
Landau v Big Bus Company, unreported, October 31, 2014 6–06
LG Blower Specialist Bricklayer Ltd v Reeves; sub nom. Gibbon v Manchester City Council [2010] EWCA Civ 726; [2010] 1 W.L.R. 2081; [2011] 2 All E.R. 258; [2010] C.P. Rep. 40; [2010] 5 Costs L.R. 828; [2010] P.I.Q.R. P16; [2010] 3 E.G.L.R. 85; [2010] 36 E.G. 120; [2010] 27 E.G. 84 (C.S.) 5–07
Libyan Investment Authority v Goldman Sachs International [2014] EWHC 3364 (Ch) 7–14
London Scottish Benefits Society v Chorley [1884] 13 Q.B.D. 872 7–17

Long v Value Properties Ltd; sub nom. 1,3 and 5 Argall Avenue, Re [2014] EWHC 2981; [2014] 5 Costs L.R. 915...2–07
Lotus Cars Ltd v Mechanica Solutions Inc [2014] EWHC 76 (QB) 4–26
Lownds v Home Office [2002] EWCA Civ 365; [2002] 1 W.L.R. 2450; [2002] 4 All E.R. 775; [2002] C.P. Rep. 43; [2002] C.P.L.R. 328; [2002] 2 Costs L.R. 279; (2002) 99(19) L.S.G. 28; (2002) 146 S.J.L.B. 86............................... 3–02, 9–33, 10–14
MacDonald v Taree Holdings Ltd [2001] C.P.L.R. 439; [2001] 1 Costs L.R. 147; (2001) 98(6) L.S.G. 45 9–14
MacLennan v Morgan Sindall (Infrastructure) Plc [2013] EWHC 4044 (QB); [2014] 1 W.L.R. 2462; (2014) 158(2) S.J.L.B. 37...4–10
Malloch v Aberdeen Corp [1973] 1 W.L.R. 71; [1973] 1 All E.R. 304; 1973 S.L.T. (Notes) 5; (1972) 117 S.J. 72..7–09
Mars UK Ltd v Teknowledge Ltd (Costs) [1999] 2 Costs L.R. 44; [2000] F.S.R. 138; (1999) 22(10) I.P.D. 22097...9–39
Mauroux v Soc Com Abel Periera Da Fonseca Sarl [1972] 1 W.L.R. 962; [1972] 2 All E.R. 1085; (1972) 116 S.J. 392 8–01
McDaniel & Co v Clarke [2014] EWHC 3826 (QB); [2014] 6 Costs L.R. 963...............10–19
Melchior v Vettivel [2002] C.P. Rep. 24 8–03
Merck KGAA v Merck Sharp & Dohme Corp [2014] EWHC 3920 (Ch)...........................5–24
Metalloy Supplies Ltd (In Liquidation) v MA (UK) Ltd [1997] 1 W.L.R. 1613; [1997] 1 All E.R. 418; [1997] B.C.C. 165; [1997] 1 B.C.L.C. 165; [1998] 1 Costs L.R. 85.......8–08
Minotaur Data Systems Ltd, Re; sub nom. Official Receiver v Brunt [1999] 1 W.L.R. 1129; [1999] 3 All E.R. 122; [1999] B.C.C. 571; [1999] 2 B.C.L.C. 766; [1999] 2 Costs L.R. 97; [1999] B.P.I.R. 560; (1999) 96(12) L.S.G. 33; (1999) 149 N.L.J. 415; (1999) 143 S.J.L.B. 98; [1999] N.P.C. 27 7–09
Mitchell v News Group Newspapers Ltd [2013] EWCA Civ 1537; [2014] 1 WLR 795; [2014] 2 All E.R. 430; [2014] B.L.R. 89; [2013] 6 Costs L.R. 1008; [2014] E.M.L.R. 13; [2014] C.I.L.L. 3452; (2013) 163(7587) N.L.J. 20 ....2–07, 4–04, 5–25
Morgan v Spirit Group Ltd [2011] EWCA Civ 68; [2011] C.P. Rep. 22; [2011] 3 Costs L.R. 449; [2011] P.I.Q.R. P9...9–18
Motto v Trafigura Ltd [2011] EWCA Civ 1150; [2012] 1 W.L.R. 657; [2012] 2 All E.R. 181; [2011] 6 Costs L.R. 1028...10–13
Moy v Petman Smith (A Firm) [2005] UKHL 7; [2005] 1 W.L.R. 581; [2005] 1 All E.R. 903; [2005] Lloyd's Rep. Med. 293; [2005] P.N.L.R. 24; (2005) 102(11) L.S.G. 31; (2005) 155 N.L.J. 218; (2005) 149 S.J.L.B. 180; [2005] N.P.C. 15..............................8–09
Multiplex Construction (UK) Ltd v Cleveland Bridge UK Ltd [2010] EWCA Civ 449; [2010] C.I.L.L. 2863 5–13
Myatt v National Coal Board [2007] EWCA Civ 307; [2007] 1 W.L.R. 554; [2007] 4 All E.R. 1094; [2007] 4 Costs L.R. 564; [2007] P.N.L.R. 25 8–14
Myers v Elman [1940] A.C. 282; [1939] 4 All E.R. 484 8–01
Nader (t/a Try Us) v Customs and Excise Commissioners [1993] S.T.C. 806, CA.........7–09
National Justice Compania Naviera SA v Prudential Assurance Co Ltd ("The Ikarian Reefer" (No.2)) [2000] 1 All E.R. 3; [1999] 2 All E.R. (Comm) 673; [2000] 1 Lloyd's Rep. 129; [2000] C.P. Rep. 13; [2000] C.L.C. 22; [2000] 1 Costs L.R. 37; [2000] I.L.Pr. 490; [2000] Lloyd's Rep. I.R. 230; (1999) 96(41) L.S.G. 35; (1999) 96(42) L.S.G. 40; (1999) 149 N.L.J. 1561; (1999) 143 S.J.L.B. 255, CA...............................8–07
Northrop Grumman Mission Systems Europe Ltd v BAE Systems (AL Diriyah C41) Ltd [2014] EWHC 3148 (TCC); [2014] TCLR 8; 156 Con. L.R. 141; [2014] 6 Costs L.O. 879; [2014] C.I.L.L. 3572 5–29
Nwoko (Ned) v Oyo State Government of Nigeria [2014] EWHC 4538 (QB)...............8–03
Onay v Brown [2009] EWCA Civ 775; [2010] 1 Costs LR 29 CA 5–04
Ontulmus v Collett [2014] EWHC 4117 (QB) 5–16
OOO Abbott v Design & Display Ltd [2014] EWHC 3234 (IPEC).............. 5–31, 5–35, 9–27

Orchard v South Eastern Electricity Board [1987] Q.B. 565; [1987] 2 W.L.R. 102; [1987] 1 All E.R. 95; (1986) 130 S.J. 956...8–01, 8–07
Owners and/or Bareboat Charterers of the Ship Samco Europe v Owners of the Ship MSC Prestige; sub nom. Samco Europe, The (Costs); MSC Prestige, The (Costs) [2011] EWHC 1656 (Admlty); [2011] 2 C.L.C. 679; [2012] B.L.R. 267; (2011) 161 N.L.J. 988 5–07
Padhiar v Patel [2001] Lloyd's Rep. P.N. 328 8–06
Palmer v Durnford Ford [1992] Q.B. 483; [1992] 2 W.L.R. 407; [1992] 2 All E.R. 122; (1991) 141 N.L.J. 591..8–07
Prince Abdulaziz v Apex Global Management Ltd; sub nom. Apex Global Management Ltd v Fi Call Ltd [2014] UKSC 64; [2014] 1 W.L.R. 4495; [2015] 1 Costs L.O. 79 4–05
PR Records Ltd v Vinyl 2000 Ltd [2007] EWHC 1721 (Ch); [2008] 1 Costs L.R. 19 8–07
R v Legal Services Commission Ex p. Wulfshon [2002] EWCA Civ 7–08
R (Bar Standards Board) v Disciplinary Tribunal of the Council of the Inns of Court and Sivanandan (Interested Party) [2014] EWHC 1570 (Admin); [2014] 4 All E.R. 759..7–17
R (Burkett) v London Borough of Hammersmith & Fulham [2004] EWCA Civ 1342; [2005] C.P. Rep. 11; [2005] 1 Costs L.R. 104; [2005] J.P.L. 525; [2005] A.C.D. 73; (2004) 101(42) L.S.G. 30; (2004) 148 S.J.L.B. 1245 6–09
R (Whitston) v Secretary of State for Justice [2014] EWHC 3044 (Admin); [2015] A.C.D. 5. 2–03
R&T Thew Ltd v Reeves (No.2) [1982] Q.B. 1283; [1982] 3 W.L.R. 869; (1982) 126 S.J. 674 8–01
Ralph Hume Garry (A Firm) v Gwillim [2002] EWCA Civ 1500; [2003] 1 W.L.R. 510; [2003] 1 All E.R. 1038; [2003] C.P. Rep. 16; [2003] 1 Costs L.R. 77; (2002) 99(45) L.S.G. 35; (2002) 152 N.L.J. 1653; (2002) 146 S.J.L.B. 237.....................................10–05
Redfern v Corby Borough Council [2014] EWHC 4526 (QB) 4–49
Redwing Construction Ltd v Wishart [2011] EWHC 19 (TCC); [2011] B.L.R. 186; [2011] T.C.L.R. 5; [2011] 2 Costs L.O. 212; [2011] Lloyd's Rep. I.R. 331; [2011] 1 E.G.L.R. 13; [2011] 15 E.G. 94; [2011] C.I.L.L. 2997; (2011) 161 N.L.J. 137 2–11
Rees v Gateley Wareing (a firm) [2014] EWCA Civ 1351; [2014] 6 Costs L.O. 953.....10–04
Ridehalgh v Horsefield; sub nom. Watson v Watson (Wasted Costs Orders); Roberts v Coverite (Asphalters) Ltd; Philex Plc v Golban; Antonelli v Wade Gery Farr (A Firm); Allen v Unigate Dairies Ltd [1994] Ch. 205; [1994] 3 W.L.R. 462; [1994] 3 All E.R. 848; [1994] B.C.C. 390; [1997] Costs L.R. (Core Vol.) 268; [1994] 2 F.L.R. 194; [1955–95] P.N.L.R. 636; [1994] Fam. Law 560; [1994] E.G. 15 (C.S.); (1994) 144 N.L.J. 231; [1994] N.P.C. 7..8–01, 8–02
Robertson Research International Ltd v ABG Exploration BV [1999] C.P.L.R. 756 8–07
Rogers v Merthyr Tydfil CBC [2006] EWCA Civ 1134; [2007] 1 W.L.R. 808; [2007] 1 All E.R. 354; [2007] 1 Costs L.R. 77; [2006] Lloyd's Rep. I.R. 759; (2006) 150 S.J.L.B. 1053 2–25
Rolf v De Guerin [2011] EWCA Civ 78; [2011] C.P. Rep. 24; [2011] B.L.R. 221; [2011] 5 Costs L.R. 892; [2011] 7 E.G. 97 (C.S.); (2011) 108(8) L.S.G. 20; [2011] N.P.C. 17... 5–30
Romer & Haslam, Re [1893] 2 Q.B. 286...10–06
Rowles-Davies v Call 24–7 Ltd [2010] EWHC 1695 (Ch); (2010) 160 N.L.J. 1043.........5–14
RTS Flexible Systems Ltd v Molkerei Alois Muller GmbH & Co AG [2010] UKSC 14; [2010] 1 W.L.R. 753; [2010] Bus. L.R. 776; [2010] 3 All E.R. 1; [2010] 2 All E.R. (Comm) 97; [2010] 1 C.L.C. 388; [2010] B.L.R. 337; 129 Con. L.R. 1; [2010] C.I.L.L. 2868; (2010) 107(12) L.S.G. 20; (2010) 160 N.L.J. 421; (2010) 154(11) S.J.L.B. 28 5–04
SB v MB (Costs) [2014] EWHC 3721 (Fam). 9–21
SC DG Petrol SRL v Vitol Broking Ltd [2014] EWHC 3900 (Comm) 8–13

SG (a child) v Hewitt (Costs) [2012] EWCA Civ 1053; [2013] 1 All E.R. 1118; [2012] 5 Costs L.R. 937 ....5–15, 5–23
Sibthorpe v Southwark LBC; sub nom. Morris v Southwark LBC [2011] EWCA Civ 25; [2011] 1 W.L.R. 2111; [2011] 2 All E.R. 240; [2011] C.P. Rep. 21; [2011] 3 Costs L.R. 427; [2011] H.L.R. 19; (2011) 108(6) L.S.G. 18; (2011) 161 N.L.J. 173; [2011] N.P.C. 11 10–04
Simmons v Castle [2012] EWCA Civ 1288; [2013] 1 WLR 1239; [2013] 1 All E.R. 334; [2013] C.P. Rep. 3; [2012] 6 Costs L.R. 1150; [2013] E.M.L.R. 4; [2013] P.I.Q.R. P2; [2013] Med. L.R. 4; (2012) 162 N.L.J. 1324; (2012) 156(39) S.J.L.B. 31 6–02
Simpkin Marshall Ltd, Re [1959] Ch 229; [1958] 3 W.L.R. 693; [1958] 3 All E.R. 611; (1958) 102 S.J. 878..................10–03
Sinclair-Jones v Kay [1989] 1 W.L.R. 114; [1988] 2 All E.R. 611; (1988) 138 N.L.J. Rep. 99; (1989) 133 S.J. 220..................8–01
Slick Seating Systems v Adams [2013] EWHC 1642 (QB); [2013] 4 Costs LR 576..................4–21, 9–20
Smith v Trafford Housing Trust (Costs) [2012] EWHC 3320 (Ch); (2012) 156(46) S.J.L.B. 31..................5–15
Solomon v Cromwell Group Plc [2011] EWCA Civ 1584; [2012] 1 W.L.R. 1048; [2012] 2 All E.R. 825; [2012] C.P. Rep. 14; [2012] 2 Costs L.R. 314; [2012] R.T.R. 24; [2012] P.I.Q.R. P9..................9–36
Sugar Hut Group Ltd v A J Insurance [2014] EWHC 3775 (Comm) 5–14, 5–28
Summers v Fairclough Homes Ltd [2012] UKSC 26; [2012] 1 WLR 2004; [2012] 4 All E.R. 317; [2012] 4 Costs L.R. 760; [2013] Lloyd's Rep. I.R. 159; (2012) 162 N.L.J. 910; (2012) 156(26) S.J.L.B. 31..................6–10
Summit Navigation Ltd v Genrali Romania Asigurare [2014] EWHC 398 (Comm); [2014] 1 W.L.R. 3472; [2014] 2 Costs L.R. 367..................4–16
Sutherland v Turnball [2010] EWHC 2699 (QB) 5–23
Symphony Group PLC v Hodgson [1994] Q.B. 179; [1993] 3 W.L.R. 830; [1993] 4 All E.R. 143; [1997] Costs L.R. (Core Vol.) 319; (1993) 143 N.L.J. 725; (1993) 137 S.J.L.B. 134..................6–21, 8–07
Tasleem v Beverley; sub nom. Bartkauskaute v Bartkauskiene [2013] EWCA Civ 1805; [2014] 1 W.L.R. 3567; [2014] C.P. Rep. 25; [2014] 4 Costs L.O. 551 ....9–31, 9–32
Tchenguiz v Serious Fraud Office [2014] EWCA Civ 1471 7–07
Ted Baker Plc v Axa Insurance UK Plc [2012] EWHC 1779 (Comm); [2012] 6 Costs L.R. 1023..................5–10, 5–23, 5–24
Tel-Ka Talk Ltd v Revenue & Customs Commissioners [2011] S.T.C. 497; [2011] S.T.I. 267 ....2–02, 10–03
TGA Chapman v Christopher [1998] 1 WLR 12; [1998] 2 All E.R. 873; [1997] C.L.C. 1306; [1998] Lloyd's Rep. I.R. 1..................6–13, 8–08
Thewlis v Groupama Insurance Co Ltd [2012] EWHC 3 (TCC); [2012] BLR 259; [2012] T.C.L.R. 3; 142 Con. L.R. 85; [2012] 5 Costs L.O. 560 5–04
Thomas Pink Ltd v Victoria's Secret UK Ltd [2014] EWHC 3258 (Ch) 9–39
Thompson v Bruce [2011] EWHC 2228 (QB) 5–23
Threlfall v ECD Insight Ltd (Costs) [2013] EWCA Civ 1444; [2014] 2 Costs L.O. 129; (2013) 163(7586) N.L.J. 18 8–10
Troy Foods v Manton [2013] EWCA Civ 615; [2013] 4 Costs L.R. 546 3–08
Trustees of Stokes Pension Fund v Western Power Distribution (South West) Plc [2005] EWCA Civ 854; [2005] 1 W.L.R. 3595; [2005] 3 All E.R. 775; [2005] C.P. Rep. 40; [2005] B.L.R. 497; [2006] 2 Costs L.R. 226; (2005) 102(30) L.S.G. 28..................5–01
Turner & Co v O Palomo SA [2000] 1 WLR 37; [1999] 4 All E.R. 353; [1999] 2 Costs L.R. 184; [1999] N.P.C. 114..................10–06
United Building and Plumbing Contractors v Kajla [2002] EWCA Civ 628; [2002] C.P. Rep. 53 7–09

Vava v Anglo American South Africa Ltd [2013] EWHC 2326 (QB); [2013] 5 Costs LR
805 6–09
Venn v Secretary of State for Communities & Local Government [2014] EWCA Civ
1539 7–05
Vestergaard Frandsen A/S v Bestnet Europe Ltd [2014] EWHC 4047 (Ch) 5–36
Wagenaar v Weekend Travel Ltd (t/a Ski Weekend) [2014] EWCA Civ 1105; [2014]
C.P. Rep. 46; [2014] 5 Costs L.O. 803; [2014] P.I.Q.R. P23...............................6–04, 9–22
Watchorn v Jupiter Industries Ltd; sub nom. Husky Group Ltd, Re [2014] EWHC
3003 (Ch)..5–12
Weatherford Global Products Ltd v Hydropath Holdings Ltd [2014] EWHC 3243
(TCC) 8–10
Webb Resolutions Ltd v E-Serv Ltd [2014] EWHC 49 (QB); [2014] 1 Costs L.R. 182.....9–15
Wheeler v The Chief Constable of Gloucestershire [2013] EWCA Civ 1791.................9–15
Wilkinson v Wilkinson [1963] P. 1; [1962] 3 W.L.R. 1; [1962] 1 All E.R. 922; (1962)
106 S.J. 219 8–01
Williams v Jervis [2009] EWHC 1838 (QB)..5–15

Table of Statutes

1934   Law Reform (Miscellaneous
          Provisions) Act (c.41) 6–04
1974   Solicitors Act (c.47) 2–02, 7–13,
                                  10–01, 10–05
          s.57 ....2–13, 10–03
             (2) 10–03
          s.59 10–03
          s.64 10–06
          s.69 10–05
          s.70 10–07
             (1) 10–06, 10–23
             (2) 10–06
             (3) 10–06
             (5) 10–08
             (9) 10–08, 10–23
          s.87 10–03
1975   Litigants in Person (Costs
          and Expenses) Act
          (c.47) 7–08, 7–09
          s.1(1) 7–08
1976   Fatal Accidents Act (c.30)..........6–04
1978   Civil Liability (Contribution)
          Act (c.47) 5–06, 6–04
1981   Senior Courts Act (c.54)
          s.51 .... 5–15, 8–07, 10–02
             (1) 8–03, 8–14
             (3) 8–14
             (6) 8–01, 8–03
             (7) 8–01
1990   Courts & Legal Services Act
          (c.41) 8–01
          s.57 10–04
          s.58 .... 2.02, 2–04, 2–06, 2–17,
                           2–30, 10–04, 10–16

          s.58(1) 2–02
          s.58(4) 2–19
          s.58(4)(c)...............................2–04
          s.58(4A) 2–02
             (b) 2–02
          s.58(4B) 2–02, 2–04, 2–06
             (b) 2–04
          s.58(5).....................2–02, 10–04
          s.58A........................2–04, 10–04
             (6) 2.02
          s.58AA............... 2–02, 2–13, 2–17,
                                  2–30, 10–04
             (4) 2–13
             (9) 10–04
          s.58C................. 2–10, 2–11, 2–25
          s.61 10–04
1990   Town & Country Planning
          Act (c.8)
          s.288 7–05
1999   Access to Justice Act (c.22)
          s.11 6–02
          s.29 2–10
          s.30 2–10
2012   Legal Aid, Sentencing &
          Punishment of Offenders
          Act (c.10) 2–01, 10–01
          s.26 6–02
          s.44 .... 2–02, 2–04, 2–31
             (6) 2–03, 2–08, 2–09, 2–19,
                      2–22, 2–29, 2–31
          s.45 2–13
          s.46 ....2–10, 6–01
          s.47 2–10

Table of Statutory Instruments

1980 Litigants in Person (Costs
      and Expenses) Order
      1980 (SI 1980/1159)...........7–08
1998 Civil Procedure Rules (SI
      1998/3132) 3–01, 4–01
      r.1.1 .... 3–02, 4–02, 4–07
        (1) 3–03
        (2)(c) 3–18
        (e) 4–51
        (f).....................4–02, 4–03
      r.1.2(f).............................. 9.03
      r.2.3 6–04
      r.3 pt 2 10–12
      r.3.4(2)(a).....................6–09, 7–01
        (b) 6–09
      r.3.8 4–05
        (4) 4–05, 4–58
      r.3.9 .... 1–03, 2–07, 3–03, 4–02,
            4–03, 4–04, 4–20, 4–35,
            4–36, 4–57, 5–33, 9–23
        (1) 4–03
      r.3.12 ...... 4–16, 4–18, 4–23, 4–28,
            6–17
        (1) 4–23, 4–52
        (1)(a) 4–15
        (b)...................................4–15
        (c) . 4–15, 4–23, 4–24, 4–52
        (1A) 4–15, 4–23, 4–56,
            4–56, 4–59
        (2) 4–01, 4–33
      rr.3.12–18 .... 4–02, 4–14,
            4–54, 4–55
      r.3.13 ...... 4–23, 4–25, 4–45, 4–46,
            4–55, 4–58, 10–13
      r.3.14 ...... 4–16, 4–24, 4–25, 4–46,
            4–58, 5–25
      r.3.15 ...... 4–15, 4–16, 4–18, 4–22,
            4–28, 4–33
        (2) 4–24, 4–54
        (3) 4–19
      r.3.17 ...... 3–03, 3–16, 4–01, 4–22,
            4–24, 4–33, 4–52
      r.3.18 ...... 3–08, 3–09, 3–17, 4–20,
            4–21, 4–32, 4–35, 4–36,
            4–40, 4–54, 9–19, 10–22
      r.3.19(5)(b) 4–59

      r.3.20 .... 4–55, 4–59
      PD 3E 4–02, 4–14, 4–55, 4–59
        para.2...............................4–23
        para.2–5 .... 4–15, 4–16
        para.5(a–f)......................4–15
        para.6..............................4–25
        para.7.2.............. 4–54, 10–24
        para.7.3 ...... 3–03, 3–06, 4–18,
            4–28, 4–41, 4–49, 4–59,
            9–19
        para.7.4 ...... 3–13, 4–18, 4–49,
            10–22
        para.7.6 ...... 3–08, 3–13, 4–11,
            4–17, 4–19, 4–33, 4–36,
            4–53, 4–55
        para.7.7...........................4–16
        para.7.8...........................4–15
        para.7.9 ...... 3–13, 4–17, 4–19,
            4–37, 4–47
      PD 3F 4–55, 4–59
        para.2..............................4–59
        para.4.1...........................4–59
      Pt 7 .... 4–45, 4–52, 9–31
      Pt 8 .... 5–04, 9–31, 9–32,
            10–07
      PD 8B 5–18
      PD 8B para.36.1.....................5–04
      r.12.4(1)..............................7–01
      r.14.4(3)..............................7–01
      r.14.5(6)..............................7–01
      r.16.3(7)..............................4–52
      r.20.3 .... 5–04, 5–32
      r.21.1(2)..............................7–03
      r.21.10 7–05
      Pt 22 4–53
      PD 22 para.2.2A..........3–17, 4–38,
            4–53, 10–14
        para.5.............................4–53
      PD 23 para.6.2(c)..................4–42
      Pt 24 7–01
      r.25.13(2)(f) 8–08
      r.26.3 .... 4–02, 4–45, 4–46, 4–58
        (1) 4–16, 4–58
        (6A) 4–58
        (7A) 4–58
        (b)...................................4–58

r.26.6(3) 4–02, 4–06, 4–07
r.26.7(3) 4–06, 4–07
r.26.8(2) 7–01
PD 26 para.12.3(2) 4–45
      para.12.4 4–45
r.27.14(5–6) 4–07
r.28.3 9–21
Pt 29 4–55
r.29.1(2) 4–02, 4–08
r.29.4 4–42
PD 29 para.8.1(1) 4–55
      para.10.5 ....9–02, 9.21
r.31.5 10–15
      (1) 4–09
      (2) 4–09
      (3–8) 4–02, 4–09
      (7) 4–17, 4–22
         (b) 4–17
r.31.6 4–09
r.32.1 4–10
r.32.2 10–15
      (3) 4–02, 4–10, 4–51
r.32.14 4–53
r.35.4 .... 4–02, 4–11, 10–15
      (2) 4–11
PD 35 para.11 .... 4–02, 4–12
Pt 36 .... 2–01, 3–17, 4–13, 4–21,
         Chapter 5, 6–02, 9.06,
         9–30, 9–36, 9–37, 9–38,
                                       10–23
      section 2 5–18
r.36.1 5–04
r.36.2 5–04
      (3) 5–04
      (5) 5–04
r.36.3 .... 5–03, 5–04
      (b) 5–14
      (c) 4–21, 5–14
      (e) 5–23
      (g) 4–21, 5–05
r.36.3(2) 5–05
      (7) 5–07
r.36.4(1) 5–04
      (2) 5–04
r.36.5 5–04
      (1) 5–05
         (e) 5–32
      (2) 5–05
r.36.7 5–05
r.36.9 5–26
      (1) 5–06
      (2) 5–06
      (3) 5–06

      (4) 5–06, 5–07
         (b) 5–06
      (5) 5–06
r.36.10 ... 5–07, 5–11, 5–26, 10–23
      (1) 5–04, 5–22
      (3) 5–26
      (4) 5–22
      (5) 5–22, 5–23
r.36.11 .... 5–03, 5–11
      (1) 5–07
      (2) 5–07
r.36.12 5–03
r.36.13 .... 5–04, 5–05
      (1) 5–22, 5–25
      (4) 5–22, 5–25
      (5) 5–22, 5–23
      (5–7) 5–23
r.36.14 .... 5–11, 5–13, 5–15, 5–24,
         5–25, 5–35, 9–27, 9–36,
                             9–37, 9–38
      (1A) 5–13
      (2) 5–24
      (3) 5–31, 5–32
         (b) 4–21
         (d) 4–02, 4–13, 5–12,
                       5–27, 9–27, 9–38
      (4) 5–15
r.36.15(1–4) 5–09, 5–10
r.36.16 .... 5–03, 5–23
r.36.17 .... 5–11, 5–13, 5–15, 5–24,
                       9–36, 9–37, 9–38
      (2) 5–13, 5–34
      (3) 5–24
      (4) 5–12, 5–31, 5–35
         (b) 4–21, 5–14
         (c) 5–14
         (d) 4–02, 4–13, 5–12,
                  5–19, 5–27, 5–31, 9–24,
                                       9–38
      (5) 5–12, 5–15, 5–23
      (6) 5–12
      (7) 5–06, 5–11
      (8) 5–11
r.36.20 5–05
r.36.21 5–11
r.31.22 7–07
r.36.23 5–25
r.36.24 5–18
r.36.25 5–18
r.36.26 .... 5–18, 5–19
r.36.27 5–18
r.36.28 5–18
r.36.29(1–4) 5–19

r.36.30 5–20
PD 36A para.2........................5–07
r.38.4 6–21
r.38.6 6–21
  (1) 6–21
r.39.4 4–51
Pt 43 1–04
r.43B 2–07
rr.43–48 2–07
PD 43 para.11.7 2–28
  para.11.8.........................2–28
Pt 44 .... 1–04, 5–34
r.44 part 2....................6–03, 6–07
r.44 part 3.................................6–16
r.44.1 9–24
r.44.2 .... 5–13, 5–29, 6–07,
                        10–07
  (4) 5–21, 5–28
  (4)(a) 3–14, 5–13, 5–28
    (b)....................3–11, 5–13
    (c) 5–13, 5–28, 10–23
  (6) 3–11, 9–30
  (7) 9–30
  (8) 7–04, 9–13
r.44.3 ....2–16, 10–07
  (1–3)......................................7–06
  (2) 3–03, 3–05, 3–06,
    3–09, 3–10, 3–15, 3–18,
    4–20, 4–21, 4–27, 9–10,
               9–18, 9–33
  (4) 7–06
  (5) 3–03, 3–05, 3–06, 3–10,
    3–18, 4–29, 4–49, 4–51,
          9–29, 9–33, 10–14
    (a) 3–11
    (d)................................9–34
  (6)(g) 5–15
  (7) 3–10
r.44.3B(1)(d) 2–07
r.44.4 3–11
  (1)(a) 3–15
    (b)................................3–17
  (2) 9–18
  (3) 3–10, 3–14, 3–17, 9–29
r.44.5 10–2
  (3) 3–02, 3–10
    (c) 7–09
r.44.6 9–02
  (a)...2–31
  (b) 7–04
r.44.11 4–35
  (1) 8–05
    (b)................................4–35

  (2) 8–05
    (a) 4–35
  (3) 8–05
r.44.13 ..... 6–04, 6–19, 6–22, 9–22
  (1) 6–01, 6–04, 9–22
  (3) 6–15
rr.44.13–17 9–22
r.44.14 .... 4–56, 6–08, 6–09, 6–15,
                 6–18, 6–22
  (1) 6–08
  (2) 6–07, 9–22
r.44.15 .... 2–07, 6–09, 6–22
  (1) 6–08
r.44.16 .... 6–08, 6–10, 6–12, 6–15,
                      6–22
  (1) 6–08, 6–11
  (2) 6–11, 6–12, 6–13
    (a) 6–12
    (b) 6–12
  (3) 6–13
r.44.17 .... 6–05, 6–06, 6–20
r.44.18 2–16
  (2)(b) 2–16
r.44.20(7) 9–22
PD 44 para.3 .... 4–55, 4–59
  para.3.6........................... 3.16
  para.3.7........................... 3.16
  para.4.1–4.2 5–11
  para.4.2 5–16
  para.9 9–02
  para.9.1 9–21
  para.9.2 9–21
    (a) 9–21
    (b) 9–21
  para.9.5 9–15
    (3)................................9–03
    (4)....................... 9–04, 9–15
  para.9.6 9–14
  para.12...............................6–11
  para.12.1 6–03
  para.12.2 6–12
  para.12.4(a)......................6–11
    (b)................................6–11
    (c) 6–11, 6–21
  para.12.5 6–13
  para.19 2–07
    (3)................................2–27
Pt 45 .... 1–04, 7–01
  section 3 7–01
  section 3A.............. 5–11, 7–01
  section 4 7–04
  section 6 7–05
r.45.1 7–01

r.45.4 7–01
r.45.9(2)..............................7–01
   (3) 7–01
   (4) 7–01
r.45.18 ....5–18, 7–03
r.45.20 5–19
r.45.24 7–04
r.45.29A 7–04
r.45.30(1)............................7–04
   (2) 7–04
   (3) 7–04
r.45.33 7–04
   (3–6)..............................7–04
r.45.34 7–04
r.45.35 7–04
r.45.36 7–04
r.45.37(1)............................7–05
   (2) 7–05
r.45.41(2)............................7–05
r.45.42 7–05
r.45.43 7–05
r.45.44 7–05
PD 45 para.1.1–1.3 7–01
   para.4.1–4.3 7–05
   para.5.1 7–05
   para.5.2 7–05
Pt 46 1–04
r.46.1 8–07
r.46.2 6–13
   (1) 8–07
   (2) 8–07
r.46.5 7–08
   (4)(a) 7–17
   (6) 7–17
r.46.8 ....8–01, 8–07
r.46.9 ..10–10, 10–12, 10–17, 10–20
   (3) 10–12
     (a) 10–12
     (b)..............................10–12
     (c) 4–38, 4–39, 10–10
   (4) 10–17
r.46.10 10–10
r.46.14 ....9–31, 9–32
PD 46 para.3 7–17
   para.5.1–5.9 8–05
Pt 47 ....1–04, 7–04, 8–05, 9–08,
                9–28, 9–32
r.47.1 4–56
r.47.6 4–56
   (1) 9–31
r.47.11 9–28
r.47.14 9–31
   (7) 9–06

r.47.15 .....9–07, 9–24, 9–32, 9–36
   (5) 9–10, 9–28, 9–30
   (6) 9–07
   (10) 9–36, 9–37
     (b)...............................9–38
r.47.16(1)............................9–28
r.47.20 ....9–06, 9–10, 9–27, 9–30,
             9–35, 9–36, 9–37,
                    9–38
   (1)(a) 9–30
     (b)...............................9–30
   (3) 4–19, 9–30
     (a) 5–33, 9–23
   (4) 5–22, 9–30
     (e) 9–35
PD 47 para.8.2 ....9–06, 9–25
   para.8.3 ....5–33, 9–06, 9–23
   para.12...........................9–25
   para.12.1 9–06
   para.13.2 9–08
   para.13.4 9–09
   para.13.6 9–09
   para.13.9 9–12
   para.13.11 9–08
   para.14...........................9–07
     (b–e) 9–07
   para.14.2............9–25, 9–28
   para.14.4(1) 9–28
     (2) 9–10, 9–12, 9–33
   para.14.5...............9–11, 9–36
   para.19...........................5–22
Pt 48 1–04
r.48.1 ....2–07, 2–27
r.48.2 ......2–29, 6–02, 6–05, 6–19,
             6–20
r.48.6(6) 7–17
r.48.8 ....10–07, 10–08, 10–10
   (2) 10–07
r.48.9 10–08
   (5) 10–19
r.48.10 10–10
PD 48 para.11.1 3–18
   para.11.2 3–18
   para.32.................2–07, 2–27
     (2).....................2–07, 2–19
   54.1 10–08
PD 51G 3–17
   para.1.3 3–08
   para.4.2 3–08
   6 10–12
r.52.9A 1–03
r.61.4(10–12) 5–07
r.63.26 7–04

2000 Conditional Fee Agreements
    Regulations (SI 2000/692)..2–14
2001 Litigants in Person (Costs and
    Expenses) (Magistrates'
    Courts) Order 2000 (SI
    2001/3438) 7–08
2010 Family Procedure Rules (SI
    2010/2955)
    Pt 28 9–21
2013 Civil Procedure
    (Amendment) Rules (SI
    2013/262)
    r.16 2–07
    r.22 9–06
2013 Conditional Fees Agreements
    Order (SI 2013/689) 2–04,
                                2–19
    art.2 2–02
    art.4 2–04
    art.5 2–04

    (1)(b) 2–05
    art.6 2–04
2013 Damages–Based Agreements
    Regulations (SI
    2013/609).................2–13, 2–17
    reg.1...........................2–14, 2–17
    reg.4...........................2–14, 2–17
    (1)(b) 2–14
    (2) 2–15
    (3) 2–14
    reg.5.....................................2–14
2013 Recovery of Costs Insurance
    Premiums in Clinical
    Negligence Proceedings
    (No. 2) Regulations (SI
    2013/739)...........................2–11
2014 Civil Procedure (Amendment
    No. 8) Rules (SI 2014/3299)
    r.18.1 5–03
    r.18.2 5–03

CHAPTER 1

Introduction

On November 3, 2008 the Master of the Rolls, Sir Anthony Clarke, announced the setting up of the Civil Justice Costs Review. The announcement stated: **1–01**

> *"The review is being undertaken as the Master of the Rolls, Sir Anthony Clarke, is concerned at the cost of civil litigation and believes that the time is right for a fundamental and independent review of the whole system."*

The objective of the review was stated to be:

> *"to carry out an independent review of the rules and principles governing the costs of civil litigation and to make recommendations in order to promote access to justice at proportionate cost".*

The terms of reference included:

> *"In conducting the review Lord Justice Jackson will:*
> - *Establish how present costs rules operate and how they impact on the behaviour of both parties and lawyers.*
> - *Establish the effect case management procedures have on costs and consider whether changes in process and/or procedure could bring about more proportionate costs."*

Sir Rupert Jackson produced his final report within the 12-month time limit which had been imposed and stated in his forward: **1–02**

> *"In some areas of civil litigation costs are disproportionate and impede access to justice. I therefore propose a coherent package of interlocking reforms, designed to control costs and promote access to justice."*

Sir Rupert very quickly found that before he could make effective proposals for promoting access to justice at proportionate cost, he would have to make fundamental changes to the procedural rules in order to address the issues which were giving rise to the problem of disproportionate costs.

In his conclusions to the final report, Sir Rupert stated:

> *"As stated in the foreword, the recommendations are interlocking. If the Government and the Civil Procedure Rule Committee see fit to implement these reforms, I believe that they will promote access to justice for all parties (both claimant and defendant) at proportionate cost".*

In the event, Parliament, the Civil Procedure Rule Committee and the judiciary introduced a raft of civil justice reforms which Sir Rupert had recommended in his final report. These included: **1–03**

- abolition of recoverable success fees and ATE premiums
- introduction of qualified one-way costs shifting ("QOCS")
- banning of personal injury referral fees
- 10 per cent increase in general damages
- authorisation of damages-based agreements
- introduction of costs budgeting/costs management
- case management reforms designed to focus factual and expert evidence upon the real issues, as well as to speed up the litigation process
- increased docketing
- revision of CPR r.3.9 to secure more effective compliance
- new disclosure rules
- "hot-tubbing" of experts
- enhanced rewards for claimants' Part 36 offers
- standard directions online
- promotion of ADR
- new definition of proportionate costs plus the reversal of *Lownds* by rule change
- restrictions upon recoverable appeal costs (new Rule 52.9A)
- provisional assessment of costs
- new template for summary assessment
- revised procedures for detailed assessment
- fast-track fixed costs
- numerous reforms to individual areas of litigation (Personal Injury, Clinical Negligence, Commercial, etc.)

Sir Rupert stated there would be five consequences if his package of proposed reforms were to be accepted:

(i)   most Personal Injury claimants would recover more damages than they did before, although some would recover less;

(ii)   claimants would have a financial interest in the level of costs being incurred on their behalf;

(iii) claimants' solicitors would still be able to make a reasonable profit;

(iv)   costs payable to claimants' solicitors by liability insurers would be significantly reduced; and

(v)   costs would also become more proportionate because defendants would no longer have to pay success fees and ATE premiums.

1–04   The recommendations made by Sir Rupert in his final report were accepted by the Government almost in their entirety. Some of the recommendations required primary legislation which is contained in the Legal Aid Sentencing and Punishment of Offenders Act (LASPOA) 2012.

Those recommendations which did not require primary legislation to bring them into force were dealt with by rule change.

A committee was set up under the chairmanship of the Senior Cost Judge with the task of revising and amending the cost rules and costs practice direction. As a direct result of the abolition of recoverable success fees and after the event insurance premiums, large gaps appeared in the existing rules and the

Costs Practice Direction. The decision was accordingly taken to re-group and streamline the rules. The decision was also taken to link the relevant parts of the Costs Practice Direction to each individual part of the rules, so that instead of having one very large Costs Practice Direction, a person looking at the rules in say, Part 47, would know that the relevant practice direction was contained in Practice Direction 47.

The result of this exercise was that the previous Part 43 ceased to exist. The new Part 44 contains the general rules about costs. Part 45 contains the rules about fixed and predictable costs, including fast track trial costs, which had previously been contained in the earlier version of Part 46. The new Part 46 deals with costs in special cases, i.e. costs payable by or to particular persons, costs relating to legal representatives, costs on allocation and reallocation and costs only proceedings. Part 47 contains the procedure for detailed assessment of costs and default provisions. Part 48 deals with Part 2 of LASPOA relating to civil litigation funding and costs and makes transitional provision in relation to pre-commencement funding arrangements. The new rules and practice directions came into force on April 1, 2013.

The vast scope of the Jackson reforms has resulted in the need for this   **1–05** book. In subsequent chapters some of the major topics are addressed. It is well understood by the editors that there are many other topics which, as a result of the reforms, also need such detailed treatment but limitations of time dictate that, for the moment, this book is limited to the following topics:

- funding litigation;
- proportionality;
- case management and cost management;
- Part 36 settlement offers and costs consequences;
- qualified one-way costs shifting;
- fixed costs, costs and different tracks, litigants in person, indemnity costs orders;
- wasted costs orders, other misconduct and costs, orders against non-parties,
- summary assessment, detailed assessment/provisional assessment; and
- the effect of the Jackson reforms on solicitor and client costs.

CHAPTER 2

Funding Litigation

Introduction

The Legal Aid, Sentencing & Punishment of Offenders Act 2012 and asso- **2–01**
ciated secondary legislation has had a significant impact on the funding of
litigation. Some aspects, in particular the greater restrictions on availability of
public funding, are beyond the scope of this section.

This section will instead focus on the changes to funding arrangements
available to litigants, in particular Conditional Fee Agreements (CFAs),
Damages Based Agreements (DBAs) and After the Event Insurance (ATE).

Lord Justice Jackson's Final Report contained detailed and inter related proposals for the means of Funding Litigation. These included:

- emphasising the benefits of public funding and stressing the 'vital neces-
  sity' to avoid any further cutbacks in its availability or eligibility[1];
- recommendations for the encouragement of take up of Before the Event
  Insurance in certain circumstances[2]; and
- perhaps most notably, a recommendation for the abolition of between
  the parties recovery of ATE premiums,[3] allied to the introduction of qualified one way costs shifting for certain litigants and the abolition of the
  between the parties recoverability of success fees on CFAs,[4] in turn allied
  to a 10 per cent increase in awards for general damages, the enhancement
  of Part 36 benefits for claimants and the capping of success fees chargeable by solicitors in personal injury claims.

Whilst broadly Jackson LJ's package of reforms in relation to CFAs, ATE, and
QOCS were adopted, his call for public funding not to be further restricted
was not, and the reforms of funding introduced did not always follow his
precise recommendations.

This can be seen in particular in relation to QOCS, where Jackson LJ's proposal for a means-tested model based on that applicable to public funding
costs protection was not adopted,[5] but also in relation to DBAs, where the
reforms introduced have not had the desired effect in practice of making a
new form of funding widely available to litigants.

The transitional provisions in relation to the abolition of between the
parties' recovery of success fees and ATE premiums have given rise to problems of their own. These have become particularly apparent in circumstances
where, for one reason or another, there is some need to vary or change the

---

[1] Final Report, p.70.
[2] Final Report, p.79.
[3] Final Report, p.89.
[4] Final Report, p.112.
[5] For further details, see Ch.6 on QOCS.

funding arrangement after April 1, 2013 in circumstances where that arrangement was first entered into prior to that date. These issues will be considered further below.

Conditional Fee Agreements

2–02   Section 44 of LASPO amended s.58A(6) of the Courts & Legal Services Act 1990 to provide that a costs order may no longer include provision requiring another party to pay part of the successful party's success fee. This was a simple reversal of the existing provision.

Whilst certain changes were made to s.58 in relation to the specific requirements for a CFA in personal injury claims[6], the basic circumstances in which a CFA could be entered into, its basic requirements and the type of cases where such an agreement was lawful were not amended.

Accordingly, the effect of the amendment to s.58A(6) was simple—where success fees had formerly been recoverable in principle between the parties, they are now no longer recoverable and, where a CFA is entered into, such success fees will have to be paid by the client with no prospect of any between the parties' recovery.

It is important to note that the fundamental principle in s.58(1) of the Act, that a CFA which does not satisfy all of the conditions applicable to it by virtue of s.58 shall be unenforceable, remains unchanged.

Equally, Lord Justice Jackson's clear recommendation that the indemnity principle should be abrogated, at least in part to limit the scope for satellite litigation in relation to issues of enforceability of retainers, was rejected. It is a call that has been repeated more recently,[7] but with no greater prospect of being heeded.

Accordingly, a failure to comply with the requirements of s.58, including the new requirements imposed by s.58(4A) and (4B) in relation to personal injury CFAs, will leave the litigant, and their solicitor, exposed to the well-rehearsed arguments that the agreement is unenforceable and that accordingly no costs under the CFA may be recovered between the parties. Whether the removal of the between the parties recovery of success fees will result directly or indirectly in a reduction in the appetite or ability of paying parties to take such points remains to be seen.

The final point to note in relation to issues of general application is that s.58(5) of the 1990 Act remains untrammelled. This is the section that provides that where the CFA is a non-contentious business agreement under s.57 of the Solicitors Act 1974, s.58(1) does not render it unenforceable. The scope of this was considered in detail by then Senior Cost Judge in 2010 in an authoritative judgment[8] and the ability to use CFAs (and now DBAs) which are not subject to the restrictions of ss.58 and 58AA for what might be

---

[6]   These are the 'specified claims' under s.58(4A)(b) by virtue of art.2 of the Conditional Fee Agreements Order 2013 (SI 2013 No.689).

[7]   *http://www.judiciary.gov.uk/wp-content/uploads/2014/10/litigation-post-jackson-world.pdf* [Accessed January 29, 2015].

[8]   *Tel-Ka Talk Ltd v Revenue & Customs Commissioners* [2010] EWHC 90175 (Costs).

termed non-contentious business is an option which is potentially a valuable one, particularly in the commercial sphere, though one which needs to be approached carefully.

Transitional provisions

The transitional provision provided for by s.44(6) states that: 2–03

> "The amendment made by [the subsection] does not prevent a costs order including provision in relation to a success fee payable by a person ("P") under a conditional fee agreement entered into before [1ˢᵗ April 2013] if—
>
> (a) the agreement was entered into specifically for the purposes of the provision to P of advocacy or litigation services in connection with the matter that is the subject of the proceedings in which the costs order is made, or
> (b) advocacy or litigation services were provided to P under the agreement in connection with that matter before the commencement day."

This ensured that the court retains its discretion to allow a between the parties success fee where the CFA was entered into before the April 1, 2013. The one proviso is that the CFA relates to a specific matter which is the subject of the proceedings before the court or advocacy or litigation services were in fact provided under the CFA before April 1, 2013.[9]

In addition, s.48 of the Act contained saving provisions allowing for the continued between the parties recovery of success fees in diffuse mesothelioma claims. On December 4, 2013 the Government announced that this exception was to be removed and success fees would cease to be recoverable between the parties in such claims. However, in October 2014 the High Court[10] ruled that the consultation process leading to that decision had been flawed and that the decision had to be quashed. Accordingly, if and when the mesothelioma exception will be lifted remains to be seen.

Implementation of s.44 was also 'suspended' in relation to publication and privacy proceedings pending further reforms initially anticipated in April 2014, but now delayed, and insolvency proceedings until April 2015.

Such specific types of cases aside, therefore, the key point was that where the CFA was entered into before April 1, 2013 the success fee continued to be recoverable in principle. If entered into on or after April 1, 2013 the success fee was irrecoverable from the paying party.

---

[9]   The latter part of this provision appears primarily directed to the position in relation to Collective Conditional Fee Agreements (CCFAs). Such an agreement may have been entered into prior to April 1, 2013, but may cover all claims of a particular type a solicitor is undertaking for a particular client or funder. The agreement may therefore cover claims in respect of matters which had not even arisen prior to April 1, 2013. If the transitional provision simply focused on the date of the funding arrangement, the CCFA could be used to ensure the ongoing recovery of additional liabilities even in respect of post-April 2013 instructions. Accordingly, in such circumstances, it is not the date of the CCFA which is relevant (because the CCFA did not relate to a specific matter which is the subject of proceedings) but rather whether the legal representative had started to provide services in respect of that specific matter before April 1, 2013.
[10]   *R (Ex parte Whitston) v Secretary of State for Justice* [2014] EWHC 3044 (Admin).

Personal injury claims—additional requirements

2–04 Section 44 of LASPO amended s.58 and s.58A of the Courts & Legal Services Act 1990 to impose additional conditions on CFAs, including the requirement that in certain classes of case, primarily personal injury claims (but for the time being excluding mesothelioma claims), the success fee does not exceed a maximum limit expressed as a percentage of certain types of damages.[11]

There is a strange circularity in the 2013 Order in that the types of cases in respect of which the cap on the success fee imposed by s.58(4)(c) applies (personal injury claims—see cl.4) are expressly specified in the Order. However, cl.6 provides that, for the time being, cl.4[12] does not apply to publications, privacy and insolvency proceedings. Given that they are not specified in cl.4, cl.4 could not apply to them in any event, so this part of cl.6 serves no purpose. It is assumed that cl.6 was phrased in this way in anticipation of the success fee cap possibly being extended to cover such proceedings if and when success fees in such claims are no longer recoverable between the parties, though why those parts of cl.6 would be needed at that point is a moot question.

The key restriction in relation to a post-April 2013 CFA for a claim involving personal injury is contained in Article 5 of the Order, which must be read in conjunction with s.58(4B) of the 1990 Act.

The success fee in any such agreement must be limited to a maximum of 25 per cent of specified classes of damages awarded in the proceedings, in respect of proceedings at first instance. Note, the express reference in s.58(4B)(b) is to 'awarded' and <u>not</u> to damages actually recovered.

The specified classes of damages are general damages for pain, suffering and loss of amenity and damages for pecuniary loss, other than future pecuniary loss, in both cases net of any sums recoverable as CRU (Compensation Recovery) (art.5(2)).

Accordingly, under such a CFA, the success fee, which cannot be recovered between the parties, cannot exceed 25 per cent of the damages for general damages and past pecuniary loss (net of CRU).

2–05 It is important not to confuse the cap on the quantum of the success fee with the percentage of the success fee itself. The maximum percentage success fee, that is to say the maximum percentage by which the solicitors' base fees may be multiplied, remains at 100 per cent, in all claims where a CFA is permissible. The 25 per cent cap operates as a financial limit on how much of the success fee the client may be charged.

If the amount of damages for general damages and past loss awarded is sufficiently high, or the amount of base fees to which the success fee is to be applied, or the percentage success fee itself is sufficiently low, then the full success fee may be payable, because it is less than the cap. Where, however, the success fee calculated at the applicable percentage on the base fees payable

---

[11] As set out in the Conditional Fee Agreements Order 2013.
[12] And cl.5, which sets the maximum percentage success fee in cases covered by cl.4 applies.

under the agreement exceeds 25 per cent of the prescribed damages, then the amount of the success fee is limited accordingly.

The interaction of the maximum limit on the percentage success fee (100 per cent) with the newly introduced cap on the maximum fee chargeable caused some confusion initially in some quarters and some errors of drafting, particularly in relation to CFAs which covered appeal proceedings.

This is because, under art.5(1)(b) of the 2013 Order, the cap on the maximum success fee is lifted from 25 per cent to 100 per cent in relation to proceedings other than at first instance. It is important to note that this is still a cap. It is merely that the effect of the cap in this situation is that the maximum success fee is limited to the full amount of the net damages for general damages and past loss, rather than only 25 per cent of that sum. This 100 per cent cap is separate and distinct from the 100 per cent limit on the success fee itself.

As a matter of practice, it would appear that many practitioners have chosen to ignore the ability to include a higher cap on the success fee where the CFA covers matters other than first instance proceedings, no doubt because of the concerns as to ensuring that the agreement is fully compliant with both caps where it covers both first instance and appellate proceedings and because of the danger of a simple error leading to the entire CFA being deemed unenforceable. Undoubtedly the simpler and safer, if potentially less remunerative, course, is to apply the 25 per cent cap alone.   2–06

The cap is intended to be inclusive of VAT—that is to say that the maximum success fee chargeable, including VAT, should not exceed the 25 per cent limit. Peculiarly, this is not specified within art.5, but rather is explained in the Explanatory Note to the Order which, as it states, is not part of the Order itself.

It is generally accepted that the cap should include any success fee payable to counsel (including VAT) under any CFA in relation to the same matter between the solicitor and counsel. However, it is fair to note that neither the 2013 Order nor s.58 of the 1990 Act, as amended, specify this. As a result, it is open to argument that reference to 'the success fee' specified under s.58(4B) of the 1990 Act, which must be subject to a maximum limit, is to the success fee (that is to say the solicitor's success fee) chargeable under the CFA, and that any success fee chargeable under any separate CFA is subject to a separate, but identical maximum limit. That does not appear to have been the intention, but appears to be an argument left open by the drafting.

Notification and advice requirements

Prior to April 2013, the between the parties notification requirements in relation to additional liabilities were contained in CPR 44.15, CPR 44 PD 19 and CPR 47 PD 32. These were replaced by substitution as part of the general substitution of CPR 44–48[13] and have no effect in relation to retainers entered   2–07

---

[13] Effected by r.16 of the Civil Procedure (Amendment Rules) 2013 (SI 2013/262).

into on or after April 1, 2013. However, they have continued effect in relation to pre commencement funding arrangements[14] (as do the former provisions of CPR 43–48 generally, for example in relation to the between the parties assessment of success fees) by virtue of CPR 48.1.

Accordingly, care must be taken in the unlikely event, for example, of a claimant who entered into a pre-April 2013 CFA where a letter before claim has not yet been sent, or, perhaps more possible, where proceedings have not yet been issued, to ensure that the proper notification is given as required by the 'old' rules. Similarly, in the more common situation of assessment of costs where the funding arrangement is a pre-April 2013 CFA (or there is a pre-April 2013 ATE premium) the requirements of old CPR 47 PD 32 must be observed if the between the parties recoverability of the additional liabilities is not to be jeopardised.

The confusion which surrounded the correct interpretation of the 'new' CPR 3.9 following the Court of Appeal's decision in *Mitchell*[15] pending clarification in *Denton*[16] led to a much stricter approach being taken towards any breaches of these notification requirements and the application of old CPR 44.3B.

That strict approach has now been moderated in light of *Denton*, as seen, for example, in *Caliendo*[17]. The existence of the strict approach did result in some clarification of the scope of the sanctions under CPR 44.3B being provided in *Long v Value Properties Ltd*,[18] which may be material in cases of such breaches in relation to pre-April 2013 funding arrangements.[19]

Implementation issues

2–08   There has not been any significant number of reported issues in relation to the implementation of the changes to the structure of CFAs, though that may largely be because it will take some time for any post LASPO CFA cases involving any substantial amounts of costs to come before the court.

However, there is a number of latent issues. Key amongst those are issues relating to the transfer and assignment of CFAs.

The common scenario where this occurs is where a personal injury claimant has entered into a pre-commencement funding arrangement, as defined in s.44(6) of LASPO, but wishes to change firms after that date. Given the existence of the pre-commencement funding arrangement, the claimant will almost certainly not be entitled to QOCS protection if he enters into a new,

---

14   As defined in CPR 48.2, which broadly means a CFA or ATE policy entered into prior to April 1, 2013 (or a CCFA where, in the individual case in which costs are being considered, work was begun in relation to that case under the CCFA prior to April 1, 2013).
15   *Mitchell v News Group Newspapers Ltd* [2013] EWCA Civ 1537; [2014] 1 WLR 795.
16   *Denton v T H White Ltd* [2014] EWCA Civ 906; [2014] 1 WLR 3926.
17   *Caliendo v Mischon De Reya LLP* [2014] EWHC 3414.
18   *Long v Value Properties Ltd* [2014] EWHC 2981.
19   In that case, it was made clear that the sanction of disallowance of the success fee under CPR 44.3B(1)(d) for late service of the relevant information in relation to the CFA in detailed assessment proceedings was limited to the loss of the success fee for the period of the default, rather than there being a disallowance of the entire success fee for the whole case, as had previously generally been thought to be the case.

post LASPO agreement with the new firm of solicitors. Equally, if he enters into such a new agreement, the success fee under the new agreement will be irrecoverable and the claimant may be exposed to a deduction from any damages in respect of that success fee.

An equally common scenario is where a firm of solicitors is changing status (for example from a partnership to LLP or ABS), or wishes to transfer a number of clients to another firm.

Perhaps the most common questions in this scenario are whether the CFAs (or indeed other retainers) may lawfully be assigned and, if so, whether they should be.

It is beyond the scope of this chapter to describe in detail the fundamen- **2–09** tal legal principles relating to assignment and novation. It suffices to note that the key argument revolves around the notion that novation results in the original agreement coming to an end, as a matter of law, and a new contract on the same terms and relating to the same subject matters, coming into being between one of the original parties and the new party, with the other original contracting party being released from the contract, whereas assignment merely transfers the existing rights under a contract from one party (the assignor) to another (the assignee).

Accordingly, it is contended that if a CFA is capable of assignment, then the effect of that assignment is that the CFA continues. It would follow, therefore, that the assignment of a pre-April 2013 CFA from, say, one solicitor to another post-April 2013 would result in the CFA still being regarded as a 'pre-commencement funding arrangement' for the purposes of s.44(6) of LASPO, CPR 48.2 and all other related provisions. Accordingly, the recoverability of the success fee would be preserved.

The correctness of that argument is likely to be the subject to detailed challenge and, ultimately, higher appellate authority. At the time of writing, there is some authority, principally Rafferty J's decision in *Jenkins*[20] which supports the principle that a CFA is capable of assignment and does not offend the usual principle that only the benefit (in general under a CFA, the solicitor's right to payment) and not the burden (in general under a CFA, the solicitor's obligation to perform) can be assigned.

However, the weight of that authority is open to question, particularly since Rafferty J expressly stated that she was not laying down any issue of general principle, but was merely deciding the case on its particular facts, but also because it is open to argument whether the analysis of the principle of conditional benefit and burden was properly analysed in that case (particularly in light of the Court of Appeal's comments in *Davies v Jones*[21] and as to whether all issues in relation to the law of assignment were fully raised or argued.

Similar difficulties may arise in the context of the need to appoint a Litigation Friend in cases where the claimant has entered into a pre-April 2013

---

[20] *Jenkins v Young Brothers Transport Ltd* [2006] EWHC 151 (QB).
[21] *Davies v Jones* [2009] EWCA Civ 1164.

CFA but has subsequently been found to lack capacity, or where the claimant was a child where a pre-April 2013 CFA was entered into with a Litigation Friend, but the claimant has subsequently attained the age of 18.

It was hoped that some general guidance on these latter issues might be forthcoming in the Court of Appeal's decision in *Blankley*, but in the end it focused on the narrow issue of whether the claimant's supervening incapacity had caused the CFA in question to be terminated by reason of frustration because the claimant could not give instructions to the solicitor.[22]

After the Event Insurance

2–10 Section 46 of LASPO introduced s.58C of the Courts & Legal Services Act 1990 with the effect of repealing s.29 of the Access to Justice Act 1999 (and s.47 LASPO repealed the similar s.30 of the 1999 Act in relation to the 'notional' premiums charged by bodies such as trade unions). These legislative changes had the effect of preventing the between the parties recovery of ATE premiums where such policies were taken out on or after April 1, 2013.

Again, this ties in (in personal injury claims) with the introduction of QOCS, in that the existence of a pre-LASPO ATE policy prevents the claimant being eligible for QOCS protection.

As with success fees, an exception exists allowing for continued between the parties recoverability in mesothelioma, publication and privacy and insolvency proceedings, such exceptions being subject to the same process of review and revocation in due course. The wording, however, is different from that in relation to CFAs, in that pursuant to s.58C of the 1990 Act, the amendments (i.e. the revocation of between the parties recoverability) does not apply "in relation to a costs order made in favour of a party who took out a costs insurance policy in relation to the proceedings before [April 1, 2013]".

Accordingly, the test is whether a' costs insurance policy was taken out in relation to the proceedings prior to April 1, 2013. The apparent effect is that the amendments (that is to say, the revocation of recoverability) do not apply at all where this is the case. It seems open to argument, therefore, that provided the claimant has taken out a single pre-April 2013 ATE policy, the claimant is entitled to seek to recover between the parties any (reasonably incurred) ATE premiums for any subsequent policies. This was probably not the intention and places too great a stress on the reference to 'a' costs insurance policy.

However, the precise limits of the section and whether, for example, it is possible to recover the costs of post-April 2013 'top up' or further staged premiums in respect of a pre-April 2013 policy will no doubt be considered in detail in forthcoming cases.

2–11 A saving provision relating to the continued between the parties recoverability of ATE premiums in very limited circumstances in relation to Clinical Negligence claims was provided by s.58C of the 1990 Act and the Recovery of Costs Insurance Premiums in Clinical Negligence Proceedings (No.2)

---

[22] *Blankley v Central Manchester Children's University Hospital NHS Trust* [2015] EWHC 18.

Regulations 2013 (finally laid before Parliament four days before the implementation date after a flawed earlier provision).

These allow for the continued recovery between the parties of ATE premiums in clinical negligence claims in certain circumstances, namely where:

- the claim has a value in excess of £1,000; and
- the insured risk relates to liability for the cost of an expert's report on issues of liability or causation

The recoverable premium is limited to the cost of such a limited policy or, if the policy is wider, to the part of the premium that can be identified as relating to that part of the risk identified above.

More generally, the changes in relation to between the parties recoverability of ATE premiums were on a more limited basis and, unlike the CFA and DBA provisions, related only to the removal of the between the parties recoverability issue and not to a fundamental change to the nature and terms of such arrangements.

Implementation issues are most likely to relate to disputes over issues such as whether a further premium paid after April 1, 2013 to 'top up' an existing policy should be regarded as part of the same pre-commencement funding arrangement (thereby being recoverable) or whether it should be regarded as a new policy.

In addition there will be issues arising out of what was, anecdotally, a rush to incept a substantial number of policies at the very end of March 2013. These might include issues such as the adequacy of funding advice given to claimants in such hurried circumstances, the suitability of the premium, and the provision of proper notification of funding, etc.

Such matters do not raise any new issues of principle and will fall to be decided on established, pre-April 2013 principles. That said, it could be argued that the revocation of the between the parties recovery of additional liabilities and the recognition that the previous scheme was flawed may, as time goes on, lead to a more robust judicial approach when it comes to questioning the reasonableness of ATE premiums in particular (and it might be said that such an approach has already started to become evidence even prior to April 2013). Cases such as *Redwing*[23] and *Black Horse*[24] offer some limited support for this theory.

Coventry v Lawrence[25]

The issues raised by Lord Neuberger in *Coventry* are strictly outside the scope of this section, since they do not arise out of the Jackson reforms. Indeed, one of the oddities of the case is that, if the arguments are correct, then these are arguments have been available to parties since the time of the introduction of between the parties recoverability of success fees and it is somewhat ironic

2–12

---

[23] *Redwing Construction Ltd v Charles Wishart* [2011] EWHC 19 (TCC).
[24] *Kelly & Another v Black Horse Ltd* [2013] EWHC B17 (Costs).
[25] *Coventry v Lawrence (No.2)* [2014] UKSC 46.

that the arguments might only come to fruition after the decision has been taken to end (in the majority of cases) such recoverability.

The arguments were heard over three days in February 2015, with a number of interveners including the Secretary of State for Justice and the Law Society. In short, the core argument was that the ability to claim success fees and ATE premiums on a between the parties basis has the effect of infringing the other party's right to a fair trial under art.6 of the European Convention of Human Rights and/or that party's property rights under art.1 of the First Protocol, and is an unjustifiable interference with such rights.

Argument is likely to focus firstly on whether or not this is correct and secondly, if so, whether the unlawful interference is a consequence of primary legislation which cannot be interpreted in a convention compatible fashion (in which case the legislation will stand, but a declaration of incompatibility would be made) or whether such interference is as a result of some form of delegated legislation which can be 'read down' without offending the primary legislation, in which case the court will be able to 'read' the applicable parts of the CPR in such a way as to disallow such additional liabilities where appropriate.

Which, if either, applies will be an important matter, since the former leaves the paying party (probably) having to pay the additional liabilities (as assessed) but with an arguable claim for damages against the Government, whereas the latter would allow the courts to take into account any infringement of convention rights when assessing the additional liabilities between the parties.

The main focus of the first respondent's case before the Court in February was that the fault lay with the secondary legislation which could be read down so as to introduce, in practice, a requirement to consider the financial position of the paying party in deciding whether, and if so to what extent, an additional liability could be recovered between the parties. If such a test was adopted, it seems unlikely to affect cases where the paying party is backed by an insurer or large public or private body, though the precise effect of such a test is unclear.

Such a test, if introduced, could potentially also affect the assessment of base costs (since the principle that the magnitude of an award of costs could infringe Article 6 appears equally applicable to both base costs and additional liabilities).

Whether any infringement at all will be found and, if so, the extent of the same and its impact on the recoverability of additional liabilities on pre-April 2013 funding arrangements, and possibly recovery of costs generally, remains to be seen.

Damages-Based Agreements (DBAs)

2–13   The introduction of DBAs was long awaited. They had, of course, been in existence for some time in relation to employment tribunal matters and the use of a contingency fee arrangement was permissible under s.57 of the

Solicitors Act 1974 in relation to non-contentious business matters, but the proposed introduction of a regulated form of arrangement whereby the solicitor's payment would be directly proportionate to the client's recovery, in general litigation, was seen by many, if not all, as a positive step in widening the available forms of funding.

Unfortunately, the precise method of their introduction has been widely criticised as being too narrow and restrictive, with the result that to date there appears to have been very limited use of DBAs in circumstances where they were prohibited prior to April 2013.

The widening of the permissibility of DBAs in contentious business was achieved by virtue of s.45 of LASPO, amending the existing s.58AA of the 1990 Act, with effect from April 1, 2013. By virtue of s.58AA(4), a DBA is now permissible in all matters save those which cannot presently be subject of an enforceable CFA (primarily criminal and family matters).

As with CFAs, a DBA must comply with the conditions imposed by the permitting statute. If it fails to do so, it is unenforceable. Again, as with CFAs, an exception exists for agreements which fall under s.57 of the Solicitors Act 1974, that is to say Non Contentious Business Agreements.

Beyond the basic requirements of the agreement being in writing and not relating to prohibited classes of proceedings, the amended s.58AA provides that for such an agreement to be enforceable it must comply with the requirements of the DBA Regulations 2013. It is therein that the problems are said to lie.

Jackson LJ had proposed that in order for a DBA to be 'valid', there should be a requirement for a client to receive specific and independent advice before it was signed.[26] The recommendation was not implemented—primarily it would appear out of concerns that it might lead to a return to the sort of between the parties arguments over enforceability and adequacy of advice which had been a feature of the Conditional Fee Agreement Regulations 2000. However, there are certain requirements for the provision of information in relation to DBAs in employment matters (set out in reg.5 of the DBA Regulations 2013) where, presumably, such advice is thought to be more desirable but, perhaps more importantly, less likely to lead to indemnity principle arguments of the type which were notoriously prevalent in relation to CFAs generally as a result, in particular, of the specific advice requirements under the (now revoked) CFA Regulations 2000, given the limited scope for between the parties costs recovery before the Employment Tribunal.

The basic provisions in relation to DBAs in employment matters have not changed and the remainder of this section will focus on the requirements in non-employment matters.

The effect of the 2013 Regulations is that a solicitor is entitled to agree with his client that he shall be paid by way of a percentage of the damages ultimately recovered by the client. Such 'payment', as defined by reg.1 of the

2–14

---

[26] Final Report, p.133.

2013 Regulations, must be net of any between the parties costs recovered by way of profit costs or counsel's fees (reg.4)—the so called 'Ontario' model. In other words, the solicitor cannot enjoy the benefit of both the 'payment' from the client and the between the parties costs recovery, but must allow such between the parties costs recovery to reduce the client's liability to pay the 'payment'.

In addition, the agreement can allow for the solicitor to charge disbursements to the client (other than counsel's fees) on top of the percentage fee (with credit being given against that charge for any between the parties costs recovered in respect of such disbursements) (reg.4(1)(b)).

The 2013 Regulations include a requirement for any DBA (other than one in relation to employment proceedings) to contain a cap on the amount of the client's recovered damages which may be used to pay the solicitor's fee under the DBA. In proceedings generally the sum is 50 per cent (inclusive of VAT) (reg.4(3)—and unlike the CFA Order, the Regulation does expressly mention VAT).

2–15   In personal injury claims there is a stricter limit, with the cap being restricted to 25per cent of the same classes of damages as apply in relation to the cap on a success fee under a CFA, namely general damages and damages for pecuniary loss other than future pecuniary loss (reg.4(2)).

This latter restriction immediately illustrates a potential, though not necessarily insuperable, obstacle to the use of a DBA in personal injury litigation. With a post-April 2013 CFA, the success fee is capped at 25 per cent of the prescribed classes of damages. However, there is no cap on base fees (other than their reasonableness) and counsel's fee can be charged in addition to the base fees and success fee (though counsel's success fee is probably included in the cap).

With a DBA, however, the total fee, including counsel's fee, is capped at 25 per cent of the same classes of damages. Whilst there will be cases where the figures are such that a DBA is still attractive, the most valuable heads of loss in a large personal injury case are usually future losses (care, loss of earnings, etc.) and not past losses or general damages and the limitation of the total fee under a DBA to a fraction of those heads of loss will limit their attractiveness and suitability in all but a small minority of cases.

This is before any more general obstacles to the use of a DBA are considered, as to which see below.

Between the parties costs recovery
2–16   CPR 44.18 provides that the fact of a DBA will not affect between the parties costs recovery and that between the parties costs shall be assessed in accordance with CPR 44.3. The rule itself is somewhat vague in this regard, and the limited use of DBA means that its scope has yet to be properly tested.

However, it is generally understood that it is intended to result in between the parties costs being assessed on a 'conventional' basis, that is to say on the basis of an hourly rate and time spent basis.

What is clear is that the between the parties costs will not be assessed by reference to the 'payment' the client is liable to the solicitor for under the DBA save that, as noted below, such payment may act as an indemnity principle 'cap' on the opponent's total liability. Accordingly, clients entering into a DBA must be made expressly aware that there is likely to be a fundamental difference (and often shortfall) between the payment due under the DBA and the equivalent sum in profit costs an opponent is likely to be ordered to pay if the claim succeeds.

The between the parties assessment will involve the court identifying a 'notional' hourly rate where none has been contractually agreed, much as occurs in between the parties assessments in publicly funded cases.

It also means that a solicitor who believed that acting on a DBA will allow the firm to avoid having to conduct detailed time recording would be wrong. Not only would a lack of detailed time recording hamper any between the parties costs recovery, it could be very unfortunate were the DBA to be challenged on a solicitor-client basis.

As noted previously, the indemnity principle has not been disapplied, despite Jackson LJ's recommendation. This is expressly reflected in CPR 44.18(2)(b) which recites that a party may not recover more by way of costs than the total amount payable under the DBA.

Accordingly, if the 'notional/conventional' between the parties costs in a case exceed the sum payable under a DBA, then the between the parties costs recovery will be limited to the DBA sum. However, if the 'notional/conventional' between the parties costs are less than the DBA sum, then because the assessment is conducted on that 'notional' basis, the between the parties costs recovery will be limited to that conventional sum.

Problems with DBAs

Some issues have already been highlighted above. Specific problems include: 2–17

- The wording of para.4 of the DBA Regulations 2013, and in particular the definition of 'payment' appears to prevent the use of hybrid DBAs. That is to say, it appears to prevent the agreement allowing the legal representative to be paid anything other than the percentage share of damages if the case is won or nothing if the case is lost. Hybrid or discounted DBAs allow for the solicitor to charge a low hourly rate win or lose, with a percentage share of damages on success. Discounted CFAs have been popular in commercial litigation, where a client is able and prepared to pay something win or lose, but wishes to share the risk with the solicitor. Hybrid DBAs would potentially be popular for offering the same opportunity whilst tying the reward directly to the amount of recovery. The present drafting appears to prevent such agreements and the wording of the regulations appears to mean that such agreements would be unenforceable. It is a moot point whether this is a deliberate decision, but it would appear to be so. That impression was emphasised by the fact that when asking the Civil Justice Council to consider some technical revisions to the DBA

Regulations in November 2014 the Ministry of Justice expressly ruled out revising them to permit (or to make clear that they already permitted) hybrid DBAs. The Master of the Rolls referred to the Government having decided to 'not permit hybrid DBAs'.[27] Lord Justice Jackson has called for the government to rethink its position in this regard and has given cogent reasons why the position should be reconsidered.[28]

- This also appears to create a problem with using a DBA in a form similar to a CFA 'lite'. That is to say a DBA which includes a provision allowing for the solicitor to retain between the parties costs in full in the event that the between the parties costs payable on the hypothetical hourly rate/time spent basis (the 'Ontario model') exceed the sum which would otherwise be payable under the agreement on a simple percentage of damages basis. There seems no particular reason why such an agreement should not be permissible if CFA lites are to remain permissible. It would not require an opponent to pay more than a reasonable and proportionate sum. At the same time, the prospect of enhanced between the parties recovery would facilitate the greater use of DBAs on a solicitor-client basis. However, such agreements do not presently appear to be permissible under the 2013 Regulations.

- The Regulations appear to require the legal representative's fee to be calculated only by reference to damages 'ultimately recovered' by the client (reg.1), whilst at the same time requiring the solicitor to give credit for any between the parties costs (profit costs or counsel's fees) which are 'paid or payable' to the client (reg.4). In other words, the legal representative bears the risk of the opponent's solvency, having to give credit for between the parties costs payable, even if not received, whilst only being able to charge the client his percentage fee where damages are actually received.

- The Regulations do not contain any provisions for payment on termination of the agreement. There appears to be nothing preventing the agreement providing that, if the client instructs another firm and subsequently wins the claim, the 'payment' under the agreement will be payable in full. However, the restriction on permitting any other form of 'payment' appears to prevent the rendering of a partial charge, on an hourly rate basis or otherwise, if the client simply 'walks away' or if the firm feels obliged to cease acting.

The limiting effect of these matters is enhanced by the continuing treatment of DBAs and CFAs in litigation as islands of legality whereby, if the requirements of s.58AA and s.58 respectively are not fully complied with, the agreement is unenforceable. In conjunction with the continued application of the indemnity principle this exposes the solicitor to a risk that if the DBA departs

---

[27] *http://www.judiciary.gov.uk/related-offices-and-bodies/advisory-bodies/cjc/working-parties/civil-justice-council-cjc-to-look-at-damages-based-agreements-revisions/* [Accessed January 29, 2015].

[28] *http://www.litigationfutures.com/news/jackson-outlines-two-pronged-strategy-promote-dbas* [Accessed January 29, 2015].

in any material fashion from the strictures of the Regulations, the agreement will be unenforceable and no payment at all will be permitted.

It is not clear to what extent these restrictions were intended (though it now seems clear that the continued non permissibility of hybrid DBAs, at least, is intentional). However, the combined effect of all of these factors has resulted in very limited use of DBAs.

Future Amendment

As mentioned above, the Civil Justice Council Working Group has been asked to look at a number of technical issues. These are:

2–18

- dividing into two sets the existing regulations with employment tribunal regulations (as per the 2010 regime) separated from regulations for civil litigation proceedings;
- changing the regulations so that defendants will be able to use DBAs, by widening the application of the regulations where the party receives a specified financial benefit (rather than restricting them to receiving a payment);
- reviewing whether the regulations should contain provisions on terminating the DBA;
- clarifying that different forms of litigation funding cannot be used during a case when a DBA is being used to fund litigation; and
- clarifying that the lawyer's payment can only come from damages, and the payment should be a percentage of the sum ultimately received (not awarded or agreed).

Of these, the first appears sensible, but of little practical effect. Second and third appear to offer some scope for the wider use of DBAs. However, the fourth and fifth appear to serve to emphasise some of the existing restrictions. It remains to be seen if this new form of funding will be used in other than a very limited number of cases.

Questions and answers

Q1. Is it possible to assign pre LASPO Conditional Fee Agreement and to retain between the parties recoverability of success fees?

This is a complex question and the answer is uncertain. The case of *Jenkins*[29]   2–19
offers some support for the argument that a CFA is capable of assignment, but is High Court appellate authority only, was decided on its own peculiar facts and may not be followed or might be capable of being distinguished in future cases. If *Jenkins* is correct, then the assignment of a CFA is at least possible in principle.

If an assignment of a CFA can validly take place then following the principle of the effect of an assignment, the existing agreement continues and accordingly there would appear to be a good argument that the assigned agreement should be regarded as being the same CFA and therefore the same 'pre-commencement funding arrangement' for the purposes of CPR 48.2 and/

---

[29]   *Jenkins v Young Brothers Transport Ltd* [2006] EWHC 151 (QB).

or s.44(6) of LASPO. However, even if the assignment is valid, there are public policy arguments which might lead a court to conclude that the agreement should not be so regarded.

These are complex issues and there will be no certainty unless and until they are resolved in an authoritative judgment.

Care needs to be taken when considering such assignments. In particular, with personal injury CFAs, if a pre LASPO CFA 'assignment' was held not to be valid, there would be an argument that there were two CFAs, a pre LASPO CFA and a post LASPO CFA, on the same terms—namely the terms of the original agreement. However, standard pre LASPO CFA terms for a personal injury CFA would not comply with the requirements for the capping of a success fee under s.58(4) of the 1990 Act and the CFA Order 2013 and it might be argued that the 'new' CFA on the 'old' terms was therefore unenforceable. This could result in all costs (and not just the success fee) under the new CFA being irrecoverable both against the client and, by virtue of the indemnity principle, between the parties.

Q2. What is the effect on recoverability of the success fee of assigning a pre-April 2013 CFA post-April 2013?

2–20 The general question of assignment is addressed in the previous question. Subject to that answer, if the assignment is effective there would appear to be a strong argument that the CFA remains a pre-commencement funding arrangement and the success fee remains recoverable in principle between the parties.

Q3. Is it possible to vary a pre-April 2013 CFA and still recover the success fee?

2–21 In principle, this seems possible. A variation does not change the date of the original agreement. However, in practice it may depend on the variation. If the variation was seen in some way to offend the broad principle against the inter parte recoverability of additional liabilities incurred after April 1, 2013 then there would be a substantial risk of it being disallowed. To take an extreme example, if the pre-April CFA had provided for a 5 per cent success fee, but was varied after the April 1, 2013 to include a 100 per cent success fee on a retrospective basis, the court might well disallow the success fee, though it could probably do so (subject to the facts) on the simple basis that even if the success fee was recoverable in principle, the increase was unreasonable on a between the parties basis.

Variation is sometimes confused with issues of construction or rectification of CFAs. Where there is some doubt as to the precise meaning of terms in a CFA, these may be resolved by reference to standard principles of construction and this simply involves identifying the true terms of the original agreement. This would have no effect on the recoverability of any success fee under the CFA. Similarly, where it can be established that the written terms do not properly record the true intention of the parties, it may be possible for the CFA to be rectified. Again, rectification is not variation—it is simply ensuring that the written document properly records the true agreed terms, and would probably not effect the recoverability of any success fee. Variation may not always be the only solution to perceived problems with a pre-April 2013 CFA.

Q4. My client instructed me prior to April 1, 2013, but I was not able to offer a CFA until later. Is it possible to backdate the CFA to the date of first instruction?
The first point is that the use of the term 'backdating' is dangerous and has **2–22** been the subject of judicial criticism. It suggests some form of deception and that the date on the written document does not reflect the date on which it was entered into. This should never happen. If an agreement is intended to have retrospective effect, it should expressly state the date on which it was entered into and expressly state the earlier date from which it is said to apply.

As to applying a CFA retrospectively so that it can benefit from pre LASPO principles of recoverability, this would not seem possible. S.44(6) of LASPO provides that the amendments do not apply if the relevant CFA was 'entered into' prior to 1st April 2013. Here, the agreement would be entered into after that date, but with retrospective effect. There seems no contractual reason why the agreement would not have retrospective effect, but it would not turn the CFA into a pre LASPO CFA and the success fee would be irrecoverable.

Q5. My client entered into a CFA prior to April 1, 2013, but has now died. I wish to offer the personal representatives a CFA to continue the claim. Will I be able to recover the success fee?
It is a moot point whether the original CFA is automatically assigned to the **2–23** personal representatives on the death of the client. Certain contracts are so assigned by operation of law on death (unless the contract provides otherwise). However, personal contracts are generally an exception to this and it is arguable whether a CFA falls into this category.

Equally, there is no reason in principle why the CFA should not expressly provide for the consequences on death of the client, including for its continuation. There is nothing preventing the (now) deceased making contractual provision to bind his personal representatives on his death, though such provision is rare in CFAs.

In addition, it was very common in CFAs, particularly personal injury CFAs, for the CFA to expressly provide that the agreement ended on the death of the client. The Law Society standard model prior to April 2013, expressly so provided. If such a CFA was used, then there is no need to consider whether it is arguable in law that the CFA persists, because the issue has been expressly addressed in the CFA and it does not.

In summary, therefore, there are certain circumstances, depending on the terms of the original CFA and how it is categorised by a court, where there may be arguments that the original CFA may continue in some way, though this could only be determined by reference to the specific terms of the CFA. If the CFA is a standard Law Society model (or one of the many variants based thereon) or if these specific circumstances do not apply, then any new CFA is likely to be seen to be a post LASPO CFA and accordingly the success fee will be irrecoverable.

Q6. Is a pre-April 2013 ATE policy premium still recoverable if the policy holder changes solicitors post-April 2013? Should the policy be 'assigned' to the new firm?

2–24   An ATE policy is a contract between the claimant and the insurer. Provided the policy is not voided or terminated by virtue of the change of solicitor (and this is often the case, particularly with policies issues by the solicitor under delegated authority) then in principle the policy remains in place and, as a pre-April 2013, the premium charged for it remains recoverable in principle between the parties.

There should be no question of 'assignment' of the policy to the new firm. Neither the new firm nor the old are likely to be parties to the contract of insurance.

Q7. If a staged premium ATE policy was incepted prior to April 1, 2013, but the further staged premiums are only incurred after that date, will the further premiums be recoverable?

2–25   Probably. Staged premiums were a common feature of litigation and their use had been expressly approved by the courts in cases such as *Rogers v Merthyr Tydfil BC*.[30] Their existence and use was well known at the time of the amendment of the rules and it would have been simple for the rule to provide that only the stages incurred prior to April 1, 2013 would be recoverable, if that had been the intention. Instead, s.58C of the 1990 Act refers to 'a policy of insurance' having been 'taken out' prior to April 1, 2013 and the taking out of a staged policy would appear to satisfy that requirement, with the effect that subsequent premiums under the policy remain recoverable in principle.

The point may be tested, however, if there has been abuse of the system with polices being incepted on a widescale basis for nominal premiums merely to get them 'on the books' prior to April 1, 2013 and then substantial premiums being later charged when the case is properly evaluated. Whether this has occurred and how the courts will approach claims for premiums in such cases remains to be seen.

Q8. Is there a long stop date whereby a party who has entered into a pre-April 2013 funding arrangement in relation to a claim must issue proceedings?

2–26   No. However, the funding arrangement must relate to the 'matter that is the subject matter of the proceedings in which the costs order is made'. Accordingly, if the claim subsequently brought is seen to relate to a different

---

[30]   *Rogers v Merthyr Tydfil BC* [2007] 1 WLR 808.

matter, then any additional liabilities will not be recoverable (and indeed there may be an issue as to what retainer in fact covers the proceedings that have been issued, with potential consequences between the parties as a result of the application of the indemnity principle and on a solicitor-client basis).

Q9. Is a notice of funding required for a Damages Based Agreement?

No. The requirements for notices of funding in (old) CPR 44 were revoked   **2–27**
with effect from April 1, 2013. They continue to apply in relation to pre-April 2013 funding arrangements (as do those relating to provision of information relating to additional liabilities on detailed assessments in CPR 47 PD 32) and should be complied with fully in respect of such arrangements (see CPR 48.1). This includes the provision under the 'old' CPR 44 PD 19.3 whereby there is a requirement to provide notice of change if the information previously provided is no longer accurate. Accordingly, if there is a change in relation to a pre-April 2013 CFA or ATE which means information provided in respect of those arrangements is no longer accurate, the opposing party should be notified accordingly.

Q10. How should the success fee be calculated in a post-April 2013 CFA?

The maximum success fee remains at 100 per cent. In setting the success fee,   **2–28**
the solicitor is entitled to have regard to those matters set out at the revoked CPR 43 PD 11.7 and 11.8. In addition, the solicitor is entitled to take into account matters such as the delay in payment under a CFA (a matter which could be used to justify the success fee on a solicitor-client basis prior to April 2013 but not on a between the parties basis). The main component of the success fee is likely to remain the risk of losing and not being paid, and in that regard the traditional 'ready reckoner' remains useful.

Ultimately, however, the issue is one of agreeing a reasonable success fee with the client in light of the terms and conditions of the CFA, the risks to which it exposes the solicitor of not being paid their base fees in whole or part, any additional financial burden placed on the solicitor, such as the arrangements for paying disbursements and the likely delay in payment overall, and the application of these matters to the facts of the case.

It is important to explain the success fee clearly and properly to the client and to ensure their informed agreement. It is vital that the client is informed that the success fee is not recoverable between the parties in any circumstances, even if the claim is won, and will remain payable by the client.

Q11. If the solicitor has entered into a pre-April 2013 CFA, but counsel's CFA with the solicitor postdates April 2013, is counsel's success fee recoverable between the parties?

It has been suggested in some quarters that this is the case. The point is proba-   **2–29**
bly arguable. However, the wording of s.44(6) refers to the between the parties recovery of a success fee under a CFA not being prevented if the agreement was entered into before April 1, 2013. It would seem to fit with the spirit and

intent of the changes and the wording of the statute (and CPR 48.2) that each agreement is looked at individually. The solicitor's success fee would be recoverable in principle, but counsel's would (probably) not be.

Q12. I wish to enter into a CFA with my client whereby in addition to the success fee being capped as required by s.58 of the Courts & Legal Services Act 1990 and the CFA Order 2013, the total costs payable under the agreement will also be capped as a percentage of the damage. I have been told that this means my agreement is a contingency fee agreement, or DBA, and must comply with the DBA Regulations 2013. Is this correct?

2–30   No, it would appear not. As a matter of pure terminology, any agreement where the payment depends on the outcome of the case is probably strictly a form of contingency fee agreement. However, that loose term has been replaced by the specific terminology used in s.58 and s.58AA.

A CFA whereby the fees payable under the CFA are not calculated by reference to the damages awarded, but whereby there is an overall cap on the amount that can be paid by reference to the damages is a CFA. It is not a DBA. The key distinction is that the cap is precisely that. If the fees payable are less than the cap, then the fees payable are those fees, as calculated. The cap merely operates as an overall limit, rather than as the method of calculation of the fees.

A DBA, by contrast, is an agreement where the fee payable is determined as a percentage of the damages recovered. It is not a cap, but rather the primary method of determination of the applicable fee.

Prior to the introduction of recoverable success fees, the Law Society model CFA used to provide for a cap on the success fee payable under the CFA. The new provisions for personal injury CFAs operate on a similar model. The agreements remain CFAs and this principle applies even if the capping effect is extended beyond the success fee to the fees generally.

Q13. What is the effect on the success fee where a CFA relating to a group claim was entered into before April 1, 2013, but some of the claimants were added after that date?

2–31   The answer to this is unclear. The transitional provisions in relation to the recoverability of success fees in s.44 of LASPO are statutory provisions and do not admit of a discretion (indeed, their express effect is to remove any discretion to allow a success fee in respect of cases covered by s.44).

Accordingly, and despite the possible temptation to do so, a court managing a GLO probably cannot simply exercise a discretion to decide how to treat such a situation but is limited to considering the particular CFA and how it interacts with the provisions of s.44(6).

Section 44(6) appears to require the court to look not merely at the date of the CFA but at whether the CFA was entered into for the purposes of providing services to a specific person in relation to the subject matter of the claim or, if not entered into for a specific person (for example, a CCFA), whether services were provided, before April 1, 2013, to the specific person in whose favour the costs order has been made.

The CCFA analogy appears the most apt here and there must be a substantial likelihood that the later joining claimants will be held not to be able to recover the success fee in respect of their claims. This may involve some question of a pro rata division of any success fee payable on common costs. The quid pro quo would be that the later joining claimants would benefit from QOCS (if it is a personal injury claim).

However, alternative approaches are possible and it is conceivable, given that the potential claimants in a GLO could be seen as being a limited and identifiable class of persons, that a court might conclude that the test under CPR 44.6(a) was satisfied in respect of all claimants when the CFA was first entered into and accordingly a success fee is recoverable in respect of all claimants.

The precise outcome will be heavily affected by the terms of the CFA, the precise circumstances of the case, the terms of any related documentation, such as costs sharing agreements, and the court's approach to the interpretation of s.44(6), which at present is uncertain.

CHAPTER 3

Proportionality

Introduction

The terms of reference for the costs review conducted by Jackson LJ[1] were "to make recommendations in order to promote access to justice at proportionate cost". The need for change was acknowledged in the foreword to the final report, which stated:

"In some areas of civil litigation costs are disproportionate and impede access to justice. I therefore propose a coherent package of interlocking reforms, designed to control costs and promote access to justice."

Inevitably, therefore, proportionality lies at the core of the package of reforms—it permeates into every aspect of the civil litigation process. The overriding objective has been amended to include specific reference to proportionality, costs and case management are determined by it and any assessment of costs is subject to it. Almost two years on from the April 2013 amendments to the Civil Procedure Rules, proportionality still provokes more debate, more controversy and more concern than any other aspect of the reforms. What does it mean, when does it arise, and what impact does it have on litigation?

Proportionality—the concept

Proportionality is not a new concept. Whilst the amended overriding objective[2] refers to "dealing with a case . . . at proportionate cost", the previous version, from introduction in 1999, defined "dealing with a case justly" by reference, amongst other things, to proportionate cost. However, in reality, prior to April 2013, proportionality only had a retrospective role at the conclusion of a case, at the time of the assessment of costs. Where it was suggested that the costs claimed were disproportionate, the Court of Appeal required the assessing judge to determine that issue at the outset of the assessment adopting the *Home Office v Lownds*[3] two-stage approach:

"In other words what is required is a two-stage approach. There has to be a global approach and an item by item approach. The global approach will indicate whether the total sum claimed is or appears to be disproportionate having particular regard to the considerations which Part 44.5(3) states are relevant. If the costs as a whole are not disproportionate according to that test then all that is

3–01

3–02

---

[1]   Review of Civil Litigation Costs: Final Report, December 2009.
[2]   CPR 1.1: "These Rules are a new procedural code with the overriding objective of enabling the court to deal with cases justly and at proportionate cost".
[3]   *Home Office v Lownds* [2002] EWCA Civ 365.

normally required is that each item should have been reasonably incurred and the cost for that item should be reasonable. If on the other hand the costs as a whole appear disproportionate then the court will want to be satisfied that the work in relation to each item was necessary and, if necessary, that the cost of the item is reasonable."

Immediately it is apparent that this approach does not genuinely meet the requirement of dealing with a case at proportionate cost. Even if the first stage of *Lownds* resulted in a finding that the costs were disproportionate, the court could not change the way it had dealt with the case procedurally. Instead all it could do was to reduce the amount of costs recoverable between the parties. Even this retrospective ability to reduce the recoverable costs did not lead to proportionality in its purest sense, as there was no certainty that necessarily incurred costs were proportionate—in essence the imposition of the 'necessarily incurred' test seemed more a sanction for incurring disproportionate costs than any genuine attempt to reduce the costs to a level that was proportionate. Indeed, in giving his judgment in *Lownds*, Lord Woolf had hinted at the purists' position on proportionality when commenting:

"If, because of lack of planning or due to other causes, the global costs are disproportionately high, then the requirement that the costs should be proportionate means that no more should be payable than would have been payable if the litigation had been conducted in a proportionate manner."

Something more was needed to ensure that cases are managed so that no more is spent as the case progresses than is proportionate.

Proportionality—what does it mean and when does it arise?

3–03   The 2013 reforms seek to provide that 'something more' by requiring the court to:
- deal with each case "at proportionate cost" (CPR 1.1(1));
- ensure that every case management decision is made taking account of the costs involved in each procedural step (CPR 3.17);
- set costs budgets that are proportionate (CPR 3 PD E 7.3);
- determine whether or not to grant relief from sanction by giving particular weight to the need for litigation to be conducted at proportionate cost (CPR 3.9); and
- undertake assessments of costs on the basis that only proportionate costs will be awarded, even if that means reasonably or necessarily incurred costs are disallowed. CPR 44.3(2) signals the demise of the *Lownds* test at assessment, reversing the timetable for consideration of proportionality. The court will assess those costs that are reasonably incurred and reasonable in amount and, having done so, step back and determine if the resultant figure is proportionate. If it is not, then the court will reduce the costs to the sum it determines is the proportionate figure.

Of course, the court can only fulfil the functions set out above by reference to the proportionate costs for a claim. How does it determine that sum? The simple answer is by reference to CPR 44.3(5), which contains the definition of proportionate costs as follows:

> *"Costs incurred are proportionate if they bear a reasonable relationship to:*
> *(a) the sums in issue in the proceedings;*
> *(b) the value of any non monetary relief in issue in the proceedings;*
> *(c) the complexity of the litigation;*
> *(d) any additional work generated by the conduct of the paying party; and*
> *(e) any wider factors involved in the proceedings, such as reputation or public importance."*

Accordingly, the court must identify which of the factors listed in CPR 44.3(5) are relevant to any case and, having done so, relate that to a costs figure. It is this step that many critics of the new approach see as unsatisfactory. They view the process as an entirely unscientific one—as the factors do not readily equal a sum in pounds and pence. The simple answer from those proponents of the process is that there is no 'absolute' answer, but, as with many exercises of judicial discretion, there is a range of answers and, provided the discretion has been exercised properly, none within that range are wrong. This is nothing new. Indeed, if different judges were asked to assess the same bill of costs at the conclusion of a claim, the likelihood is that there would be as many different figures as there were judges assessing the bill, but, again on the proviso that those judges had properly exercised their discretion, none of the assessments would be 'wrong'.

It is for this reason that in the 15th Implementation Lecture on May 29,   **3–04**
2012 the Master of the Rolls Lord Neuberger stressed the case-sensitive nature of proportionality and anticipated little case law on the topic:

> *"While the change in culture should reduce the scope of costs assessments at the conclusion of proceedings, it will not obviate the need for a robust approach to such assessments. Again the decision as to whether an item was proportionately incurred is case-sensitive, and there may be a period of slight uncertainty as the case law is developed.*
> *That is why I have not dealt with what precisely constitutes proportionality and how it is to be assessed. It would be positively dangerous for me to seek to give any sort of specific or detailed guidance in a lecture before the new rule has come into force and been applied. Any question relating to proportionality and any question relating to costs is each very case-sensitive, and when the two questions come together, that is all the more true. The law on proportionate costs will have to be developed on a case by case basis. This may mean a degree of satellite litigation while the courts work out the law, but we should be ready for that, and I hope it will involve relatively few cases."*

It is hard to see what further guidance is either necessary or likely other than in extremely general terms. Unnecessary because the very flexibility of the definition makes it hard to think of any case where relevant features impacting on costs do not fall to be taken into account within one of the five factors. Unlikely because each case is fact sensitive, the ambit of judicial discretion is broad and any decision falling outside the parameters would only define proportionality in a very broad sense in that specific case. Beyond that, any comments will be of a general nature, e.g. in *CIP Properties (AIPT) Ltd v Galliford Try Infrastructure Ltd*[4] where Coulson J commented that:

> "*Costs budgets are generally regarded as a good idea and a useful case management tool. The pilot schemes (including the one here in the TCC) have worked well. They are not automatically required in cases worth over £2 million or £10 million, principally because the higher the value of the claim, the less likely it is that issues of proportionality will be important or even relevant. A claimant's budget of £5 million might well be disproportionate to a claim valued at £9 million, but such a level of costs is probably not disproportionate to a claim worth £50 million.*"[5]

Those seeking certainty are, in effect, wishing for something akin to a form of fixed fee regime for all cases. Given the variety of claims it is almost inevitable that any regime of fixed fees would be set with a very broad brush. Be careful for what you wish.

Proportionality—the effect on litigation

3–05   For a more detailed consideration of the effect on litigation see **Chapter 4— Case and Costs Management**. In essence, though, proportionality will arise at all stages of a case, as any case management decision engages the overriding objective, which now includes the obligation to deal with a case at proportionate costs, regardless of any additional burdens imposed by specific provisions. This applies to all claims, regardless of track and regardless of value where there is no fixed cost regime in place. The court, and the parties, should have proportionality in mind whether they are dealing with the lowest value small claim or the highest value multi track.

The discretion offered by the flexible definition of proportionality means that it can be adapted to meet the diverse considerations of all claims, which is just as well as, despite Jackson LJ's recommendation, fixed fees have yet to be introduced for non personal injury fast track claims. Indeed Jackson LJ regards this as a serious omission because the CPR 44.3(5) was not designed as a mechanism to control costs in the fast track. Without fixed fees and costs management in fast track a significant emphasis in fast track claims remains on proportionality after the costs have been spent under CPR 44.3(2) at assessment.

---

[4]   *Properties (AIPT) Ltd v Galliford Try Infrastructure Ltd* [2014] EWHC 3546 (TCC).
[5]   The reference to £2 million and £10 million being to the respective versions of CPR 3.12 in place from April 1, 2013 and April 22, 2014.

Questions and answers

Q1. Is there any distinction between proportionality and reasonableness in reality?

The answer, as an exercise of semantic interpretation of the CPR, is yes, because   3–06
throughout the CPR the two are referred to separately—see for example CPR 3PDE.7.3 which requires the court to approve budgets for phases that are *"reasonable and proportionate"* and CPR 44.3(2) which clearly draws a distinction between the two. Indeed it is the latter provision that makes it clear that some costs may be reasonable, but not proportionate.

In practice, there will be cases where the court, having assessed the reasonable costs, then applies the CPR 44.3(5) factors to the proportionality cross check under CPR 44.3(2) and determines that those costs are <u>also</u> proportionate—indeed the court's assessment of proportionality might be at a higher figure than the reasonable costs for a variety of reasons (e.g. because of limits imposed by the contractual retainer). There will also be cases where the same cross-check reveals the reasonable costs are still disproportionate. Perhaps the better answer, therefore, is, not necessarily so.

Q2. Is there not a risk that similar claims will have different outcomes because of the determination by separate case managing judges of what is proportionate in a particular case?

Yes—there is such a risk. The determination of proportionality will dictate what   3–07
case management directions are given. Different determinations will lead to different directions, e.g. permission for an expert in one case and not in another. However, that does not mean that the judges are necessarily 'wrong', simply that one has exercised discretion in another way from the other. Of course, that happens, and legitimately so, regardless of proportionality, on a daily basis in all courts—not just on procedural matters, but on factual disputes of a similar nature. Whilst there is judicial discretion there will be instances where there are a number of outcomes—none of which are 'wrong'. This question ought to be linked, however, with consideration of whether the risk is justified as an attempt to curb disproportionate costs and to promote access to justice. It is too early to say whether the drive to introduce proportionality will achieve this aim.

However, it is surely unarguable that a system that provides transparency of the 'recoverable costs' at large at an early stage will focus the attention of the parties and enable them to make decisions and give their legal representatives instructions on a more informed basis as to how they wish a claim pursued or defended, than a system where they find out the exact extent of the other party/parties' costs only when they are ordered to pay them and find out the shortfall between their legal fees and the exact amount of those that they may recover from the other party at assessment, after the costs have been spent.

Q3. Is proportionality a 'fixed sum' throughout the life of a claim?

This depends entirely on the specific features of any claim, e.g. an assess-   3–08
ment of proportionality is made at the costs management stage in a claim

where two heads of loss are pursued, each with a considerable value. After disclosure it becomes apparent that one head of loss is unsustainable and the claimant discontinues that part of the claim. At that stage plainly the sum in issue has altered. In those circumstances there has been a significant development for the purposes of CPR 3 PD E 7.6 and we would expect the parties either to agree revised budgets or, in the absence of agreement, to seek the approval of the court to revised budgets on the basis that what was proportionate for the claim as originally presented is not for the claim that then remains. In other words, the proportionality of a claim may alter throughout its course.

However, this does not mean that as a matter of routine the court will revisit earlier decisions on proportionality. Many saw the decision to grant permission to appeal in *Troy Foods v Manton*[6] as opening the door to revisiting proportionality in costs managed cases at subsequent assessment. This interpretation overlooks some important points as follows:

- This was simply a decision on whether or not to permit an appeal. As such it is not a binding authority.
- The case was under the pilot scheme at what was CPR 51 PD G. At para.4.2 of the practice direction, the objective of costs management was said to be "to control the costs of litigation in accordance with the overriding objective". The overriding objective was in its pre-April 2013 form without specific reference to dealing with a case at proportionate costs. Whilst para.1.3 of the Practice Direction makes a reference to proportionate costs it does so in the context of the relevance of costs already incurred. Nowhere in the Practice Direction does it state that the court is expressly charged with setting the budget by reference to proportionality.
- The costs managing judge appeared to have applied a test of approving the budget "provided it was not so unreasonable as to render it obviously excessive or, as he put it, 'grossly disproportionate'". Accordingly, permission was given on the basis that it was arguable the judge had applied the wrong test and been overgenerous as a result.
- When setting a budget under the costs management provisions of CPR 3 and 3 PD E, the court is required to budget phases by reference to what is 'reasonable and <u>proportionate</u>'. In other words, the court has assessed the proportionality of any phases budgeted already.
- CPR 3.18 could not be clearer—on a standard basis assessment the court will not depart from the last approved or agreed budget for each phase of the proceedings unless it is satisfied that there is 'good reason' to do so. To do otherwise would be to adopt no more than an inappropriate appellate function.

Accordingly, unless there is 'good reason' to depart from the last budget, the court will not revisit the proportionality determination of any phase of the claim that has been budgeted (see **Chapter 4** for consideration of 'good reason'

---

[6]   *Troy Foods v Manton* [2013] EWCA Civ 546.

in this context). Indeed, were the reverse to be correct, then the purpose of costs management would be defeated.

Q4. If there is no 'good reason' to depart from the budget on assessment, how does the court apply the proportionality 'cross check' under CPR 44.3(2) at the end of the assessment?

At the end of the assessment the court will have determined the reasonably incurred and reasonable in amount of non budgeted costs (i.e. those incurred before the costs management order) and these must then be added to the budgeted sum. The proportionality cross check is then applied, <u>but</u> on the basis that this cannot reduce the overall costs to less than the budgeted sum, for, as is set out above, those costs were subject to a determination of proportionality at the time the budget was set and the wording of CPR 3.18 precludes departure from this sum. Accordingly, if the total of the assessed costs is not proportionate, then the court must reduce the costs to a level that is proportionate, but that cannot be less than the budgeted costs. For example, if the total of the budget for the phases budgeted, whether by agreement between the parties, approval of the court or a combination of both, is £50,000 (and there is no 'good reason' to depart from this) and the total for the assessed non budgeted costs is £30,000, but the court determines that the combined sum of £80,000 is disproportionate, then the proportionate figure that the court assesses under CPR 44.3(2) is somewhere between £50,000 to £80,000. It cannot be less than £50,000.

3–09

Q5. How do the transitional provisions relate to proportionality at assessment?

Three possible scenarios arise—two of which are straightforward and the other presents some practical difficulties.

3–10

CPR 44.3(7) makes it clear that the 'new' proportionality provisions—namely the new definition of proportionality at 44.3(5) and the cross check at 44.3(2)—do not apply to:

- a case at all where it was commenced before April 1, 2013; and
- those bits of work done on a case prior to April 1, 2013, where the case was issued after March 31, 2013.

This transitional provision leads to three scenarios as follows:

1) In cases issued before April 1, 2013, *Lownds* still applies and if proportionality is challenged at assessment it must be dealt with at the outset, by reference to what were the 'seven pillars of wisdom' at 44.5(3) and which are now the first seven of eight 'pillars' at 44.4(3). The outcome will be that the costs are either assessed against a necessarily or reasonably incurred test.

2) In cases which are issued after March 31, 2013 and <u>no</u> work is done on that case prior to that date, then the new provisions apply to all the costs.

3) In cases where the claim is issued after March 31, 2013, but <u>some</u> work is done before that date, the *Lownds* approach must be adopted in respect

of the work done prior to April 1, 2013 and the new test to all the work after March 31, 2013.

It is the last of the three scenarios above that presents challenges. Parties seeking assessment of costs, whether by summary or detailed assessment, will need to ensure that the costs pre and post April 1, 2013 are clearly separated (this is likely to mean two Forms N260 or separate parts in a bill)—experience suggests that this is not being done for assessments, whether summary or detailed. The risks then are that:

- It is not proportionate to adjourn off the summary assessment to another date or for written submissions and the court may be forced to do the best it can on the information available. This may result in the court concluding that if a party has not troubled to separate out the two periods, the sanction (and proportionate way forward) is to assess all the costs under the new test.
- The court does adjourn and demands a re-drawn bill, but does not permit any recovery of costs for so doing.

If there are separate Forms N260 or separate parts of the bill, the court's function is invidious. It must do one proportionality determination at the beginning (for the pre April 1, 2013 costs) and one at then end (for the post March 31, 2013 costs). However, both exercises are artificial, because the court cannot aggregate the costs of both parts to do the exercise under each discrete test. To do otherwise would be to ignore the clear language of CPR 44.3(7). Instead the court will have to identify the work undertaken in each period and apply the relevant test to determine the proportionality of that work.

Q6. Does the court look at the sums reasonably claimed or the sums recovered when determining 'the sums in issue in the proceedings' under CPR 44.3(5)(a)?

3–11   Obviously at the time that proportionality is considered for the purposes of budget setting and case management, the court does not know what sums will ultimately be recovered. At that stage the determination must be based on what is claimed. If there is an argument, namely that the claim is exaggerated, then all that does is confirm that the sums claimed are in issue.

At the conclusion of the claim the court will know what sum was recovered. The fact that the sum may be less than was claimed does not, of itself, necessarily alter the determination of proportionality. The fact that one sum was claimed and one was recovered does not mean that the original sum was not in issue. However, this does assume that it was reasonable to pursue the claim as stated.

If, for example, it emerges that the claim was exaggerated, but the claimant still obtains an award of some costs, then in cases costs managed, this may well be a 'good reason' to depart from the budget as that will have been set on a basis that the claimant knew was wrong. In non budgeted cases conduct can be considered when assessing the reasonable costs under CPR 44.4 and the 'real' value is likely to apply on the proportionality 'cross check'.

In contrast, if the claimant recovers a lower sum than that claimed, but it was reasonable to pursue the higher sum, e.g. if there was a complicated causation argument where the defendant's expert evidence was preferred or where the case turned on a factual dispute and the court preferred the evidence of the defendant's witnesses, then it is likely that will not alter 'the sums in issue' for the purpose of proportionality and so will not represent a 'good reason' to depart from the budget in costs managed cases and will not influence proportionality in non budgeted cases.

In practice, in both scenarios the limited recovery is likely to sound in the award of costs itself, with something less than a full costs order being made under CPR 44.2(4)(b) and 44.2(6). The court must be astute to avoid 'double jeopardy', although as is clear from *Drew v Whitbread*[7] conduct may be considered both on the award and the assessment of costs.

Q7. Why is only the conduct of the paying party included in the definition?
This question really arises at two stages—at case/costs management and 3–12 at assessment. It is important, though, when considering the question to remember the full wording of this factor. It is not conduct generally, which falls to be considered, but only conduct of the paying party which generates additional work.

At the case/costs management stage
At the costs management stage the rationale is that the past conduct of 3–13 the parties (for at this stage it is not clear who will be the receiving and who the paying party) is not relevant. This is because the court can only budget the costs "to be incurred". As such, the court can control conduct going forward by proportionate costs and case management. In other words, the court's directions should preclude the possibility of conduct generating additional work. The court sets and manages the progression of the case. If a party persists in conduct that is likely to generate additional work, then the other party may always apply under CPR 3 PD E 7.6 to vary the budget as a result of that conduct or seek discrete costs sanctions on any applications that arise outside the budget under CPR 3 PD E 7.9, relying on the stark warnings given by the Court of Appeal about non co-operation in *Denton v T H White*,[8] which resonate beyond the specific scenario which was under consideration:

> *"The court will be more ready in the future to penalise opportunism. The duty of care owed by a legal representative to his client takes account of the fact that litigants are required to help the court to further the overriding objective."*[9]

In any event, CPR 3 PD E 7.4 requires the court to take incurred costs into account when considering the reasonableness and proportionality of the costs

---

[7] *Drew v Whitbread* [2010] EWCA Civ 53.
[8] *Denton v T H White* [2014] EWCA Civ 906.
[9] para.43.

to be budgeted. So, if unreasonable and/or disproportionate costs have been incurred by a party as a result of its conduct up to costs management, it may find its budget going forward suffers as a result.

At the assessment stage

3–14   The reason that the conduct of the receiving party does not form part of the definition at assessment seems more complicated. Whilst it is likely that such conduct will already have been taken into account by the court when making the award of costs—see CPR 44.2(4)(a)—that is by no means certain as it may not always be obvious at that stage whether certain conduct has generated additional costs. However, conduct is also taken into account at the assessment—see CPR 44.4(3). Both these provisions, though, relate to the conduct of <u>the parties</u>. So if the argument is that conduct has already been considered, then that ought also to apply to the conduct of the paying party.

The explanation may be that it is difficult to imagine a situation where any additional costs of the receiving party generated by the conduct of that party survive the test of whether they are reasonably incurred or reasonable in amount and, as such, have already been disallowed out by the time that the court does the proportionality cross check. In contrast, the receiving party's additional costs caused by the paying party's conduct will survive the test of whether they were reasonably incurred and reasonable. If the court does not remind itself that these reasonably incurred and reasonable in amount costs include those extra costs, there is a danger that the overall sum is deemed disproportionate and the paying party escapes the consequences of its actions.

Q8. If the effect of CPR 44.3(2) is that the sum to be allowed on an assessment is that which is proportionate, why does the court trouble first with undertaking an assessment of what is reasonably incurred and reasonable in amount?

3–15   There are a number of reasons why the court must first assess the reasonable sum. These are:

- Because that is what the combined effect of CPR 44.4(1)(a) and 44.3(2) require of the court.
- The effect of the indemnity principle. The increasing use of fixed fee solicitor and client retainers and pressure on hourly rates means that there may well be cases where the proportionate sum exceeds the reasonable sum. However, to proceed straight to the proportionality assessment would lead to the assessment of a sum that exceeds the permitted recovery under the retainer. Linked to the point above is that it is also not sufficient in such a situation to say that as the costs claimed are less than the proportionate sum, they then should be allowed in full. This is because, as said above, proportionality does not necessarily equal reasonableness. The court must be satisfied under CPR 44.4(1)(a) that the costs are <u>both</u> proportionate <u>and</u> reasonable. There may still be items of costs that were unreasonably incurred or unreasonable in amount even if the overall sum is proportionate. Those

items should not be allowed, even if that means the eventual sum assessed is reduced still further from what may be the proportionate sum. In these cases proportionality acts as a cap and not as fixed costs.
- That, as seen under **Q7** above, the question of the conduct of the parties demands an assessment of what is reasonable by looking at items where it is said that this has generated additional costs. It is only the assessment of reasonableness that introduces the conduct of the receiving party and informs the court as to whether the conduct of the paying party sounds in the proportionality determination.

Q9. Is proportionality to be applied in all cases, or, as some wish to suggest, is it really for the small to medium value claims, where disproportionate costs are more likely?

Whilst costs management is limited to those claims specifically referred to in CPR 3.12, and any other claims where the court orders it, this does not limit the all encompassing relevance of proportionality. It is part of the overriding objective and, as such, all case management decisions must be made against the obligation on the court to deal with cases at proportionate cost. This is reinforced by CPR 3.17, which provides that:

3–16

> *"When making any case management decision, the court . . . will take into account the costs in each procedural step."*

Even in those cases where the filing of Form H is required and the court chooses not to make a costs management order, the rules on the relevance of that budget at assessment have been strengthened. CPR 44 PD 3.6 and 3.7 reiterate and expand previous provisions. They enable the assessing court, where there is a difference of 20 per cent or more between the costs claimed and those shown in a budget, to:
- Restrict the recoverable costs where reliance has been placed on the budget by the paying party to what is reasonable <u>even if</u> that results in a sum less than that which would otherwise be proportionate and reasonable.
- Regard the difference between the costs claimed and those in the budget as evidence that the costs claimed are unreasonable or disproportionate, even where no reliance on the budget is established.

Expect the court to be more robust in applying these provisions, than it was before April 1, 2013.

Proportionality also has a role to play in non fixed fee fast track and small claims track cases. Indeed, cases that might previously have been allocated to multi track (e.g. because the time estimate for trial exceeded one day) may now be allocated to fast track with directions targeted to reduce the time estimate to one day and cases that are over the small claim track limit may now be allocated to that track as the consent of the parties to this is no longer required. In both these tracks, directions will be targeted to ensure that the cases are dealt with proportionately (and that includes the amount of court time that they occupy).

Q10. What relevance, if any, does proportionality have in cases where an order for costs is made on the indemnity basis?

3–17 Proportionality is still relevant before the costs order is made, as the court will have case managed on a proportionate basis. Where the order for indemnity costs has significance is on the assessment of the amount of costs. When conducting an assessment on the indemnity basis under CPR 44.4(1)(b), the court must decide whether costs were unreasonably incurred or unreasonable in amount—it is not required to consider proportionality. Albeit that the rule number may have changed (from CPR 44.4(3)) this does not alter the provision in place before April 2013. However, where the change in outcome is marked is in cases where a costs management order has been made. This is because CPR 3.18, which provides that the court will not depart from the last approved or agreed budget at assessment unless there is 'good reason', expressly only applies to cases where the court is assessing costs on the 'standard basis'.

Whilst Coulson J in *Elvanite Full Circle Ltd v AMEC Earth & Environment*[10] suggested that even where there was an order for indemnity costs, the budget should be the starting point, it must be remembered that he was considering a budget prepared under CPR 51 PD G. The budget form (Form HB) did not require any certification suggesting that the budget was constrained in any way by proportionality—in other words it was probably a fair reflection of all the costs that the client was likely to incur and so represented an approximation of indemnity costs. Now the budget does require a certification linking the sums included to those that are proportionate as is set out in CPR 22 PD 2.2A:

> *"This budget is a fair and accurate statement of incurred and estimated costs which it would be reasonable and <u>proportionate</u> for my client to incur in this litigation."*[11]

As a result the link between the budget sum and indemnity costs relied upon by Coulson J is no more. If there was still any vestige of doubt, that has been dispelled by the Court of Appeal in the judgment of Dyson MR and Vos LJ in *Denton v T H White*.[12] The relevant section of the judgment was considering sanctions in costs for non co-operation between the parties. It dealt with indemnity costs as a possibility and said this:

> *"If the offending party ultimately loses, then its conduct may be a good reason to order it to pay indemnity costs. Such an order would free the winning party from the operation of CPR rule 3.18 in relation to its costs budget."*

It is clear from this that there is a greater benefit to a receiving party of an order for indemnity costs than was the case before the 2013 reforms. However, the

---

[10] *Elvanite Full Circle Ltd v AMEC Earth & Environment* [2013] EWHC 1643.
[11] para.43.
[12] *Denton v T H White* [2014] EWCA Civ 906.

test for whether or not an order for indemnity costs is merited has not altered. However, as Akenhead J observed in *Courtwell Properties Limited v Greencore PF (UK) Limited*,[13] where a party entitled to an automatic standard basis costs order under Part 36 sought an order for indemnity costs instead:

" ... *parties must act in a proportionate way ... Where the indemnity costs application depends on evidence which is likely to involve material conflicts of evidence, the applicant party needs to think long and hard about whether it is appropriate to pursue the application.*"

Q11. Is the effect of proportionality that in a case about money, the costs cannot exceed the sums in dispute?

Before April 1, 2013, there was an acceptance within the CPR that there were **3–18** cases where the proportionate cost would exceed the sum in issue. Section 11 of the then Costs Practice Direction expressed it in these terms:

"*11.1 In applying the test of proportionality the court will have regard to rule 1.1(2)(c). The relationship between the total of the costs incurred and the financial value of the claim may not be a reliable guide. A fixed percentage cannot be applied in all cases to the value of the claim in order to ascertain whether or not the costs are proportionate.*
11.2 In any proceedings there will be costs which will inevitably be incurred and which are necessary for the successful conduct of the case. Solicitors are not required to conduct litigation at rates which are uneconomic. Thus in a modest claim the proportion of costs is likely to be higher than in a large claim and may even equal or possibly exceed the amount in dispute."

What is immediately clear is that 11.2 accords precedence to 'necessary' costs. Work that was necessary informed the assessment of proportionality. This is no longer the situation, for CPR 44.3(2) expressly gives primacy to proportionality, even if that means that necessary costs (and by implication necessary work) are not recoverable. This does no more than codify the comments at Ch.3 para.5.10 of Jackson LJ's Final Report[14] under the bold heading 'Costs do not become proportionate because they were necessary'.

Does this mean that costs can never exceed the amount in dispute? The answer must surely be no, but not because a certain amount of work is necessary in any given claim, but, instead, because CPR 44.3(5) does not limit the relationship between proportionality and costs solely to the amount in issue. If there are other relevant factors then those inform the determination of the proportionate sum. This, again, illustrates the flexibility of the definition that enables it to apply to all circumstances. The Final Report concluded, when making the recommendation for the new definition of proportionality, that:

[13] *Courtwell Properties Limited v Greencore PF (UK) Limited* [2014] EWHC 184 (TCC).
[14] Review of Civil Litigation Costs: Final Report, December 2009.

> *"Proportionality of costs is not simply a matter of comparing the sum in issue with the amount of costs incurred, important though that comparison is. It is also necessary to evaluate any non-monetary remedies sought and any rights which are in issue, in order to compare the overall value of what is at stake in the action with the costs of resolution."*[15]

However, where the only relevant factor under CPR 44.3(5) is the sum in issue, it is difficult to envisage a court determining that it is proportionate for the parties to spend more than this sum in determining the dispute.

---

[15]   Ch.3 para.5.5.

CHAPTER 4

Case and Costs Management

Introduction

Although the title of this chapter suggests that case and costs management   **4–01**
are two separate exercises, in reality they are two sides of the same coin. As
Jackson LJ commented in his Final Report:

> *"First, case management and costs management go hand in hand. It does not
> make sense for the court to manage a case without regard to the costs which it
> is ordering the parties to incur. The Rubicon was crossed on 26th April 1999,
> when the court assumed under the CPR wide powers and responsibilities for case
> management."*[1]

The April 2013 amendments to the CPR inextricably linked both in CPR
3.12(2) when defining the purpose of costs management as being "that the
court should manage both the steps to be taken and the costs to be incurred
by the parties to any proceedings". CPR 3.17 strengthens the link between
the two by requiring the court to have regard to any available budgets and to
take account of costs when making any case management decision. In fact, it
may be artificial to talk of both case and costs management as, in those cases
where costs management orders are standard (see below), the latter is simply
part of the former.

In this chapter we shall consider the procedural changes made to the existing case management provisions of the CPR and the costs management rules
that were introduced in April 2013 separately, and then illustrate how they
combine in a seamless practical application.

In his Final Report Jackson LJ asked if costs management was worth the
candle. He answered the question in the affirmative giving two reasons in
support of that answer. The first is set out above. The other reason was:

> *"Secondly, I am in full agreement with the Law Society's view that costs manage-
> ment, if done properly, will save substantially more costs than it generates."*[2]

It is clear that the changes made to case management cannot work in isolation and 'proper' costs management is essential to the success of the reforms.

The changes made to the existing CPR case management provisions

The principal procedural change that affects and informs all case manage-   **4–02**
ment decisions (and informs costs management decisions) is the change to

---

[1]   Review of Civil Litigation Costs: Final Report, December 2009, Ch.40 para.7.1.
[2]   Review of Civil Litigation Costs: Final Report, December 2009, Ch.40 para.7.1.

the overriding objective at CPR 1.1 to introduce the obligation to deal with a case "at proportionate cost". All the other changes are designed to achieve this objective. These are:

1. Enforcing stricter compliance with court orders, rules and practice directions (both in CPR 1.1(2)(f) and 3.9).
2. Replacing allocation questionnaires with directions questionnaires designed to provide more relevant case information (CPR 26.3).
3. A greater discretion to the court when determining the track to which to allocate claims and an increase to the small claims limit (CPR 26.6(3) and the removal of what was CPR Pts 26.7(3), 27.14(5) and (6)).
4. The encouragement to use standardised directions to ensure consistency and facilitate the production of orders (CPR 29.1(2)).
5. More targeted disclosure provisions (CPR 31.5(3–8)).
6. More prescriptive powers in respect of witness statements (CPR 32.2(3)).
7. The provision of more information about any expert evidence proposed (CPR 35.4).
8. The option to hear the oral evidence of experts concurrently (CPR 35 PD 11).
9. Increasing the incentive for claimants to make realistic settlement proposals (CPR 36.14(3)(d) which will become CPR 36.17(4)(d) from April 6, 2015).
10. The introduction of costs management (CPR 3.12–3.18 and CPR 3 PD E).

1. Enforcing stricter compliance with court orders, rules and practice directions (both in CPR 1.1(2)(f) and 3.9)

4–03 In the Final Report, Jackson LJ identified the change of culture that was required, commenting:

> "First, the courts should set realistic timetables for cases and not impossibly tough timetables in order to give an impression of firmness. Secondly, courts at all levels have become too tolerant of delays and non-compliance with orders. In so doing they have lost sight of the damage which the culture of delay and non-compliance is inflicting upon the civil justice system. The balance therefore needs to be redressed."[3]

In the pre-April 2013 case of *Fred Perry (Holdings) Ltd v Brands Plaza Trading Ltd*,[4] the Court of Appeal gave an indication of the imminent alteration of emphasis, leaving no doubt that a wind of change was blowing:

> "The Rule Committee has recently approved a proposal that the present rule 3.9(1) be deleted ... It is currently anticipated that this revised rule will come into force on 1st April 2013. After that date litigants who substantially disregard court

---

[3] Review of Civil Litigation Costs: Final Report, December 2009, Ch.39 para.6.5.
[4] *Fred Perry (Holdings) Ltd v Brands Plaza Trading Ltd* [2012] EWCA Civ 224.

orders or the requirements of the Civil Procedure Rules will receive significantly less indulgence than hitherto."[5]

Whether the warnings went unheeded or whether some practitioners failed to appreciate quite how much less indulgence was to be afforded by the court is unclear, but from November 2013, and the decision in *Mitchell v News Group Newspapers Ltd*,[6] until July 2014, and the clarification provided in *Denton v T H White*[7] the court reverberated to the sounds of applications for relief from sanctions and the disappointed cries of those whose applications were dismissed. *Denton* has clarified that the court should approach these applications in three stages: **4-04**

- **Stage 1** requires an evaluation of the breach. The Court of Appeal made it clear that this must be looked at in isolation—concentrate solely on the seriousness and significance of this breach. If there have been other failures/misconduct by the defaulting party, those must be ignored at this stage, but may merit consideration at stage 3. The court then moves on to stages 2 and 3. If it has concluded that there is not a serious or significant breach, then stages 2 and 3 may not occupy much court time, but if there has been a serious or significant breach then the final 2 stages take on a greater importance.
- **Stage 2** involves consideration of whether there was good reason for the breach. The Court of Appeal declined to produce an 'encyclopaedia' of what might constitute 'good reason'. This will be fact specific. However, *Mitchell* at para.41 sets out some examples.
- **Stage 3** At this stage the court considers "all the circumstances of the case", but, remembering that the two factors specifically mentioned in CPR 3.9 carry 'particular weight' (although Jackson LJ dissented, on the basis that the two factors were mentioned to draw attention to them, but that they carried no weight above any others). It is worth noting that the Court of Appeal specifically drew attention to the fact that the importance of complying with rules, practice directions and orders had received insufficient emphasis in the past stating:

"The court must always bear in mind the need for compliance with rules, practice directions and orders, because the old lax culture of non-compliance is no longer tolerated."

It is clear from the extract above that those who think that the position has reverted to what it was on March 31, 2013 remain due for an unpleasant shock. If further evidence of a shift towards compliance was required, it was provided in *HRH Prince Abdulaziz Bin Mishal Bin Abdulaziz Al Saud v Apex Global Management Ltd*,[8] where the Supreme Court, whilst at pains to reiterate **4-05**

---

[5] Jackson LJ, para.4.
[6] *Mitchell v News Group Newspapers Ltd* [2013] EWCA Civ 1537.
[7] *Denton v T H White* [2014] EWCA Civ 906.
[8] *HRH Prince Abdulaziz Bin Mishal Bin Abdulaziz Al Saud v Apex Global Management Ltd* [2014] UKSC 64.

that generally case management and CPR was the domain of the Court of Appeal, confirmed that:

> "*The importance of litigants obeying orders of court is self-evident. Once a court order is disobeyed, the imposition of a sanction is almost always inevitable if court orders are to continue to enjoy the respect which they ought to have . . . One of the important aims of the changes embodied in the Civil Procedure Rules and, more recently, following Sir Rupert Jackson's report on costs, was to ensure that procedural orders reflected not only the interests of the litigation concerned, but also the interests of the efficient administration of justice more generally.*"[9]

So, whilst the change may not be as dramatic as *Mitchell* suggested, relief will still be granted more sparingly than previously.

Hand in hand in *Denton* with guidance on relief was:

i) an entreaty by the Court of Appeal (coupled with costs threats if ignored) for parties to co- operate and not use court rules as technical trip wires. This links to the amendment made to CPR 3.8 in April 2014 to add a provision at 3.8(4) enabling parties to agree extensions to the period for compliance with orders, rules and practice directions that specify the consequences of a failure to comply, provided that this does not jeopardise any hearing; and

ii) a reminder to members of the judiciary to ensure that "the direc- tions that they give are realistic and achievable". The Court of Appeal acknowledged that it was of no use to set a timescale so tight that it was obvious that it could not be met, stressing that "the court must have regard to the realities of litigation in making orders in the first place". This harks back to the extract from Jackson LJ's Final Report quoted above, in which he stressed that the court should set realistic timeta- bles for cases and not impossibly tough timetables in order to give an impression of firmness (see above and the Final Report Ch.39 para.6.5).

2. Replacing allocation questionnaires with directions questionnaires designed to provide more relevant case information (CPR 26.3)

4–06   Directions questionnaires should assist the court with determining proportion- ate case management decisions. More information is required about proposed expert evidence and, unless there is a valid explanation for being unable to do so, expect the court to police the requirement to provide details of witnesses <u>and</u> the issue(s) to which their evidence will be addressed. Questionnaires that suggest that this information is 'to be advised' are likely to receive short shrift and their authors may find themselves the recipients of orders, includ- ing 'unless orders' to provide the information or a satisfactory explanation of why it cannot be provided or face the consequences (e.g. being unable to rely upon any witness evidence).

---

[9]   paras 23–25.

3. A greater discretion to the court when determining the track to which to allocate claims and an increase to the small claims limit (CPR 1.1 and 26.6(3) and the removal of what was CPR Parts 26.7(3), 27.14(5) and (6))

The court must take account of proportionality when allocating. Accordingly   **4–07**
those claims that might previously have been allocated to the multi track simply because of time estimate (e.g. where the value is within fast track limits, but there are a number of witnesses) are now likely to be allocated to fast track with a restriction on the evidence that may be adduced to ensure the claim is disposed of within a day. Similarly the omission of CPR Part 26.7(3), which prevented a court allocating a claim to the small claims track if the value exceeded the limit for that track without the agreement of all parties, seems designed to enable the court to allocate more claims to the limited 'fixed fee on issue' regime of that track.

This aim is bolstered by the removal of previous provisions (CPR 27.14(5) and (6)), which enabled parties agreeing to allocation to the small claims track to include an agreement that fast track costs would still apply and that any appeal would carry the costs consequences as if it had been a fast track claim. These provisions are no more and so whether a claim with a fast track value is allocated to the small claims track with or without the consent of the parties, the limited small claims track costs allowances prevail.

At the same time the proportion of claims proceeding in the small claims track has been increased as the financial scope of that track has been doubled to £10,000 (save for personal injury and housing disrepair claims that remain unaltered at £1,000).

4. The encouragement to use standardised directions to ensure consistency and facilitate the production of orders (CPR 29.1(2))

The proliferation of different forms of directions up and down the country   **4–08**
was identified by Jackson LJ as a source of unnecessary cost. If the same form of order is used in all courts, then the parties can use them as a starting point when discussing proposed directions as they will not be confronted by 'local' variations, there will be consistency of orders produced, less risk that a direction will be overlooked or that a direction will be phrased ambiguously (not to be underestimated given the potential sanction for non compliance) and the final order will be easier for the court to generate. Accordingly he recommended that:

> " . . . a menu of standard paragraphs for case management directions should be
> prepared for each type of case of common occurrence and made available to all
> district judges both in hard copy and online. These standard directions should
> then be used by district judges as their starting point in formulating initial case
> management directions."[10]

---

[10] Ch.39 para 5.3.

CPR 29.1(2) was introduced to achieve this by linking to a raft of standard orders. However, the uptake appears to have been distinctly lukewarm. The directions are under review, but in the meantime, some courts are insisting that draft directions are filed adopting the standard template orders and others are not. It is hard to see how practitioners can be faulted by the court if they use the standard orders under CPR 29.1(2) as the provision does state that these *'should'* be taken as the starting point.

5. More targeted disclosure provisions (CPR 31.5(3–8))

4–09 In the 7th Implementation Lecture,[11] Jackson LJ referred to the costs of the disclosure process in these terms:

> *"Even in medium sized actions where all the documents are in paper form, disclosure can be a major exercise which generates disproportionate costs."*

The resultant attempt to curb the costs of this phase of litigation can be found at CPR 31.5. This introduces the 'disclosure report' (Form N263), which is designed to facilitate discussion between the parties as to the appropriate disclosure order prior to the first case management conference and to inform the court, in general terms, of the types of documents involved, by whom and where they are held, how electronic documents are stored, the costs of 'standard disclosure' and what disclosure order is suggested. CPR 31.5(7) then sets out a menu of possible disclosure options. It is no surprise that other than a catch-all provision, 'standard disclosure' is listed as the last of the disclosure options. The pre-amble to the menu stresses that the court will decide which option to order 'having regard to the overriding objective and the need to limit disclosure to that which is necessary to deal with case justly'. The reference to the overriding objective plainly imposes the requirement for proportionality.

CPR 31.5(1) and (2) combine to exclude personal injury claims from the new provisions. Standard disclosure remains the 'norm' in these claims, but with a residual discretion to the court to order otherwise.

The 7th Implementation Lecture left little doubt as to the importance of the new disclosure provisions:

> *"The order made at the first CMC concerning disclosure will have a profound impact on the future course of the case and also upon the final costs of the litigation. Therefore this issue merits careful thought and analysis when the parties initially and the court ultimately are making their selection from the menu of possible disclosure orders."*

Notwithstanding the exhortation to select from the menu after careful thought and analysis, anecdotal evidence suggests that 'standard disclosure' is the type most generally suggested in the N263, perhaps unsurprisingly, as the requirement to cost this form of disclosure, steers parties towards it. Even if standard disclosure is to remain more routinely used than had

---

[11] 7th Implementation Lecture: Controlling the Costs of Disclosure, November 24, 2011.

been envisaged under the reforms, the definition of standard disclosure that appears at CPR 31.6 merits repetition as it is far narrower than many appear to think:

> *"31.6 Standard disclosure requires a party to disclose only —*
> *(a) the documents on which he relies; and*
> *(b) the documents which —*
> > *(i)   adversely affect his own case;*
> > *(ii)   adversely affect another party's case; or*
> > *(iii)   support another party's case; and*
> *(c) the documents which he is required to disclose by a relevant practice direction"*

Tales of trial judges inundated with bundles based on 'standard disclosure' from which they are taken to only a few pages may be apocryphal, but do not be surprised if some judges add to an order for standard disclosure "as defined by CPR 31.6".

6.   More prescriptive powers in respect of witness statements (CPR 32.2(3))

The court has always had the power to control evidence under CPR 32.1.   **4–10** However, the specific reference in CPR 32.2(3) to the ability of the court to give directions identifying and limiting the issues upon which factual evidence is to be given, identifying specific witnesses and limiting the length and format of statements, gives the court the ability to case manage factual evidence in a proportionate way.

An early illustration of the use of this provision was in *MacLennan v Morgan Sindall (Infrastructure) Plc*.[12] The court was concerned with a significant claim for loss of earnings in a severe brain injury claim. This element of loss raised four broad issues upon which the claimant wished to call 43 witnesses. The defendant sought an order under CPR 32.2(3) limiting the number to 8. In the end the court made an order restricting the number of witnesses to 28 and identifying those issues with which the witnesses would deal.

7.   The provision of more information about any expert evidence proposed (CPR 35.4)

It is curious that almost two years after the introduction of CPR 35.4, parties   **4–11** are still completing directions questionnaires and attending subsequent case management conferences, indicating that they require expert evidence without details of the expert, the issues that the expert will address and the likely cost of the expert. Curious because:

- This information is a pre-requisite to the court giving permission for expert evidence. CPR 35.4(2) makes the provision of this information

---

[12]   *MacLennan v Morgan Sindall (Infrastructure) Plc* [2013] EWHC 4044 (QB) Green J.

> mandatory (qualified to the extent that the name is required where reasonably practicable) when applying for permission to rely upon expert evidence in any type of claim.
> - Notwithstanding the failure to provide this information, some parties still feel able to complete the costs budget providing details of what the reasonable and proportionate expenditure on the expert phase will be—inserting figures for the expert—at a stage when the expert has not even been identified and the extent of that expert's remit not determined.

There is a real risk that if this information is not available, the court will simply not give permission. This means that in those cases that are costs managed, they will be costs managed without provision for permission for that/those expert(s) whom the party in default seeks to rely upon, with inevitable implications on the expert phase of the budget. If the party in default sees the way the wind is blowing and does not pursue the application for permission at the case management conference, but instead, seeks to rely on a subsequent free standing application, it is likely to confront difficulties as the rectification of a previous failure is unlikely to be viewed as a 'significant development' for the purpose of budget variation under CPR 3 PD E 7.6. Even if the court were minded to entertain the subsequent application and permit the expert evidence, this would mean consequential recasting of the directions and variations of costs budgets at considerable expense. It is not difficult to envisage what the costs order in respect of that additional expenditure would be!

8. The option to hear the oral evidence of experts concurrently (CPR 35 PD 11)

4–12   CPR 35 PD 11 provides the court with the option of taking expert evidence concurrently and sets out, subject to judicial discretion to alter the process, the procedure to adopt. In reality though, the process is inevitably case and judge specific.

There was a pilot run in the Manchester 'Construction and Technology' and 'Mercantile' Courts. The feedback from that was limited, inevitably due to the small number of cases involved prior to the pilot report. However, there seemed to be a consensus that in the right case utilising this option could save court time and facilitate the evidential process. There has yet to emerge any authority that sheds light on the potentially challenging issue of ensuring that the parties feel they have had a sufficient opportunity to advance the expert evidence that they wish in this format. Albeit in a different scenario (that of experts and site inspections), the case of *Hatton v Connew*[13] is a timely reminder of the need for the court to take expert evidence in an appropriate fashion which is fair to the parties.

---

[13]   *Hatton v Connew* [2013] EWCA Civ 1560.

9. *Increasing the incentive for claimants to make realistic settlement proposals (CPR 36.14(3)(d)) (which from April 6, 2015 will be CPR 36.17(4)(d))*

Giving the lead judgment in *Fox v Foundation Piling Ltd*,[14] Jackson LJ high-lighted one of the major reasons that cases that ought to resolve without the expense of a trial failed so to do:

4–13

> *"A not uncommon scenario is that both parties turn out to have been over-optimistic in their Part 36 offers. The claimant recovers more than the defendant has previously offered to pay, but less than the claimant has previously offered to accept."*[15]

Therefore, it was not a surprise that CPR Pt 36 was amended to increase the incentive for the parties to adopt more realistic valuations to encourage earlier settlement. That amendment comes in the form of CPR 36.14(3)(d) (from April 6, 2015 CPR 36.17(4)(d)). If a claimant makes a relevant Part 36 offer, then in addition to the 'established' consequences (an entitlement to indemnity costs and increased interest on both the substantive award and the costs), there will be an award of an additional amount, unless the court thinks it unjust to make such an award. The additional amount is 10 per cent of the damages awarded up to £500,000 and that sum plus 5 per cent of the damages awarded that are over £500,000 and up to £1,000,000, with a cap on the additional amount of £75,000. This wording left the surely unintended consequence that an award of over £1,000,000 attracts no 'additional amount'. Amendments to CPR 36 coming into force later this year (April 6, 2015) will, amongst other matters, remove this anomaly and simply provide for 10 per cent of damages up to £500,000, with a further 5 per cent for damages over £500,000 with a cap of £75,000. In other words, anyone awarded over £1 million is entitled to an additional amount capped at £75,000.

Part 36 is considered in more detail in **Chapter 5**.

10. *The introduction of costs management (CPR 3.12–3.18 and CPR 3 PD E).*

In the Final Report, Jackson LJ described costs management in these terms:

4–14

> *"(i) The parties prepare and exchange litigation budgets or (as the case proceeds amended budgets).*
> *(ii) The court states the extent to which those budgets are approved.*
> *(iii) So far as possible, the court manages the case so that it proceeds within the approved budgets.*
> *(iv) At the end of the litigation, the recoverable costs of the winning party are assessed in accordance with the approved budget."*[16]

---

[14] *Fox v Foundation Piling Ltd* [2011] EWCA Civ 790.
[15] para.46.
[16] Review of Civil Litigation Costs: Final Report, December 2009, Ch.40 para.1.4.

In essence these four characteristics form the basis of the regime introduced at CPR 3.12–3.18 and at CPR 3 PD E. However, the implementation and regulation of costs management has proven, and is proving, more challenging than the simple assertion of the regime's principles. To facilitate the understanding and practical application of the regime, it is simplest to approach it under the following five headings:

A.   Which cases are subject to costs management?
B.   What procedural requirements are imposed on the parties in respect of costs management?
C.   How does the court 'costs manage'?
D.   Variation of budgets
E.   The effect of a costs management order on subsequent assessment

A. Which cases are subject to costs management?

4–15   Although costs management is less than two years old, there has already been substantial revision of the rules regulating which types of cases are covered by the regime. The current provisions relate to those cases issued after April 22, 2014. In summary, the regime applies to:

*   All CPR Part 7 where the amount claimed or the limit in the statement of value is less than £10,000,000 (CPR 3.12 (1)(a) and (b)).
*   Any other proceedings (including applications) where the court so orders (CPR 3.12(1A)). CPR 3 PD E 2–5 'Other cases' sets out both the procedure that will apply where costs management is proposed by either the court of its own motion or the parties in cases not otherwise within the scheme and the types of case that are particularly suitable (the types of case are set out in CPR 3 PD E 5(a)–(f)).

If the initial form of CPR 3.15 was deemed less than prescriptive as to when the court should costs manage, the current version leaves little room for doubt. The court <u>will</u> make a costs management order in cases where a costs budget has been filed and served unless it can be satisfied that the litigation can be conducted justly and at proportionate costs in accordance with the overriding objective without such an order being made. Given that the court cannot make this assessment until it has seen the budgets, it is hard to imagine why the court will not always be making costs management orders, because either the budgets are plainly disproportionate immediately triggering court concern or they are obviously proportionate in which case, to ensure that they stay that way, and as it will take no time to do, it seems prudent that the court would make a costs management order in the terms of those parts of the Form H that it is permitted to budget. Whilst there remains an 'opt out' for the court in CPR 3.12(1)(c), this is surely a provision to be used sparingly, otherwise it risks undermining the regime and may result in both forum shopping (for those keen to avoid budgeting) and the suggestion of 'local practice directions'. To that extent, agreements between the parties to avoid the costs management regime will need to be well reasoned to survive the rigorous consideration that they merit.

However, litigants in person are exempted from the obligation to file and exchange costs budgets (CPR 3 P DE 7.8), although they must be served with the budget of any other represented party and clearly are entitled to make representations about the budget at any costs management hearing.

B. What procedural requirements are imposed on the parties in respect of costs management?

In general terms the parties in receipt of a notice of provisional allocation   **4–16** to the multi track should exchange and file a budget in Form H by the date stated in that notice (CPR 26.3(1)). In cases where no date is specified in the notice, then Form H must be exchanged and filed seven days before the first case management conference or, if the case is one not automatically subject to costs management under CPR 3.12, the budget must be exchanged and filed by any date specified by the court. Failure to comply results in the automatic sanction under CPR 3.14, namely that the defaulting party is treated as having filed a budget comprising only applicable court fees. The effect of this for any party subject to a costs management order on this basis is that only future court fees may be budgeted, but costs incurred at the time of the order are still recoverable, subject to assessment, as a costs management order only relates to "the costs to be incurred" (CPR 3.15).

The budget must be in the form of precedent H attached to CPR 3 PD E. There have been two cases already that seek to test the prescription of this requirement. In *The Bank of Ireland v Philip Pank Partnership*[17] the claimant failed to include the full wording of the statement of truth, although the budget was signed and dated by the legal representative. The court found that this omission did not render the budget a nullity and as such, the claimant had complied with the requirement to file and exchange its budget. Instead the Form H was simply subject to an irregularity. In the second case, *Americhem Europe Limited v Rakem Limited*,[18] the same judge found that the failure to have a budget signed by a senior legal representative (it was signed by a costs draftsman) also did not render a budget a nullity, again amounting to no more than an irregularity. The judge, having noted that this was the second occasion when he had to deal with a mere irregularity in budget form, took the opportunity to cite from the judgment of Leggatt J in *Summit Navigation Ltd v Genrali Romania Asigurare*[19] as follows:

> *"But, as the Master of the Rolls emphasised . . . it is not the aim of the reforms to turn rules and compliance into 'trip wires' . . . "*

If the court makes a costs management order then CPR 3 PD E 7.7 requires a party to re-file and re-serve the budget in the form approved by the court. In fact some courts are budgeting electronically using the first page of the

---

[17]   *The Bank of Ireland v Philip Pank Partnership* [2014] EWHC 284 (TCC) Stuart-Smith J.
[18]   *Americhem Europe Linited v Rakem Limited* [2014] EWHC 1881 (TCC) Stuart-Smith J.
[19]   *Summit Navigation Ltd v Genrali Romania Asigurare* [2014] EWHC 398 (Comm) Leggatt J.

budget in a self calculating form, so that the budget recalculates as the hearing progresses. In those cases the courts are simply attaching the first page of each budget as costs managed to the directions order and dispensing with the requirement at 3 PD E 7.7, saving the time and resource of re-filing and re-serving.

4–17 The preparation of the Form H itself is assisted by a guidance note on what work to insert in which phases within the form. The guidance is brief, some would say too brief, but, in general terms, it does identify the allocation of work within Form H. All costs incurred, even those pre-action, that are attributable to a phase of the budget should be inserted in the 'incurred' columns in the specific phase and all work to be incurred should be inserted in the 'estimated' columns in the specific phases.

One obvious lacuna in the guidance relates to work that has already commenced, such as on an interim application, which by definition is not contingent, but which does not fit neatly into any of the phases, e.g. applications for interim payments, security for costs, etc. Remembering that the budget should inform the other parties and the court, there is a danger that the exercise becomes one of form over substance. So long as this work is clearly identified, and the budget attributes incurred and estimated expenditure transparently, does it really matter if it is included as a contingency even though it is already a reality?

The guidance also contains the occasional oddity:

- Under the Case Management Conference ("CMC") phase the suggestion is that any subsequent CMC should not be included in this phase. This begs two obvious questions—why have an 'estimated' column for this phase and where does any budget for a subsequent CMC ordered by the court fit in the budget? Anecdotally, it seems that some courts are budgeting for the cost of a later CMC in the 'estimated' columns of Form H. Certainly this provides ready clarity when the budget comes to be examined against expenditure later.

- Why is specific disclosure excluded from the disclosure phase when it is one of the types of disclosure order mentioned in the menu of orders at CPR 31.5(7)? The answer, presumably, is that the guidance form pre-dated the change to CPR 31.5(7). However, this seems unhelpful when the court is encouraging parties to move away from the default position of standard disclosure. As Jackson LJ saw disclosure as one of the most expensive phases of litigation, it makes no sense that if the guidance is followed when the court makes an order under CPR 31.5(7)(b), it does not budget the costs. If, as with non party disclosure, this is deemed a contingent cost, this too appears illogical. This is because CPR 31.5(7)(b) envisages a request for specific disclosure being made with disclosure of a party's own list. Accordingly, the time between case management order and compliance with the disclosure order is minimal. The notion that at the CMC this might be only a contingency is not credible. However, even if it is a contingency the court must budget it, so uncertainty over the proportionate expenditure cannot be the reason for it being excluded· from the phase. As the court has to budget it anyway, why not do it within the phase within which it most naturally arises—namely disclosure? Another option is to regard specific disclosure as so uncertain as to fall within CPR 3 PD E 7.9. However, it is hard to argue that something is uncertain when it is what the court is ordering to take place. The final option is to treat any subsequent request for specific disclosure as a 'significant development in the litigation' justifying a budget variation. Again, it is difficult to see the occurrence of something the court has ordered as a 'significant development'.

- Why is mediation (which is a form of ADR) specifically excluded from the ADR/Settlement phase and is to be included as a contingency? One answer may be so that the court can readily identify the costs attributable for this discrete form of ADR. However, if that is the case, this would sit more happily as a named phase rather than as a contingency.
- Why is there reference to 'paragraph 4.7' in paragraph 3 of the guidance? This is a legacy of the pilot schemes for which the guidance was originally prepared. It would be helpful if the guidance specifically referred here to CPR 3 PD E 7.6 (variation) and 7.9 (interim applications not reasonably included within the budget).
- The PTR phase refers to "preparation of updated costs budgets and reviewing opponent's budget". However, budgets only need to be updated once set by the court in the event of 'significant developments in the litigation' under CPR 3 PD E 7.6.

C. How does the court 'costs manage'?
The only provisions in respect of the form of the budgeting exercise itself are in CPR 3.12, 3.15 and 3 PD E 7.3 and 7.4. These provide that: **4–18**

- The court cannot budget costs already incurred. In fact, CPR 3 P DE 7.4 seems to countenance a situation where costs incurred between the date of the budget and the date of the costs management hearing may be budgeted. However, both CPR 3.12 and 3.15 use the words 'costs to be incurred'. As the rule takes precedence over the practice direction, only future costs may be budgeted. If there is significant delay between the preparation of the budget and the costs management hearing, parties may consider filing and exchanging updated budgets and making an application to be heard at the costs management for permission to rely on the updated budgets at that hearing. However, in this situation the court is likely to expect to see the same figure in the grand total on p.1 as in the earlier budget—for all that has changed is the passage of time means that some costs that were estimated in the future have now been incurred and so the incurred costs have gone up, <u>but</u> by the same amount as the estimated costs have gone down. Any other alteration is hard to justify simply on the basis of the delay between first budget and hearing.
- When undertaking the budgeting exercise, the court is only charged with

setting a total sum which is reasonable and proportionate for each phase of the proceedings. The court is expressly not required to do a detailed assessment and, whilst it 'may have regard to the constituent elements of each total figure', it is not compelled to do so. In other words, the court simply sets one figure per phase for the future costs of that phase.

- The parties may agree budgets or discrete phases of the budgets. If they do this, then the court either makes a costs management order in respect of these costs recording the extent of the agreement or elects not to make a costs management order. Some see this as a curious provision. Whilst parties are to be encouraged to co-operate and narrow issues, the apparent inability of the court to interfere with agreement of what it may see as disproportionate costs seems an odd fetter in the pursuit of proportionality. If the court manages the case on a different basis from that upon which the parties have based their agreement of budget, then the court will expect the parties to revisit the budgets (as the basis upon which agreement has been reached has been altered). If, however, the case management directions are in line with those upon which agreement of budgets was reached, then the court either makes a costs management order on the basis of the agreement or makes no costs management order. Remember that costs (and costs liabilities to another party) are those of the client. Any agreement of all or part of a budget requires client approval, which is why access to the client during, or very specific instructions from the client before, a costs management hearing is essential.

In other words the precise mechanics of costs management are not prescribed. However, it is imperative that the exercise itself does not become disproportionate. The adoption of the broad brush of setting one total sum per phase as required under CPR 3 PD E 7.3 combined with the avoidance of arguments that are of the type routinely raised at the assessment stage, seems to meet this requirement, both in respect of the proportionality of the exercise for the parties and for the court in allocating its resources between cases.

D. Variation of budgets

4–19   There is an apparent tension between CPR 3.15(3), which requires the court to control the parties' budgets once a costs management order has been made, and CPR 3 PD E 7.6, which suggests that where there is a significant development in the litigation that necessitates a variation to the budget, the parties should seek to agree this between themselves and only involve the court if agreement is not possible.

What is clear is that the budget may only be varied if there is a significant development in the litigation. Perhaps the dissipation of the tension lies here. It is hard to imagine a 'significant development' that does not require consequential case management. If further case management directions are proportionate, then inevitably, budgets will have to be re-visited and it is no surprise that the parties are encouraged to agree these. Of course, the court may take the view, informed by the revised budgets, that the directions sought are disproportionate and refuse them and the budget variation that accompanied them.

CPR 3 PD E 7.6 envisages both downward and upward budget revision. Examples of the former may be where a claimant discontinues part of a claim or where a defendant withdraws part of a defence and of the latter where a final prognosis in a personal injury claim provides a bleaker outlook than expected with a significant increase in future loss and the evidence in support of this. Clearly all of these are significant developments and respectively should result in lesser or increased costs being expended. A failure to seek a variation in respect of additional costs means that a receiving party has to rely upon 'good reason' to depart from the budget at any subsequent standard basis assessment. A cross application of *Mitchell* suggests that an oversight is unlikely to be a 'good reason'. If a party fails to vary downwards when it should there is no obvious 'sanction'. However, plainly if costs have to be assessed simply because a party has failed to vary downwards when it ought to have done that raises issues in respect of the costs of the assessment under CPR 47.20(3).

CPR 3 PD E 7.9 makes it clear that discrete applications that were reasonably not included in the budget shall be treated as additional to the budgets. In such cases, the court will make an award of costs and, if that is for one party to pay the costs of another, undertake a summary assessment and order payment in the usual way (subject to any consideration of qualified one way costs shifting or indemnity issues deferring an immediate entitlement to costs) with this having no impact on the budget. If the order is for 'costs in case', then these costs fall outside the budget at any subsequent assessment once an award of the costs of the case is made.

E. The effect of a costs management order on subsequent assessment

CPR 3.18 clearly sets out that on a standard basis assessment, the court will not depart from the last approved or agreed budget for each phase without 'good reason'. Accordingly:

    4–20

- This provision applies to summary and detailed assessments.
- Unless there is 'good reason', the budgeted costs will be assessed as budgeted and any assessment will focus on the non-budgeted costs. What constitutes 'good reason'? There is no guidance in the rules. The only assistance so far comes from the comments made by the Court of Appeal in *Mitchell* (see above), in the context of CPR 3.9 and the earlier comments of Moore-Bick LJ in *Henry v News Group Newspapers Ltd*,[20] a case within the defamation pilot. The former suggests that 'good reason' will present a challenge to those trying to show it. The latter steers towards the same conclusion:

    " . . . *although the court will still have the power to depart from the approved or agreed budget if it satisfied that there is 'good reason' to do so . . . I should expect*

---

[20] *Henry v News Group Newspapers Ltd* [2013] EWCA Civ 19.

it to place particular emphasis on the function of the budget as imposing a limit on recoverable costs."[21]

The provision does not apply to costs assessed on the indemnity basis. There was initially some suggestion within the pilot schemes that the budgets still formed the starting point for an assessment on the indemnity basis (see *Elvanite Full Circle Ltd v Amec Earth & Environmental (UK) Ltd*,[22] which advanced this proposition and *Kellie v Wheatley & Lloyd Architects Ltd*[23] which disagreed with that approach). This is not the position as proportionality has no place in an indemnity basis assessment and budgets have been produced and set by specific reference to proportionality. Any doubt was resolved by the Court of Appeal in *Denton v T H White*.[24] When referring to the consequence of an indemnity-based costs order, the Master of the Rolls described it as follows:

> *"If the offending party ultimately loses, then its conduct may be a good reason to order it to pay indemnity costs. Such an order would free the winning party from the operation of CPR rule 3.18 in relation to its costs budget."*[25]

The intention is plain—assessments, whether of a summary or detailed nature, will be both less time-consuming and more proportionate, because the court will be concerned only with determining the reasonableness of those costs that have not been budgeted and the overall proportionality cross check under CPR 44.3(2). An illustration of the ease of summary assessment where a budget has been set can be found in *Slick Seating Systems v Adams*,[26] where the trial judge concluded that the sum sought was within the budget for each phase, assessed in that sum and commented that detailed assessment had been rendered 'otiose'.

4–21   The fact that an order for indemnity costs sees 'escape' from the constraints of the budget is not a reason for an increase in applications for such orders. The principles surrounding when the court will make an order for indemnity costs have not altered (save by the identification in *Denton* of a specific type of conduct that might merit such an award).

However, an indemnity costs award arising under CPR 36.14 (3)(b) (CPR 36.17(4)(b) from April 6, 2015) presents unique challenges. A claimant is entitled to indemnity costs from "the date on which the relevant period expired" (relevant period is defined in CPR 36.3(c) and from April 6, 2015 becomes CPR 36.3(g)). However, this means that for some part of the litigation costs are constrained by the budget (absent 'good reason') and for another part the budget becomes irrelevant. However, the chance of the date when this transition takes place falling neatly at the end of a phase of Form H so it is clear which parts of the budget remain wholly relevant is slim (not non-existent,

---

[21]   para.28.
[22]   *Elvanite Full Circle Ltd v Amec Earth & Environmental (UK) Ltd* [2013] EWHC 1643 (TCC) Coulson J.
[23]   *Kellie v Wheatley & Lloyd Architects Ltd* [2014] EWHC 2886 (TCC) HHJ Keyser QC.
[24]   *Denton v T H White* [2014] EWCA Civ 906.
[25]   para.43 majority judgment.
[26]   *Slick Seating Systems v Adams* [2013] EWHC 1642 (QB) HHJ Simon Brown QC.

e.g. if the relevant period expired just before trial it may be possible to identify the phases clearly).

What happens in this situation where only part of the phase falls to be assessed on the standard basis? Sadly the answer is not clear (and it seems that the Civil Procedure Rules Committee is looking at this). It is arguable that as the court is not looking at a phase exclusively on the standard basis, then CPR 3.18 has no application or if it does then this is a 'good reason' to depart from the budget. However, this potentially presents a windfall to the receiving party beyond the ordinary benefit of an indemnity costs order. Even if this is the position, the court is still required to undertake an assessment in part on the standard basis and in part on the indemnity basis and the proportionality cross check pursuant to CPR 44.3(2) continues to apply to the standard basis costs. Does this mean that bills where there is a relevant CPR 36 offer will need to be split between dates as well as, within the new format bill, phases matching the Form H? At the moment questions abound and there are no clear answers.

Those accepting a CPR Pt 36 offer, but then seeking an order for costs on the indemnity basis (in order to escape from the confines of a budget) should take note of the decision in *Courtwell Properties Ltd v Greencore PF (UK) Ltd*,[27] in which Akenhead J stated:

> "*In cases where the parties have settled through the Part 36 procedure or otherwise but leave the judge to decide costs, particularly where indemnity costs are claimed, parties must act in a proportionate way. There can be few if any cases in which there should in effect be a trial of all or some of the settled issues in the case. Where the indemnity cost application depends on evidence which is likely to involve material conflicts of evidence, the applicant party needs to think long and hard about whether it is appropriate to pursue the application.*"[28]

Case and costs management in harmony

Having identified the key case management amendments and the costs management provisions, the practical link between the two becomes obvious. By requiring the court to costs manage by phases (which broadly equate to the procedural steps on the way to trial), the court is able to tailor the directions to the reasonable and proportionate cost of the respective phases. This may result in:

4–22

- Controlling the number of witnesses, the issues they may address and the length of their statements.
- Selecting the appropriate form of disclosure from the options at 31.5(7), which includes the possibility of dispensing with disclosure altogether.
- Controlling the extent of expert evidence by number, by reliance on jointly instructed experts, by specific identification of the issues upon which they may report and by the use of concurrent evidence at trial.

---

[27] *Courtwell Properties Ltd v Greencore PF (UK) Ltd* [2014] EWHC 184 (TCC) Akenhead J.
[28] para.42.

- Ongoing costs management preventing claims changing fundamentally in nature without court intervention. Any variation in the budget is linked to 'significant developments in the litigation'. It is hard to imagine any such developments that do not require further court case management directions. At such a stage the ongoing control of the parties' budgets required by CPR 3.15 and the requirement at CPR 3.17 for the court to take account of the costs in each procedural step, combine so that the court must determine the extent, if at all, to which it is prepared to permit the claim to change course.
- Limiting the trial length. In a sense one should start here, for the assessment of proportionality dictates the trial length and all other directions must then be crafted to ensure that the trial can be completed within that period. Inevitably this informs the court's decisions on the matters listed above.
- A summary rather than detailed assessment at the conclusion of the trial. In some cases the 'costs of the costs' are disproportionate. One way to avoid this is for the court to undertake more assessments on a summary basis.

What is clear from the consideration of case and costs management above is that this presents new challenges to both the judiciary and court users. All must now be astute to ensure that rules, practice directions and orders are followed and to 'cut the cloth' proportionately. For the court this may mean deciding cases on more limited evidence than might previously have been available. For the professions this, inevitably, places a far greater emphasis on compliance with timetables and the management of client expectations. For the parties they have to co-operate with timescales and temper their expectation of a case being dealt with justly to what outcome can be achieved at a proportionate cost.

Questions and answers

Q1. How prescriptive is the wording of CPR 3.12(1) and (1A)? In particular can the court costs manage cases that fall within the definition of those outside the scheme and when may the court exclude cases from the regime under CPR 3.12(1)(c)?

4–23   The wording of 3.12(1) and (1A) allows the court flexibility, both of an inclusionary and exclusionary nature.

Under CPR 3.12(1A) it may bring into the costs management regime other proceedings. Although a case involving consideration of the provisions in force from April 1, 2013 until April 22, 2014, Coulson J considered the question of extension of the regime in *CIP Properties (AIPT) Ltd v Galliford Try Infrastructure Ltd*.[29] In this case the claim was put in the region of £18,000,000— so in excess of both the £2,000,000 cut off in place until April 22, 2013 and the £10,000,000 cut off since that date. He concluded that the provision at

---

[29]   *CIP Properties (AIPT) Ltd v Galliford Try Infrastructure Ltd* [2014] EWHC 3546 (TCC) Coulson J.

CPR 3.12(1A), and in particular the reference to 'any other proceedings', did indeed extend to multi track claims worth £10,000,000 or more, stating:

> *"I take the view that the exercise of the court's discretion under CPR 3.12(1) is unfettered. There is nothing in the CPR to suggest otherwise. This discretion extends to all cases where the claim is for more than £2 million (old regime) and £10 million (new regime) There is no presumption against ordering budgets in claims over £2 million or £10 million, and no additional burden of proof on the party seeking the order."*[30]

Coulson J recognised that to have concluded otherwise would have left the court's hands tied and the system open to abuse by claimants wishing to avoid the costs management regime simply valuing their claims at £1 more than the cut off.

The fact that the regime is sufficiently flexible to permit costs management in cases not strictly within the provisions is, in any event, borne out by the express provision in CPR 3 PD E 2. This allows the court, whether on the application of a party or of its own initiative, to costs manage in those cases where the parties are not required to file budgets under CPR 3.12 and 3.13. CPR 3 PD E 5 sets out examples of cases strictly outside the regime where it may be particularly appropriate to costs manage. The fact that the £10 million limit is not a bar is reinforced by the inclusion in CPR 3 PD E 5 of personal injury and clinical negligence cases where the value exceeds that sum.

The reverse position is envisaged by CPR 3.12(1)(c), which permits the **4–24** court to disapply the regime in multi track Part 7 claims that would otherwise fall within the provisions.

If the court does not do so prior to the deadline for filing and exchanging budgets then the court must make a decision not to costs budget based on CPR 3.15(2)—namely that it is satisfied that the litigation can be conducted justly and at proportionate cost in accordance with the overriding objective without a costs management order.

Cases where the court disapplies the regime before the filing and exchange of budgets ought to be rare. The reason for this is that it is hard to see how the court can reconcile the obligation imposed on it by the overriding objective and, more specifically by CPR 3.17 (to take into account the costs of each procedural step) without any information about costs.

If the parties wish to persuade the court that a case is not suitable for costs management then they should apply <u>before</u> the expiry of the time for filing and exchanging budgets both to disapply the regime and, in the alternative, for an extension of time to file and exchange budgets until a date after the determination of the application in the event that the primary application is refused. If they do this and the court dismisses the application to disapply the costs management provisions, then the parties are dealing with an application to extend time and not an application for relief from

---

[30] para.27.

the sanction under CPR 3.14 (see consideration of *Hallam Estates v Baker*[31]in Q2 below).

Q2. Should a party file its Form H on the basis of the way in which it thinks the claim should progress, e.g. if it thinks a split trial is appropriate should the budget be completed on that basis?

4–25   CPR 3 PD E 6 is clear on this. The court may direct that budgets are limited initially to part of the proceedings and subsequently extended to cover the whole of proceedings. Accordingly, unless the court has so directed, the budget must cover the entire proceedings. This means that any party which proposes to seek costs management of part only of the proceedings has two options. The first is to file and exchange a budget of the whole proceedings and then seek a direction before the case management conference that budgets are filed and exchanged on the additional alternative basis. The second is to apply before the time expires for budgets to be filed and exchanged under CPR 3.13 for an extension of time to file budgets and for a direction that budgets should be limited initially to a discrete part of the proceedings.

The advantage of the first approach is that the party has complied with CPR 3.13 and does not face sanction under CPR 3.14. The disadvantage is that if the court agrees that the claim proceeds with budgeting of part only, then the parties may have incurred the cost of preparing two budgets instead of one.

The advantage of the second approach is that if the court agrees with it, then one or both parties may have saved the cost of preparing two budgets at this stage. The disadvantage is that whilst a prospective application will be treated as one for an extension of time and not as one involving relief from sanctions (see *Hallam Estates v Baker*[32]), in this age of robust case management, it is a brave course to adopt. However, there is no doubt that it is better than filing and exchanging a full budget and raising the possibility of limited costs management only at the case management hearing when the court will then have difficulties deciding whether that is proportionate (without knowing the cost of so doing) and costs managing if it agrees (e.g. the court accepts that it is just and proportionate that there should be a preliminary trial on liability, but the budgets are not readily divisible between costs on liability and costs on quantum).

Interestingly, the Form H guidance suggests that the trial of a preliminary issue may be dealt with as a contingency in the budget. In practical terms it is hard to see how this could be done in an informative way, as to do so would have the court budgeting one figure under one contingency phases for all the work to be incurred to the end of the preliminary point, rather than by the identified phases in Form H. As such it would be difficult, if not impossible, for the court to determine the proportionality by phases to enable it to manage the steps to be incurred proportionately.

---

[31]   *Hallam Estates v Baker* [2014] EWCA Civ 661.
[32]   *Hallam Estates v Baker* [2014] EWCA Civ 661.

Q3. If a defendant brings an additional claim against a party other than the claimant, does the defendant need to produce two budgets—one for the defence of the claim and one for the pursuit of the additional claim—or will one total budget suffice?

There is no clear guidance upon this. However, the situation did arise and was considered by Coulson J in *CIP Properties (AIPT) Ltd v Galliford Try Infrastructure Ltd*[33] (see **Q1** above). In that case one of four additional parties suggested that the defendant should provide separate costs budgets for the defence of the claim and for the discrete claims against each additional party. The response of the defendant was that the costs overlapped, with some costs being common costs, and that to do separate budgets would be "unworkable, impractical and expensive". Coulson J concluded that as it was a case where it would be difficult to identify what of the overall costs would be spent on the defence and what on the additional claims, it would be unfair and disproportionate to order separate budgets. He cited with approval the judgment of Master Kaye QC in *Lotus Cars Ltd v Mechanica Solutions Inc*.[34] In multi party litigation the Master had concluded that:

$\qquad$ 4–26

" . . . *where the management of cases is to be treated as common and is dealt with accordingly, there is no sensible reason why the costs budgeting should always be considered separately and some good reasons why it should not".*

What seems clear is that each case is likely to be fact specific, but that where the issues overlap inextricably then the court is unlikely to order separate budgets.

Q4. Does the court give the directions first and subsequently costs manage?

As costs management and case management go hand in hand, the two cannot be separated. If the case management directions are set without reference to the costs, with the budgeting exercise conducted afterwards, then all the court is doing when costs managing is pricing directions that have been given. The consequence is that if the court subsequently determines that a particular direction cannot be budgeted proportionately, there is nothing it can do as the direction has already been given. In contrast, if the two are done hand in hand the proportionate expenditure informs the appropriate direction. In simple terms, the danger of setting the directions and then costing them is that the directions ordered are those that the court determines are needed in the particular case. However, CPR 44.3(2) makes it clear that proportionality trumps need and the overriding objective 'to deal with a case at proportionate cost' applies to any case management decision. The court should be giving directions that see the case dealt with proportionately and that assessment can only be made by dealing with the directions and the relevant phase of the budget simultaneously.

$\qquad$ 4–27

---

[33] *CIP Properties (AIPT) Ltd v Galliford Try Infrastructure Ltd* [2014] EWHC 3546 (TCC) Coulson J.
[34] *Lotus Cars Ltd v Mechanica Solutions Inc* [2014] EWHC 76 (QB) Master Kaye QC.

Q5. Should the court set hourly rates as part of the budgeting exercise?

4–28   There appears to be a divergence of approach on this topic. The straightforward answer is that the court is not required to set hourly rate when costs managing because CPR 3 PD E 7.3 specifically states that the court sets 'total figures for each phase of the proceedings'. Those who favour the setting of hourly rates suggest that the court can only set a total figure by reference to an hourly rate. However, hourly rate in isolation is worthless. It is only relevant if it is multiplied by an amount of time. However, hours multiplied by time smacks of what is 'needed', which brings us back to CPR 3 PD E 7.3 as the court is <u>not</u> charged with setting a budget to allow necessary work—instead it is charged with setting a budget for each phase that is reasonable and proportionate.

There are a number of other reasons why setting the budget by reference to an hourly rate appears inappropriate. These are:

- It is too prescriptive. It is for the legal representatives and the client to determine how to spend the sum budgeted for a phase. If the budget is set by a specific hourly rate, then the court is effectively saying that that particular fee earner must do that amount of work. This is micro management taken to an extreme. Setting a total figure enables the representatives and, more importantly, the client, to decide who does what work and what work is contracted out to counsel.
- If the budget is set by reference to hourly rate it opens doors for arguments at assessment as to whether, in fact, a fee earner commanding that rate actually undertook the phase work in question. If the answer is no, then that may be 'good reason' to depart from the budget. These arguments do not arise if the budget is simply a total sum for the phase.
- If an hourly rate is set and at the end of the case, on assessment a different hourly rate is set for the non budgeted work (as the hourly rate set for the budget cannot be determinative in respect of the non budgeted costs as the court has no power to budget them under CPR 3.12 and 3.15), then immediately that opens the door to one or other party to argue 'good reason' to depart from the budget, submitting that the budget was set on the 'wrong' hourly rate.
- Setting rate and then determining the time by which to multiply it has all the hallmarks of a detailed assessment, which CPR 3 PD E 7.3 specifically cautions the court against undertaking when costs managing.
- The amount of court time taken to determine rate and then the time by which to multiply it renders the budgeting exercise disproportionate—both for the parties and for the court.
- There is a very real risk that parties/representatives will 'forum shop' in cases with no requirement to proceed in a particular court venue.

In summary, CPR 3 PD E 7.3 does not require the court to set hourly rates. The emphasis is on a far simpler, less time-consuming and more proportionate process. One aim of costs management is to reduce the incidence of, and time taken on, subsequent assessments of costs. Setting a rate within the budget seems designed to encourage more contested assessments and to defeat this aim.

Q6. How can the court set the budget without assessing prospectively the work that is required and the appropriate hourly rate(s) at which that work should be done?

The court is not charged when setting a budget with 'assessing', giving the word its customary meaning in a costs context. The court is also not charged with determining what work is required. What the court is charged with doing, is determining the proportionate case management directions and whether the budgeted costs for a phase of these directions 'fall within the range of reasonable and proportionate costs'. This inevitably involves a decision based on the definition of proportionality at CPR 44.3(5). It is against the backdrop of this definition that the court determines whether the sum sought for a phase is reasonable and proportionate and, if it is not, whether there is a more suitable case management direction and what total sum should be substituted. When looked at in these stark terms, it is clear why a detailed analysis of hourly rate and time does not inform the outcome. The court simply determines the work to be done by reference to proportionate expenditure. It is for that reason that case and costs management have to go hand in hand, so that the directions ordered only permit work that can be undertaken at proportionate cost.

4–29

Q7. If the court is budgeting only be reference to a global sum and not taking account of the respective hourly rates, surely this means that a party who has agreed a lower hourly rate retainer will be able to do more work than one with a higher hourly rate? If so this appears unfair.

Yes—a party with a lower hourly rate retainer is, in theory, able to undertake more work than one with a higher hourly rate. However, there are relevant factors that militate against the apparent unfair consequence:

4–30

- The court determines the appropriate proportionate case management directions. These inevitably define the extent of work that may be undertaken, e.g. limits on the number of factual witnesses, the amount of disclosure, the length of trial, etc.
- If the budget is set globally, then it is for a party to determine how to spend that money. Remember, costs are the client's and the budget is the client's to spend. The budget 'set' by the court will have to be explained to the client. Professional obligations on legal representatives may dictate that the way that sum is spent necessitates that the case plan is re-visited (e.g. does the client wish the work to be done by a lower level fee earner or is the client happy to have the higher level fee earner for less time or for the same amount of time, but in the knowledge that some of that cost will, inevitably be irrecoverable from the other party? Does the client want a less expensive expert/counsel or lesser input from the expert/ counsel?). In certain instances this may mean that the client seeks alternative representation. What this does highlight is the importance of the

retainer, both at the outset and on any variation, in defining precisely what work will be done for what remuneration. There is no doubt that the introduction of budgets reiterates the ongoing importance of managing client expectation, particularly in terms of any restraints that the case and costs management orders impose on a client's instructions.

However, at the end of the day it is for each client to negotiate the retainer with the legal representatives. If one negotiates a lower rate than another, then any consequences based on the differential rate stem from the choice of retainer and not from any costs management order.

Q8. If the court does set the hourly rate in the budget what happens if, at assessment, the assessing court sets a different hourly rate for the non budgeted work?

4–31   See the answer to **Q5** above. This may open the door to arguments that there is 'good reason' to depart from the budget. The possible consequences are that the length of summary assessments may be increased, that this persuades the trial judge to order a detailed assessment instead of assessing summarily in a fraction of the time and at a fraction of the cost and that there is an increased incentive for a paying party to take its chances on a detailed assessment. All fly in the face of a desire to make decisions about 'the costs of the costs' simpler and proportionate.

Q9. Is the budget 'without prejudice' to any subsequent assessment?

4–32   CPR 3.18 is clear. On a subsequent standard basis assessment (whether summary or detailed) in a case where the receiving party's costs have been subject to a costs management order, then the court will not depart from the budgeted sums for those phases budgeted unless there is 'good reason' to do so.

There is no provision in the rules for applying a 'without prejudice' qualification beyond 'good reason' to a costs management order, it is not part of the costs management regime and seems, simply to add time and costs to the case management process for no purpose—other than possibly assisting the court to identify the proportionate case management directions that should be given (by virtue of setting the budget in the normal way), but in a thoroughly disproportionate way if the budget is qualified other than by CPR 3.18.

Adopting this approach seems to deprive the parties of the certainty that CPR 3.18 provides, involves everyone in an exercise that may well prove futile and seems to act as a clear encouragement to pursue costs issues further at assessment. Accordingly, such an approach seems contrary to the specific costs management provisions and the overriding objective.

Q10. What, if anything, can the court do when the parties agree budgets or phases of the budgets in sums that the court thinks are disproportionate?

4–33   This is one of the curiosities of the costs management regime. CPR 3.15 clearly envisages that the parties may agree all or part of the budgets and that if they do so, the court is left with the options of making no costs management order at all or making a costs management order recording the extent of the agreement (and setting a budget in respect of those phases not agreed).

However, CPR 3.12(2) makes it clear that the function of the court is to manage both the steps and the costs to be incurred. Accordingly, if the court takes the view that the case management approach of the parties upon which the budget agreement is based is not proportionate, then the court must give proportionate directions. This is reinforced by the duty on the court imposed by CPR 3.17 to take account of the cost of any procedural step and by the overriding objective.

It is unlikely that an agreed budget will remain so if the assumptions upon which the agreement was reached are altered, e.g. if the disclosure phase is agreed on the basis of an order for standard disclosure, but the court permits only a more limited form of disclosure, is a party really likely to maintain the agreement? This means that representatives at court must have ready access to the client during the case management hearing (if the client is not present) so that further instructions may be taken. Of course, if the parties have agreed what the court perceives to be proportionate case management directions, but have simply agreed figures more than the court thinks are proportionate, then there genuinely is nothing that the court can do to interfere with the agreement.

The position becomes even more curious if there is a variation of the budget. CPR 3 PD E 7.6 provides that in such circumstances the parties need only involve the court if they cannot agree the budget variation. This seems to sit unhappily with CPR 3.15(3), which imposes on the court the obligation to control the parties' budgets once it has made a costs management order. How can it do so if the parties may vary the budget by agreement (and, it seems, without any requirement that the agreed varied budget is even filed at the court)? The answer, perhaps, lies in the first sentence of CPR 3 PD E 7.6. The parties may only revise budgets if 'significant developments in the litigation warrant such revisions'. It is hard to think of such developments that will not require consequential case management directions. As already stated, as soon as the court is concerned with case management CPR 3.17 applies and the court must determine whether the procedural step is worth the candle. This may mean that if court determines that the costs the parties have agreed as a consequence of the further directions necessitated by the 'significant developments' are disproportionate, then the directions will not be given. This leaves the parties with the options of proceeding on the basis of the case that was originally budgeted or revisiting the varied budget to try to reach a figure at which the court will determine the significant developments can be dealt with at proportionate costs.

Q11. Can the parties agree to vary their budgets from that recorded by the court in a costs management order, where there has been no 'significant development' in the litigation, but both are unhappy with the amount budgeted by the court?
No. Once a costs management order has been made by the court, it may only   **4–34**
be varied where there are significant developments. The fact that all parties

may be unhappy with the costs management order made is not a significant development. The remedy of the parties in such a situation would be to seek to appeal the costs management order.

Q12. What effect will a 'costs sanction' for unreasonable conduct, as suggested by the Court of Appeal in Denton v T H White,[35] have on a costs budget?

4–35 At para.42 of the majority judgment the Court of Appeal said this:

> *"The court will be more ready in the future to penalise opportunism . . . Heavy costs sanctions should, therefore, be imposed on parties who behave unreasonably in refusing to agree extensions of time or unreasonably oppose applications for relief from sanctions. An order to pay the costs of the application under rule 3.9 may not always be sufficient. The court can, in an appropriate case, also record in its order that the opposition to the relief application was unreasonable conduct to be taken into account under CPR rule 44.11 when costs are dealt with at the end of the case. If the offending party ultimately wins, the court may make a substantial reduction in its costs recovery on grounds of conduct under rule 44.11. If the offending party ultimately loses, then its conduct may be a good reason to order it to pay indemnity costs. Such an order would free the winning party from the operation of CPR rule 3.18 in relation to its costs budget."*

Accordingly, it is clear that the 'costs sanction' envisaged may be relevant to budgets set in two scenarios:
1) If the offending party subsequently becomes the receiving party on an assessment, then the unreasonable opposition may be a 'good reason' to depart from the budget relying upon the provisions at CPR 44.11(1)(b) and 44.11(2)(a).
2) If the offending party subsequently becomes the paying party, then an award of costs on the indemnity basis may follow and, as has already been stated, this means that the provisions of CPR 3.18 do not apply (as that rule is limited to where the court is assessing on the standard basis).

In both situations the effect may be substantial—in the first limiting and in the second increasing costs recovery.

Q13. What guidance is there on what may constitute 'good reason' under CPR 3.18 to enable a departure from a budget at assessment?

4–36 At the moment there have been no reported authorities on the current provisions in respect of what might constitute good reason. However, as is clear from the text of this chapter, Moore-Bick LJ in *Henry v News Group Newspapers Ltd*,[36] a case within the defamation pilot scheme, clearly envisaged that 'good reason' was intended to present a high hurdle and that the court would not lightly permit departures from the budget. Although in a different context

---

[35] *Denton v T H White* [2014] EWCA Civ 906.
[36] *Henry v News Group Newspapers Ltd* [2013] EWCA Civ 19.

(CPR 3.9), the Court of Appeal has already reinforced the view that the 'good reason' definition bar is set high.

Some 'good reason' departures from the budget are obvious, e.g. where a budgeted contingency does not arise or where a claim is resolved before a specific phase has commenced. Beyond these, counsel of caution must be to seek prospective variation under CPR 3 PD E 7.6 whenever it is appropriate, rather than to run the gauntlet of arguing 'good reason' at assessment.

Q14. Will the introduction of 'J-Codes'[37] lead to Form H being completed to include all costs—including those of a solicitor/client nature?
No. The court has no role in budgeting solicitor and client costs—those   **4–37** remain a matter of contractual retainer. J-Codes will enable representatives to record time against the specific phases of the Form H and should simplify the management of any budget set by a costs management order. So far as the court is concerned the use of these codes should enable easier comparison of the budget and the sum spent on each phase budgeted if there is a challenge on any subsequent assessment—although this may require practitioners to separate out 'solicitor and client' costs from costs recoverable 'between the parties'.

J-Codes should also make it easier for a party to identify the costs attributable to any free standing application that falls outside a budget under CPR 3 PD E 7.9.

At the time of writing, J-Codes and new format bills are to be piloted.

Q15. Does the statement of truth on the budget prevent a solicitor recovering more than the budget from the client?
No. Subject to the appropriate wording of any specific solicitor and client fee   **4–38** retainer (the qualification is because in County Court proceedings, s.74(3) of the Solicitors Act 1974 limits costs to those which could have been recovered from another party in the absence of any agreement to the contrary).

CPR 22 PD 2.2A makes it clear that the budget is concerned with reasonable and proportionate costs. Proportionality has no place in solicitor/client assessments (which are effectively on the indemnity basis).

However, plainly a solicitor should inform the client of the budgeted sum so that the client is aware of the limit on those costs that may be recovered from another party in the event a costs order is made in the client's favour. This should enable the client to give informed instructions after the budget has been set. CPR 46.9(3)(c) makes clear that on any assessment of solicitor and client costs, costs are assumed to be unreasonably incurred if they are of an unusual nature or amount and the solicitor did not tell the client that as a result they might be irrecoverable.

---

[37] For more information on J-Codes, see Jackson Review Drafting Group, *Civil Litigation J-Code Set Overview and Guidelines*, August 4, 2014.

Q16. What if a client still wants the legal representatives to incur costs that the court has not allowed within the budget?

4–39   Remember that the costs management exercise is concerned with recoverable costs 'between the parties' only. The basis of retainer remains a contractual issue between the solicitor and the client. To that extent, provided that the retainer permits it and the expenditure is agreed, the client is not constrained in what costs are actually incurred by the budget set by the court. So, for example, the client may still choose to engage counsel whose brief fees will mean that the client inevitably exceeds the budgeted sum for the trial phase. This is entirely the prerogative of the client provided /he/she realises that there will be a shortfall between expenditure incurred and recovery of costs even if he/she is awarded the costs—see **Q15** and the reference to CPR 46.9(3)(c) above.

However, clearly the case management directions that the court has given do impose an inevitable constraint. For example, if the court has limited a party to a set number of named expert witnesses, then there is no purpose in the client insisting upon the instruction of further experts as their evidence cannot be relied upon in court.

In summary, as Jackson LJ stated in his *Preface and Guide to the Civil Justice Reforms* in the White Book 2014:

> *"Within the confines of the directed procedure any party is free to waste its own money, if it wishes to do so."*

Q17. Can the budgeted sum exceed the sum due from that party to the solicitor under the contractual retainer, and, if so, is this a permitted breach of the indemnity principle?

4–40   The budgeted sum may exceed the sum provided for within the retainer. However, the fact that the court makes a costs management order does not mean that those costs are recoverable from another party regardless of the indemnity principle. Indeed the amendment to the statement of truth on Form H was, in part at least, to address the problem where specific fee retainers made completion of the budget difficult (e.g. in house lawyers, fixed fee cases, etc.).

Breach of the indemnity principle would be a 'good reason' under CPR 3.18 to depart from the budget. However, this may prove a more challenging exercise than it seems at first sight. Imagine the case where the fee retainer is a fixed fee for all work or a Damages Based Agreement where there is simply 'the payment' which cannot be calculated until the end of the claim. How does the solicitor apportion between the phases of Form H in those situations? Client retainers may need to be drafted in creative fashion to enable this apportionment and to meet any challenge under 'good reason', e.g. that apportionment of the overall fixed fee/the payment is a matter for the solicitor provided that the work that has been agreed to be done under the retainer is undertaken. It is likely that as these cases work through the system, the court will be confronted with the challenges that they present and authority will emerge.

Q18. How important is the breakdown between disbursements and solicitors' fees in an approved/agreed budget?

Whilst the format of Form H requires a division between profit costs and various types of disbursement, CPR 3 PD E.7.3 simply requires the court to set the budget for a phase by way of a total figure. Accordingly, many courts are not breaking down the sum budgeted for a specific phase between profit costs, counsel, experts and other disbursements, and for good reason. The rationale for this is that it is for the solicitor and the client to agree how the sum for a phase is to be spent. Solicitors may model this in many ways for the client to choose, e.g. where the proposed budget has been reduced by the court, the client may agree to place less reliance than had been envisaged on counsel or the same amount of reliance, but with the solicitors then using a less expensive fee earner.

4–41

Another difficulty of the court being too prescriptive about how the total sum for a phase is spent, is that it reduces the flexibility for the solicitor and client, e.g. if the budget for the pre-trial review is based on a division between solicitor and counsel on the assumption that counsel will attend the PTR and, in fact, the solicitor and the client agree that the solicitor will conduct that hearing, is that then 'good reason' to depart from the budget that was based on counsel attending? As one aim of costs budgeting is to reduce the number of assessments, this is better achieved by the court setting one figure for each phase and leaving the solicitor and client to decide how to spend that sum. Remember that the court is not sanctioning, for example, use of counsel or a fee earner with a set hourly rate at a specific stage, it is instead simply determining what is the reasonable and proportionate sum for each phase

Having said all the above, there is no doubt that the breakdown in the Form H further informs the court of the case plan upon which the filed budget is predicated.

Q19. Does the introduction of costs management mean that the court is rarely likely to dispense with a case/costs management conference and deal with directions and budgets as a paper exercise?

Clearly having a case/costs management hearing introduces delay and expense to cases. If the court is able to undertake this work as a paperwork exercise that would be the preferable course (indeed Jackson LJ in the final report was at pains to stress that only case management hearings that had a purpose should be listed). However, unless the case management directions and budgets are agreed and the court is prepared to approve both, then it is difficult to envisage how a hearing can be dispensed with at this stage. Even the optional provisional paper budget scheme introduced for certain work in the Manchester Civil Justice Centre envisages an oral hearing if any party wishes after the provisional setting of the budget. It is hoped that as the regime settles in and

4–42

the experience of practitioners and judges alike grows, then an increasing number of budgets and proposed directions will lend themselves to a paper determination. In the meantime, parties should seek to narrow as many issues as possible and inform the court of any measure of agreement that will reduce the required hearing time for a case management conference as that is likely both to expedite the listing of the hearing (as a shorter time estimate ought to lead to earlier court availability) and reduce the cost of the hearing. Parties should remember that they are under a duty to endeavour to agree appropriate directions anyway (CPR 29.4).

Where it is not possible to dispense with a hearing, the parties should, at least, consider whether a telephone case/costs management hearing is feasible (subject to the court being prepared to accommodate this). In many cases there is an argument to be made that a hearing by telephone is more proportionate (e.g. where the advocates are not local to the hearing centre). However, whilst CPR 23 PD.6.2(c) suggests that a case management conference will be by telephone unless the court orders otherwise, this is in respect of hearings up to an hour long. Many case/costs management hearings are listed for longer than this.

Q20. How detailed should be the assumptions upon which the budget is based?

4–43 This must depend upon the specific demands of any given case. The assumptions are clearly important as they set out a party's case plan. However, assumptions with attached breakdowns of the costs that render the Form H far more akin to a bill for a prospective detailed assessment are clearly contrary to the requirements of the rules and are likely to be disproportionate in preparation. The purpose of the assumptions is so that other parties and the court can readily understand the case plan upon which the budget is predicated, e.g. how many witnesses, what type of disclosure, how many experts and whether partly or jointly instructed and the length of trial. Ideally the assumptions should be on p.1 of the Form H so that this page provides a clear summary of a party's procedural and cost plan for the claim for ease of reference.

Q21. The guidance for completion of Form H is brief and it is not always clear where certain items of work should be included. Is there any sanction for inserting items in what the court may regard as the wrong phase of the budget?

4–44 The decisions in *Bank of Ireland v Philip Pank Partnership*[38] and *Americhem Europe Ltd v Rakem Ltd*[39] suggest that the court may treat insertion of items in the wrong place in the budget as irregularities rather than things that render the budget a nullity.

Obviously parties should follow the Form H guidance but where it is not

---

[38] *Bank of Ireland v Philip Pank Partnership* [2014] EWHC 284 (TCC) Stuart-Smith J.
[39] *Americhem Europe Ltd v Rakem Ltd* [2014] EWHC 1881 (TCC) Stuart-Smith J.

clear there is a real danger that the process of completing the Form H becomes one of form rather than substance. The document should inform the parties and the court to enable the parties to reach agreement or raise any issues of contention and to enable the court to case and costs manage properly. If it is not clear where to insert specific work and the cost incurred and to be incurred on that (e.g. on an interim application that has already been made and so arguably is not a contingency, but does not fit happily into any other phase) the key is to ensure that wherever it is included it, and the costs attributable to it, are clearly identified. In the example given, it may be best to insert the application as a contingency, even though it creates the oddity that work has already been undertaken and costs spent on something that comes in a phase that the guidance refers to as 'anticipated'. At least by so doing the expenditure is in the budget and the costs attributable to it are set out separately—assisting the court under CPR 3 PD E 7.4 as what has already been spent informs what costs should be budgeted going forward.

Q22. Does costs management apply to the disposal stage of a claim after the entry of a default judgment for damages to be decided by the court?
Strictly a disposal hearing is defined in CPR 26 PD 12.4 as a hearing that will **4–45** not exceed 30 minutes and at which the court will not take oral evidence. Such claims are not allocated to track (unless they are within the small claims limit and are allocated to that track —see CPR 26 PD 12.3(2)). Accordingly, claims listed for disposal are not allocated to the multi track and they do not fall within the costs management regime under CPR 3.12.

However, parties often refer to a disposal hearing when, in fact, they mean a trial on quantum where the final hearing will exceed 30 minutes and at which oral evidence will be given. These cases should be allocated. If they are allocated to the multi track, then, as CPR 7 multi track cases, the costs management provisions apply. In such cases there may not be any notice under CPR 26.3. Instead the file may be referred to the District Judge on entry of the judgment for damages to be decided to give directions. Prior to the introduction of costs management, the District Judge might have ordered the filing of directions questionnaires, listed the claim for case management conference or given directions as a paper exercise. The likelihood now is that the last of those options is unlikely to occur in cases where allocation is to the multi track. Accordingly, parties should be astute to when a Form H is triggered under the provisions of CPR 3.13 in these cases.

Q23. What should parties do when the notice of provisional allocation under CPR 26.3 is to the multi track, but one or more parties believe that the appropriate allocation is to the fast track?
The risk of ignoring the consequence of the provisional allocation to multi **4–46** track and simply filing a directions questionnaire with proposed directions seeking allocation to the fast track but without a Form H, is that if the court concludes that the provisional allocation was appropriate, then there is a

71

breach of CPR 3.13 and the consequences of CPR 3.14 apply. A more prudent approach is to file a consent application (if all parties agree that the provisional allocation is inappropriate) or an on notice application (if all parties do not agree that the provisional allocation is inappropriate) prior to the date for filing and exchanging costs budgets, seeking an extension of the time for so doing until a date to be fixed after determination of the appropriate track at an allocation hearing. This avoids the potentially wasted expense of producing a Form H if subsequently the court allocates other than to the multi track, but means that the argument is one of extension of time for compliance under CPR 3.13 and not relief from the sanction of 3.14 if the court maintains the provisional allocation to multi track.

Q24. What sort of applications fall within the provisions of CPR 3 PD E 7.9? How does this link with the provision for contingencies in the budget?

4–47   The guidance gives a very clear steer in respect of those costs that will fall outside the budget and are to be dealt with under CPR 3 PD E 7.9. It states that this provision relates to those "costs which are not anticipated but which become necessary later". This links to the definition of contingencies as relating to "anticipated costs that do not fall within the main categories set out in the form" (for categories read phases). So, if something is not anticipated at the time of the budget, e.g. an application to enforce compliance with directions, then that is outside the budget and the costs of that application fall to be determined and then assessed as part of the determination of the application, which is entirely free standing and independent of the budget. The inevitable consequence of the guidance on contingencies is that parties should apply common sense. Is something genuinely anticipated or not? If it is, then include it in the budget, if it is not, then deal with it outside of the budget if it ever arises. The court is unlikely to be impressed with endless contingencies that are no more than flights of fantasy at the budget stage. The risk of asking the court to budget such costs is that decisions on whether or not to do so inevitably extend the time estimate for the case management conference and, if the court is persuaded to do so, increase the risk that at the end of the case the parties may overlook that some of the contingencies never came to fruition for the purpose of 'good reason' to depart from the budget (as the fact that a contingency for which budgetary provision was made did not occur, must surely be a 'good reason' for departing from the budget).

Q25. Do the costs allocated to contingencies count when determining whether or not a budget exceeds £25,000 and, in consequence, in determining whether only page 1 of the Form H needs to be completed?

4–48   As the budget is in Form H and that includes contingencies and, as any contingencies that the court includes in the costs management order it makes plainly form part of the budget, it follows that the sums included by parties as contingencies in Form H count towards the total budget and even if, absent these, the budget would be less than £25,000, the full Form H must be completed.

Q26. If there has been a significant front loading of the costs so that by the time of the costs management hearing the costs already spent exceed what the court regards as the proportionate expenditure on the claim, can the court set a budget going forward of nil?

No. The reason for this is that the budget is not set as an overall sum. It is set   **4–49**
by phase under CPR 3 PD E 7.3. Accordingly, even if the court concludes that the incurred sum to date exceeds that which is proportionate to have dealt with the entire claim, it must look at the budget on a phase by phase basis. This may mean that the budget for certain phases may be set at nil if the court thinks the incurred sum under that phase already equals or exceeds the reasonable and proportionate cost for the entire phase. This is because CPR 3 PD E.7.4 requires the court to take costs already incurred "into account when considering the reasonableness and proportionality of all subsequent costs". However, there will be other phases, such as PTR, trial preparation and trial, where plainly there will be no incurred costs at that stage and it would be wrong, as the budget is set by reference to the reasonable and proportionate costs for each phase, for the court to budget these phases at nil.

The link between 'incurred costs' and the budget set was considered in the case of *Redfern v Corby Borough Council*.[40] Although this case appears to overlook the reviewing and revisionary function in the court when discussing the court's approval,. rather than setting, of budgets, this judgment appears to endorse the general relevance attributed to 'incurred costs' set out above. However, it is not clear from the judgment whether the incurred costs were viewed as a whole (both at first instance and on appeal), as opposed, as suggested above, to the specific sums attributable to each phase of the budget. If the former, then this decision is hard to reconcile with the CPR 3 PD E 7.3 requirement to set budgets by phases. In so far as the case also deals with the damages/costs ratio (para.15), it is important to remember that the definition of proportionality at CPR 44.3(5) is not restricted solely to monetary value of the claim.

Of course, the court may also record its comments on the costs incurred before the date for any budget to assist the court at any later assessment when it considers the non budgeted costs.

Q27. Does the fact that a party has a contractual right to indemnity costs against the other party mean costs management is not applicable or pointless because the claimant has a contractual right to claim costs under Gomba Holdings (UK) Ltd v Minories Finance Ltd (No.2)?[41]

Whilst the position of the contractual costs of a mortgagee may be some-   **4–50**
what different from those parties holding contractual rights to costs in other

[40]   *Redfern v Corby Borough Council* [2014] EWHC 4526 (QB).
[41]   *Gomba Holdings (UK) Ltd v Minories Finance Ltd (No.2)* [1993] Ch 171.

situations, this question seems directed to those cases where, in one form or another, there is a contractual right to costs on an indemnity basis between the parties in favour of one party, which is known about at the time that costs management would ordinarily arise.

The position is really a matter for the court. Whilst there is merit in avoiding the time and expense of budgeting by not costs managing the costs of the party who will rely upon the contractual obligation, the court still has a duty to case manage proportionately. Knowing what that party sees as the proportionate expenditure for the directions it advances will assist the court in determining the proportionate procedural approach to adopt. By so doing the court may, incidentally, reduce the costs due under the contract, as the directions proposed may not be proportionate and the effect of a different procedural route to trial may well limit what is reasonably incurred and reasonable in amount under the contractual entitlement.

Q28. Does the emphasis on proportionality impact on the situation where a claim falls within fast track financial limits, but the number of witnesses is such that the time needed for trial exceeds one day?

4–51 Indeed it does. Many of these cases would have been allocated to the multi track based on the trial time estimate prior to April 1, 2013. Since that date, allocation must be viewed against the revised overriding objective and the court must determine whether allocation to the multi track is proportionate. It will do so by reference to the CPR 44.3(5) factors. The mere fact that the number of witnesses that the parties wish to call would mean that the trial will exceed one day is not determinative in isolation. If there is that number of witnesses because of the complexity of the claim or because there are issues of public importance or reputation, then that may justify allocation to the multi track as proportionate. If no such factors exist, then the court is likely to allocate to the fast track. This will be in conjunction with case management using the powers that the court has under CPR 32.2(3) to control the extent of witness evidence permitted and its powers under CPR 39.4 to timetable the trial to ensure that the trial does not exceed one day. In such a case parties may expect the trial timetable to limit the time allocated for opening the case (if permitted), cross examination, closing submissions and judicial consideration, judgment delivery, award of costs and summary assessment under any award. In other words, parties may have to select their 'best' evidence and their 'best' cross examination points. As Jackson LJ stated in the Final Report:

> *"The essence of proportionality is that the ends do not necessarily justify the means."*[42]

Remember that not only will allocation to the multi track incur the parties in further expenditure, but also that CPR 1.1(2)(e) expressly includes in the definition of "dealing with a case justly and at proportionate cost" the allocation

---

[42] Ch.3.para 5.3.

of court resources and the express requirement to take account the resource needs of other cases. Allocation to multi track simply to accommodate a longer trial time erodes the judicial time available for other cases.

Q29. What is the position if a Part 7 claim commences as a fast track claim, but subsequently it becomes apparent that the claim is undervalued and needs to be re-tracked to the multi track, but it is not within one of the costs management exceptions in CPR 3.12(1)?
This is not an uncommon scenario—particularly in personal injury proceedings where the prognosis is uncertain at the time of allocation. Whilst the court is not constrained by a statement of value or allocation as to what sum it may award (see CPR 16.3(7)), plainly the claimant must apply to amend the statement of value and to seek re-allocation. In any event, the increase in value is likely to result in a need to be linked with an application for further substantive directions (e.g. change of trial time estimate/trial window/further expert evidence, etc.).   4–52

As the costs management provisions apply to all multi track CPR 7 claims (subject to the exceptions detailed in CPR 3.12(1)), then the effect of any re-allocation is to bring the claim within the costs management provisions. As such, it would be prudent for the claimant to attach a Form H to the application (and if the application is by consent for the defendant to do likewise). In any event, expect the court to order Forms H to be filed and exchanged when listing the application or before it considers any consent order if the parties have not already provided them. This is not only because the court wishes to consider costs managing, but also because of the provisions of CPR 3.17. Re-allocation is a case management decision and the court will need to know the cost consequence of any decision it takes.

If the application comes very late in the claim and the only variations to the existing case management directions are the amendment to statement of value, re-allocation and fresh trial window, it may be appropriate to include in the application a request that the court exercises its power under CPR 3.12(1)(c) not to costs manage. This would be on the basis that the cost of the exercise may, in context, be disproportionate as the costs and steps to be incurred at that stage are limited. Of course this argument is something of a double-edged sword, as the court may take the view that as such, the costs management exercise will not occupy much court time and can be dealt with promptly and proportionately and as preparation for trial and trial are usually two of the most expensive phases of the budget (if not the most expensive), the exercise is still worthwhile and necessary. However, as trial preparation and trial are often the most expensive elements of a claim, even a limited costs management order in respect of these phases may be appropriate. In the case of *Hegglin v Person(s) Unknown, Google Inc.*[43] the court was confronted with an application to cap costs ten days before the commencement of the

---

[43]   *Hegglin v Person(s) Unknown, Google Inc.* [2014] EWHC 3793 (QB) Edis J.

trial. Edis J declined to do so, based on the late stage of the proceedings and the procedural threshold for making such orders, but, instead, exercised costs management powers under CPR 3.15 to budget the trial and some outstanding work on an expert's report.

Q30. Is it better for a party to over-estimate costs in the budget filed and exchanged, on the basis that it is then likely to see a higher budget set and less likely to need to go back to the court asking for the budget to be varied under CPR 3 PD E 7.6? Conversely, if a party recognises that it is likely to be the paying party is underestimation better, trying to persuade the court to reduce the budgets of all parties to that level to limit the potential liability for costs or limit the work that can be undertaken, making the outcome of the claim less certain as a result?

4–53   The simple answer to the related questions above is that the parties must complete Form H in a fashion that enables them to sign the statement of truth set out in CPR 22 PD 2.2A. As is clearly set out in CPR 22 PD 5 and, by cross reference, CPR 32.14, the consequence of verifying the budget by statement of truth knowing that the Form H does not give a fair and accurate statement of incurred and estimated costs that it would be reasonable and proportionate for the client to incur, is possible proceedings for contempt of court. Representatives should be extremely wary of adopting 'tactical budgets'— whether high or low.

Q31. To which sum do the percentages in CPR 3 PD E 7.2 apply—the total sum in the Form H after the budget has been set or just those parts of the Form H that the court has budgeted?

4–54   There appears to be some debate about this, with anecdotal evidence that some take the view that the percentage is to be applied to the 'Grand Total' sum in the bottom right hand box of page 1 of the Form H after the budget has been set and others taking the stance that the percentage applies only to the sums set for costs to be incurred in those phases of the budget that have been costs managed. CPR 3 PD E 7.2 states:

> *"i) that the costs of initially preparing Form H are the greater of £1,000 or 1% of the approved and agreed budget;*
> *ii) all other recoverable costs associated with the budgeting and costs management process shall not exceed 2% of the approved or agreed budget."*

Those arguing for the former interpretation point to the fact that 'budget' is not defined in the rules and that throughout CPR 3.12–3.18, and the accompanying CPR PD E, the budget is described as being in the format of Form H. As such reference to the budget is to the entire Form H. Whilst these points have some resonance, they seem to miss the point that CPR 3 PD E 7.2 refers to the percentage as being set by reference to the 'approved or agreed budget'. The only costs within Form H that can be approved by the court or agreed by the parties as part of the costs management exercise are those <u>to be incurred</u>. Indeed the specific reference to approval or agreement of the budget is in CPR 3.15(2) and is directly linked to costs to be incurred. This leads inexorably to the conclusion that the percentage can only apply to those parts of the budget in respect of which the court makes a costs management order.

There are three other valid reasons why the interpretation adopted above may be preferred: the first two are by specific reference to the rules and the third is one of common sense:

i)   CPR 3.18 expressly uses the words 'approved or agreed budget' and it is clear that in doing so it refers <u>only</u> to those parts of the Form H in respect of which the court has made a costs management order, suggesting that there is a difference between the respective definitions of 'budget' and 'last approved or agreed budget'.

ii) If the words 'approved or agreed budget' apply to the entire Form H total after the costs management exercise then, for the purpose of continuity under CPR 3.18, the court has costs managed incurred costs (which is impermissible) and the CPR 3.18 provisions would apply to all the costs in the Form H and so any subsequent assessment would be on 'good reason' alone.

iii) There would be nothing that the court could do to prevent a party over-estimating 'incurred' costs within the Form H to ensure that whatever happened on those parts costs managed, the percentage still came to an inappropriately high sum, even if, at a subsequent assessment of the 'incurred' costs, most were assessed to be irrecoverable as unreasonable and/or disproportionate. It seems utterly illogical that in rules designed to ensure both reasonableness and proportionality of costs, the percentage should be set by reference to a figure, over much of which the court has no control.

Q32. Is a further Form H required with a pre-trial checklist ("PTCL") as CPR 29 imposes no such requirement and yet the wording of the PTCL requires one?

CPR 29 PD 8.1(1) requires a PTCL to be in Form N170. Form N170 does refer   **4–55** to a budget at **Section F**. However, the wording at **Section F** is not mandatory. It refers to a party attaching an estimate of costs if appropriate. This in turn is qualified by guidance at the beginning of the N170 which suggests that in cases not costs managed an estimate of costs is required. However, it is clear from the wording used (reference to costs estimates and reference to these being provided in accordance with the provisions of the CPR) that the guidance is an unhappy and unwelcome failure to take account of the revised CPR. As we shall see under **Q36** below, the only provisions relating to budgets are to be found at CPR 3.12–3.18, 3.20, 3 PD E, 3 PD F and CPR 44 PD 3. These do not contain any requirement for an estimate at the time of PTCL (and neither does CPR 29—other than in the PD as referred to above).

The only requirement to file a further budget actually arises in costs managed cases where a party seeks revision of the budget and cannot agree that revision and so applies to the court.

Whether because of the confusion in the wording of Form N170, because the parties have not understood the significance of CPR 3 PD E 7.6 or because of the reference in the Form H guidance on the PTR phase, most Forms H filed under CPR 3.13 contain within the assumptions in the PTR phase 'Updating of the budgets'. This is wrong as there is no automatic right to update. The only provision is CPR 3 PD E 7.6 which permits revision in specific circumstances. Expect the court to examine the PTR phase closely and reduce it where it contains the assumption set out above as work updating the budget is not time routinely reasonable and proportionate. There is also a danger that including this will make the court concerned as to what else has been included in the budget that ought not to have been and lead to a far closer scrutiny of all of the assumptions.

Q33. Can the court costs manage detailed assessment proceedings?

4–56   Some see it as curious that claims worth £25,001 are subject to the full rigour of the costs management regime and yet detailed assessments, where the costs claimed may run into many millions, fall outside the provisions. We say 'fall outside' as Form H specifically excludes the costs of detailed assessment (although this does not seem to stop some parties including these costs as a contingency).

However, there seems to be no reason why the court cannot exercise its power under CPR 3.12(1A) to costs manage detailed assessment proceedings where that is appropriate. CPR 47.1 clearly implies that the substantive proceedings are over by the time of assessment and CPR 47.6 expressly refers to detailed assessments as 'proceedings'—both suggesting that detailed assessments are 'proceedings' in their own right (an interpretation supported by *Crosbie v Munroe*[44]) and capable of consideration under CPR 3.12(1A).

The difficulty with costs management of detailed assessment proceedings is when and how it is undertaken. This raises many of the same arguments as to the inability of the court to costs manage 'incurred costs' (and particularly pre-action costs) in substantive proceedings. Does the court decide to budget whenever it makes an order for detailed assessment so that costs are managed from the inception of the process even though this will require a significant time and costs investment when most costs are settled without there even being a request for a detailed assessment hearing under CPR 47.14? If not there is a real danger in most cases, that by the time the court does step in all that remains is the assessment hearing itself and significant costs have already been incurred in settlement skirmishes, preparation of the bill, drafting of the Points of Dispute and any Replies to them. This is against a backdrop of repeated concern expressed by the judiciary about the 'costs of the costs'.

Inevitably, the consideration above leads to the conclusion that costs

---

[44]   *Crosbie v Munroe* [2003] EWCA Civ 350.

management is an option in detailed assessment proceedings, but that its suitability is entirely case specific. It will require robust costs and case management by the costs judge or costs officer and an early identification of those cases where costs management is purposeful—which essentially means that it is, in context, a proportionate exercise. In practice complex assessment proceedings are already the subject of robust case management, with the resolution of preliminary issues often leading to settlement.

Q34. Does the decision of the Court of Appeal in Denton v T H White[45] mean that relief from sanction will be granted provided that there is no prejudice to any other party that cannot be compensated by a costs order and that a trial date can still be met?
No, not necessarily. All cases will be fact specific. The Court of Appeal has set out a clear three-stage approach to applications under CPR 3.9 and it is the application of that which will determine the outcome of each specific application for relief. As such that may mean that in some cases the fact that there is no prejudice to the other party and a trial date can be met will, in all the circumstances, result in relief and in others it will not.   **4–57**

Whilst *Denton* clearly provides those seeking relief with a greater prospect of success than *Mitchell*, it is clear from the phraseology adopted by the court in *Denton* that there is not to be a return to the approach of pre April 1, 2013 as set out in the quote from the judgment in the text. Instead, as is stated in the judgment of the majority, what is required "is a more nuanced approach . . . Anything less will inevitably lead to the court slipping back to the old culture of non-compliance which the Jackson reforms were designed to eliminate"[46]. It is also important to remember that whilst *Denton* may have clarified and amplified the judgment in *Mitchell*, much of what that latter case determined remains pertinent and the actual facts of *Mitchell*, and the conclusion reached on those facts, still represents a far more robust approach to non compliance than prior to April 1, 2013.

Q35. What is the position in respect of CPR 3.13 where a directions questionnaire ("DQ") is not filed within the time specified in the notice of provisional allocation under CPR 26.3(1), but is filed accompanied by a Form H within the further time provided by the court under CPR 26.3(7A)? Is CPR 3.8(4) of any relevance in this situation?
CPR 3.13 seems inflexible in this context and the link with CPR 26.3 generally contains a procedural trap for the unwary. A Form H must be filed and exchanged by the date set under CPR 26.3(1). There is nothing in CPR 3.13 that automatically extends this period to the date set in the notice under CPR 26.3(7A). Accordingly on a strict interpretation, it seems that a represented party that fails to respond to the CPR 26.3(1) notice, but complies with the   **4–58**

[45] *Denton v T H White* [2014] EWCA Civ 906.
[46] para.38.

CPR 26.3(7A) notice, avoids the striking out of its statement of case under CPR 26.3(7A)(b), but falls foul of CPR 3.14 and is treated as having filed a budget comprising applicable court fees only.

CPR 26.3(6A) states categorically that the time for compliance with a notice under CPR 26.3(1) may not be varied by agreement between the parties. A consequence of failure to comply with the notice is specified in CPR 26.3(7A) (namely that a notice requiring compliance within seven days will be served on the defaulting party and in default of compliance with that further notice the statement of case will be struck out). However, does CPR 3.8(4) permit the parties to extend the time specified within the CPR 26.3(1) notice? It seems that the answer is not straightforward.

Firstly, CPR 3.8(4) only applies where a party is required to do something within a time specified by a rule and that rule imposes a sanction for failure to comply. In this situation there has been non compliance with 26.3(1) and the sanction is imposed by 26.3(7A). Is the rule CPR 26.3 and are 3(1) and 3(7A) sub-rules. The answer seems to be yes. Although there is no definition of 'rule' in the CPR, when it refers to a rule it seems to do so to, for example, all of 26.3.

However, does the provision permitting agreement under CPR 3.8(4) take precedence over the bar to agreement in CPR 26.3(6A)? The answer is that specific rules take precedence over general rules. CPR 26.3(6A) is a specific rule and CPR 3.8(4) is a general rule. As such it would seem that the period cannot be extended by agreement and that CPR 3.8(4) does not apply to the time for compliance with CPR 26.3(1).

Q36. Will cost capping be ordered more rarely?

4-59 It is difficult to see how costs capping has a future in those cases where the costs management regime applies (see *Hegglin v Person(s) Unknown, Google Inc.*[47]). By definition, a costs management order ensures that the costs budgeted are proportionate, as that is the basis upon which they have been set under CPR 3 PD E 7.3. As the court in the costs capping regime can only apply a cap to future costs, then in such a case a party will never be able to satisfy the requirement of CPR 3.19(5)(b), that without a cap there is a substantial risk that costs will be disproportionately incurred.

It would be nonsensical to look at costs capping in those cases where the court exercises its discretion under CPR 3.12(1A) to exclude cases that would otherwise fall within the costs management regime. This would fly in the face of the decision not to costs manage in the first place.

The relevance of costs capping in cases where the court chooses not to make a costs management order or which fall outside the regime is, at first blush, unaltered by costs management. However, in cases outside the regime where the court is concerned at the level of costs and the likelihood of these being adequately controlled by case management and subsequent assessment, the court may choose to exercise its discretion under CPR 3.12(1A) to costs

---

[47]   *Hegglin v Person(s) Unknown, Google Inc.* [2014] EWHC 3793 (QB) Edis J.

manage, rather than to costs cap. As the budget to be filed and served in an application for costs capping will be in the format of Form H (see CPR 3 PD F 2) and as the court will have to assess the quantum of the costs for the purpose of imposing a cap anyway (CPR 3 PD F 4.1), it may determine that costs management is preferable to costs capping. This also avoids the difficulty presented by the 'exceptional circumstances' threshold set for costs capping. As a result it may be that a party seeking a costs cap may wish to link the application to one for costs management.

Obviously, if the court is to consider costs management as an alternative to costs capping it will require Forms H from all parties and will need to exercise its discretion under CPR 3.20 to ensure that this is the case when dealing with a multi party claim.

A point of interest arises in respect of the subsequent relevance of budgets where a claim is not subject to the costs management regime, but where, in the course of an unsuccessful application for costs capping, Forms H are filed and served. Are these budgets of relevance at any subsequent assessment of costs? Strictly under CPR 44 PD 3.1 only budgets filed under 3 PD E are relevant when considering the provisions relating to a 20 per cent or more difference between budget and eventual costs claimed. As the budget in a costs capping application has been filed under CPR 3 PD F it seems that these provisions do not apply. It does seem curious that the provisions of CPR 44 PD 3 have been limited and do not apply to all budgets filed under any rule, practice direction or court order.

CHAPTER 5

Part 36 Settlement Offers and Costs Consequences

Background to Part 36

Part 36 has undergone significant changes in recent years. With effect from April 6, 2007, CPR Pt 36 was completely revised. Payments into court were no longer permitted. These reforms came about following two Court of Appeal decisions: *Crouch v Kings Healthcare NHS Trust*[1] and *Trustees of Stokes Pension Fund v Western Power Distribution (South West) Plc.*[2]

    The changes foreshadowed by these decisions were brought about by the Civil Procedure (Amendment No.3) Rules 2006 which came into force on April 6, 2007. The earlier version of Part 36 was replaced by an entirely new Part 36, together with a new Practice Direction. The Civil Procedure (Amendment No.8) Rules 2014,[3] which come into force on April 6, 2015, contain another entirely new version of Part 36 in Sch.1. There are also consequential amendments to other Parts.

5–01

Reform of Part 36

The Civil Procedure Rule Committee (CPRC) set up a sub-committee to consider reforms to Part 36 with a view to simplifying and clarifying it by, for example, allowing offers by counterclaiming defendants and discouraging "cynical claimant offers". The Forum of Complex Injury Lawyers (FOCIS) reacted to the sub-committee's report in relation to "cynical claimant offers" and suggested that wider amendments could risk undermining the Jackson Reforms and create greater disparity. The CPRC's sub-committee examining Part 36 felt that it was too technical and offers under it were failing on technical grounds. The intention of the new Part 36 is to align the rules with the case law developed since the Part was last amended. Given this situation there are no cases on the new rules. This work refers to the new rules and necessarily concentrates more heavily on those rules than on case law. The order of the rules has been re-arranged which has led to numerous consequential amendments. The sub-committee may well recommend still further amendments.

5–02

---

[1] *Crouch v Kings Healthcare NHS Trust* [2004] EWCA Civ 1332; [2005] 1 W.L.R. 2015.
[2] *Trustees of Stokes Pension Fund v Western Power Distribution (South West) Plc* [2005] EWCA Civ 854; [2005] 1 W.L.R. 3595.
[3] SI 2014 No.3299.

Transitional provisions

5–03   The new Part 36 applies only in relation to Part 36 offers made on or after April 6, 2015, save that rr.36.3 (definitions), 36.11 (acceptance of a Part 36 offer), 36.12 (acceptance of a Part 36 offer in a split trial case) and 36.16 (restriction on disclosure of a Part 36 offer) also apply in relation to any Part 36 offer where the offer is made before April 6, 2015, but a trial of any part of the claim or any issue arising in it starts on or after April 6, 2015.[4]

CPR Part 36 after April 5, 2015

5–04   Section I of Part 36 contains a self-contained procedural code about offers to settle made pursuant to the procedure set out in Part 36. Section I contains general rules about Part 36 offers. Section II contains rules about offers to settle where the parties have followed the Pre-Action Protocol for Low Value Personal Injury Claims in Road Traffic Accidents ("the RTA Protocol") or the Pre-Action Protocol for Low Value Personal Injury (Employers' Liability and Public Liability) claims ("the EL/PL Protocol") and have started proceedings under Part 8 in accordance with Practice Direction 8B.[5]

Under Section I, any party to an action may make an offer to settle in whatever way that party chooses, but if the offer is not made in accordance with r.36.5 (form and content of a Part 36) it will not have the consequences specified in Section I.[6] Where an offer does not comply with the requirements set out in r.36.2, it is not a Part 36 offer.[7]

A Part 36 offer may be made in respect of the whole or part of any issue that arises in a claim, counterclaim or other additional claim, or an appeal or cross-appeal from a decision made at a trial.[8] Counterclaims and other additional claims are treated as claims and references to a claimant or a defendant include a party bringing or defending an additional claim.[9]

In proceedings following a road traffic accident, the defendant, who alleged contributory negligence, made an offer, under the previous regime, to settle that issue on the basis of a 25 per cent reduction, three weeks before the trial was due to start. The claimant accepted the defendant's offer one week before trial. Neither the offer nor the acceptance made any mention about the costs of the contributory negligence issue. The Judge at first instance found that the defendant was in fact the claimant for the purposes of the contributory negligence issue, and ordered the claimant to pay the defendant's costs in relation to it. On the claimant's appeal, it was held that the defendant's offer amounted to an offer solely in relation to liability. It fell within old r.36.2(5) (which provided that "An offeror may make a Part 36 offer solely in relation to liability"—this provision has been omitted from the new rule, presumably because it was superfluous), and the fact that the context was contributory

---

[4]   Civil Procedure (Amendment No.8) Rules 2014, rr.18(1) and (2).
[5]   r.36.1.
[6]   r.36.2.
[7]   See *Thewlis v Groupama Insurance Co Ltd* [2012] EWHC 3 (TCC); [2012] BLR 259.
[8]   r.36.2(3).
[9]   rr.20.2 and 20.3.

negligence did not affect that. The defendant's offer was, and was intended to be, a Part 36 offer and the claimant's entitlement to costs arose under old r.36.10(1) (now r.36.13). In the light of the settlement at 75 per cent to 25 per cent, it was wholly artificial to describe the claimant as anything other than the winner.[10]

Except where a Part 36 offer is made in appeal proceedings, it has effect only in relation to the costs of the proceedings in respect of which it is made and not in respect of any appeal in those proceedings. If a Part 36 offer is made in appeal proceedings the references in the rules to, e.g. claimant/defendant are replaced by corresponding terms, e.g. appellant/respondent (r.36.4(1) and (2)).

The Court of Appeal held that an appeal is an independent regime, so far as Part 36 is concerned. In an appeal where the defendant chose to resist a claimant's new point without having made any offer, the defendant was at risk of paying the costs of the appeal. On the facts it would not be right to order the defendant to pay the costs of the claimant's new point when considerable costs were expended fighting the preliminary issue on a different basis in the court below, and those costs had been reserved to the trial Judge. It would be better if the costs were looked at in the round after the trial had taken place. The costs of the appeal were accordingly reserved to the trial Judge as well.[11]

The definition section of Part 36 makes it clear that a trial means any trial in a case whether it is a trial of all the issues or a trial of liability, quantum or some other issue in the case. A trial is in progress from the time when it starts until the time when judgment is given or handed down. A case is decided when all issues in the case have been determined, whether at one or more trials.[12]

Form and content of a Part 36 offer

A Part 36 offer must: 5–05
(a) be in writing;
(b) make clear that it is made pursuant to Part 36[13];
(c) specify a period of not less than 21 days within which the defendant will be liable for the claimant's costs where a Part 36 offer is accepted in accordance with r.36.13 or, where Section IIIA of Part 45 applies, in accordance with r.36.20 if the offer is accepted;
(d) state whether it relates to the whole of the claim or part of it or to an issue that arises in it and if so, to which part or issue; and
(e) state whether it takes into account any counterclaim.[14]
Where a defendant had made what purported to be a claimant's Part 36 offer in respect of the defendant's counterclaim, "the proceedings in respect of

---

[10] *Onay v Brown* [2009] EWCA Civ 775; [2010] 1 Costs LR 29 CA.
[11] *RTS Flexible Systems Ltd v Molkerei Alois Muller GmbH & Co AG* [2009] EWCA Civ 26.
[12] r.36.3.
[13] This is a change from the earlier version of the rule which required the offer to "state on its face if it was intended to have the consequences of Section I of Part 36".
[14] r.36.5(1).

which" it was made included the claim and the proposed counterclaim, but were not restricted only to the counterclaim. A Part 36 offer may be made before the commencement of proceedings (under old r.36.3(2), now r.36.7) so the fact that the defendant's counterclaim had not been formulated or pleaded did not of itself matter.[15]

A Part 36 offer may be made at any time including before the commencement of proceedings. Such an offer is made when it is served on the offeree.[16] The period of 21 days specified in (c) above or such longer period as the parties agree, in the case of an offer made not less than 21 days before trial, is known as "the relevant period". Where an offer is made less than 21 days before a trial, the relevant period is the period up to the end of the trial.[17]

Withdrawing or changing the terms of a Part 36 offer generally

5–06   There was a considerable body of case law dealing with offers which were purportedly withdrawn or the terms of which were changed. The new rules codify the position.

A Part 36 offer may only be withdrawn or its terms changed if the offeree has not previously served notice of acceptance. The offeror may withdraw the offer or change its terms by serving written notice of the withdrawal or change of terms on the offeree.[18] Rule 36.10 makes provision about when permission is required to withdraw or change the terms of an offer before the expiry of the relevant period. Subject to that, notice of withdrawal or change of terms takes effect when it is served on the offeree.[19]

Provided that the offeree has not previously served notice of acceptance, after expiry of the relevant period the offeror may withdraw the offer or change its terms without the permission of the court, or the offer may be automatically withdrawn in accordance with its terms. Where the offeror changes the terms of the offer to make it more advantageous to the offeree, the improved offer will be treated not as the withdrawal of the original offer, but as the making of a new Part 36 offer on the improved terms, and provided that the new offer is not made less than 21 days before the start of the trial, the relevant period will be 21 days or such longer period (if any) identified in the written notice of change of terms.[20]

r.36.9(4)(b) provides that an offer may be automatically withdrawn after the expiry of the relevant period in accordance with its terms. This is both the effect and apparent intention of 36.9(4)(b)—a Part 36 offer can now include within it a provision by which the offer is automatically withdrawn (and therefore time limited)—though it must still usually be open for a minimum of 21 days and 36.9(4)(b) cannot be used until that relevant period has passed.

This alters the position under the previous version of Part 36, as confirmed

---

[15]   *AF v BG* [2009] EWCA Civ 757.
[16]   r.36.7.
[17]   rr.36.3(g) and 36.5(2).
[18]   See r.36.17(7) as to the costs consequences following judgment of an offer which is withdrawn.
[19]   r.36.9(1), (2) and (3).
[20]   r.36.9(4) and (5).

in *C v D*.[21] Part 36 is to be treated as prescriptive. Its requirements have to be complied with clearly by a party seeking to secure its benefits. A Part 36 offer can only be withdrawn by a notice in writing by the offeror to the offeree (or, after the expiry of the relevant period, automatically in accordance with its terms (r.36.9(4)(b)). It is irrelevant whether the offer has been rejected or even ignored by the offeree. Withdrawal cannot be implied by conduct. It does not automatically follow that a claimant's costs should be payable by a third party in the same proportion as any apportionment of liability established by the Court as between a defendant and a third party. The Court has an overall discretion which is not circumscribed by the Civil Liability (Contribution) Act 1978.[22]

Withdrawing or changing the terms of a Part 36 offer before the expiry of the relevant period

Where the offeree has not previously served notice of acceptance and the offeror serves notice of withdrawal of the offer or changes in its terms to be less advantageous to the offeree before the expiry of the relevant period, if the offeree has not served notice of acceptance of the original offer by the expiry of the relevant period, the offeror's notice has effect on the expiry of that period; if the offeree serves notice of acceptance of the original offer before the expiry of the relevant period, that acceptance has effect unless the offeror applies to the court for permission to withdraw the offer or to change its terms within seven days of the offeree's notice of acceptance, or, if earlier, before the first day of trial. If such an application is made, the court may give permission for the original offer to be withdrawn or its terms changed if satisfied that there has been a change of circumstances since the making of the original offer and that it is in the interests of justice to give permission.[23]

5–07

Where the offeror seeks permission of the court to withdraw a Part 36 offer or to change its terms to be less advantageous to the offeree before expiry of the relevant period, the permission of the court must unless the parties agree otherwise, be sought by making a Part 23 application which must be dealt with by a judge other than the trial judge or at a trial or other hearing provided that it is not to the trial judge.[24]

A building contractor sued a householder for work done. The householder counterclaimed for losses alleging poor workmanship. The defendant made a Part 36 offer, inclusive of interest, and subsequently made increased offers. The claimant made counter-offers, but the parties did not reach agreement. The defendant withdrew all the offers, except the original one. At trial before the District Judge the claimant recovered some £300 more than the defendant's original Part 36 offer. The defendant appealed against the costs order, arguing

---

[21]   *C v D* [2011] EWCA Civ 646.
[22]   *Carillion JM Ltd v PHI Group Ltd, Carillion JM Ltd v Robert West Consulting Ltd* [2011] EWCH 1581 (TCC); 2011 BLR 504, Akenhead J.
[23]   r.36.10.
[24]   Practice Direction 36A, para.2.

that the judgment was not materially more advantageous to the claimant than the original Part 36 offer. On appeal the Court of Appeal held that the provisions of Part 36 state clearly how an offer may be made, how it may be varied and how it may be accepted. Unlike ordinary common law principles they do not provide for an offer to lapse or become incapable of acceptance on being rejected by the other party. Once made, a Part 36 offer remains open for acceptance until the start of the trial or its withdrawal in the manner set out in previous r.36.3(7) (now r.36.9(4)). Where a party makes several offers in different terms, a later offer does not revoke or vary an earlier offer, and all of them may be capable of acceptance at any one time.[25]

Following a collision at sea, the claimant offered to settle liability 60/40 in favour of the claimant. The offer was said to be made in accordance with CPR Part 61.4(10)–(12) and/or Part 36. The offer was subsequently withdrawn two months before trial, when the claimant offered to settle on the two thirds/one third basis. At trial, liability was apportioned 60/40 in favour of the claimant. In relation to costs, the court decided that there was a line of authority starting before the CPR but continuing after it, indicating that where an offer had been withdrawn which should have been accepted, it would not be unjust to award the offeror all of its costs, because, had the offer been accepted, no further costs would have been incurred thereafter (see *Bristol and West Building Society v Evans Bullock & Co*[26]). The mere fact that an offer had been withdrawn did not necessarily deprive the offer of effect on the question of costs. The defendant should have accepted the offer when it was available, or should have appreciated the costs risk and taken protective steps by making a realistic Part 36 offer itself. The fact that the offer was withdrawn two months before trial did not make it unjust to order that the claimant should get all their costs from 21 days after the offer was made. Prior to that the defendant should pay 60 per cent of the claimant's costs, and the claimant should pay 40 per cent of the defendant's costs.[27]

Acceptance of a Part 36 offer

5–08   Acceptance of a Part 36 offer is effected by serving written notice of acceptance on the offeror. Except where the permission of the court is required (see below) and acceptance of an offer in a split trial case, a Part 36 offer may be accepted at any time unless it has already been withdrawn, whether or not the offeree has subsequently made a different offer.[28]

A claimant who was already in breach of an unless order requiring him to serve certain documents purported to accept a Part 36 offer. On appeal it was held that a claim that had been struck out (under the unless order) was at an end, therefore the claimant could not have accepted the Part 36 offer once he

---

[25]   *LG Blower Specialist Bricklayer Ltd v Reeves* [2010] EWCA Civ 726.
[26]   *Bristol and West Building Society v Evans Bullock & Co* Unreported February 5, 1996 CA.
[27]   *Owners and/or Bareboat Charterers and/or Sub Bareboat Charterers of the Ship Samco Europe v Owners of the Ship MSC Prestige* [2011] EWHC 1656 (Admlty) Teare J.
[28]   r.36.11(1) and (2).

was in breach of the order, as his claim had in substance been brought to an end.[29]

Acceptance of a Part 36 offer made by one or more but not all defendants

In the case of Part 36 offers made by one or more, but not all, of a number of defendants, if they have been sued jointly or in the alternative the claimant may accept the offer, if he discontinues his claim against those defendants who have not made the offer, and those defendants give written consent to the acceptance of the offer. If the claimant alleges that the defendants have a several liability, the claimant may accept the offer, and continue with his claims against the other defendants if he is entitled to do so. In any other case the claimant must apply to the court for an order permitting acceptance of the Part 36 offer.[30]

5–09

Unaccepted offers
Restriction on disclosure of a Part 36 offer

A Part 36 offer is treated as being "without prejudice except as to costs". The fact that such an offer has been made must not be communicated to the trial judge until the case has been decided. This restriction does not apply where the defence of tender before claim has been raised; where the proceedings have been stayed following the acceptance of a Part 36 offer; where the offeror and offeree agree in writing that it should not apply; or where, although the case has not been decided, any part of it or issue in it has been decided, and the Part 36 offer relates only to parts or issues which have been decided. Where a part or issue has been decided, the trial judge may be told whether or not there are Part 36 offers other than those relating to the parts or issues which have been decided, but must not be told any of the terms of the other offers unless any of the above exceptions apply to them.[31]

5–10

Costs consequences following judgment

Save where Section IIIA of Part 45 applies,[32] where, upon judgment being entered, a claimant fails to obtain a judgment more advantageous than the defendant's Part 36 offer, or judgment against the defendant is at least as advantageous to the claimant as the proposals contained in the claimant's Part 36 offer, the court must, unless it consider it unjust to do so, order that the defendant is entitled to costs (including any recoverable pre-action costs) from the date on which the relevant period expired, and interest on those costs.[33] The provision does not apply to a soft tissue injury claim to which

5–11

---

[29] *Joyce v West Bus Coach Services Ltd* [2012] EWHC 404 (QB) Kenneth Parker J.

[30] r.36.15(1)–(4).

[31] r.36.16(1)–(4). For cases which led to the revision of this Rule, see *Experience Hendrix LLC v Times Newspapers Ltd* [2008] EWHC 458 (Ch) Warren J; *Beasley v Alexander* [2012] EWHC 2715 (QB) Sir Raymond Jack; *Ted Baker Plc v Axa Insurance UK Plc* [2012] EWHC 1779 (Comm) Eder J.

[32] See r.36.21.

[33] In relation to any money claim or any money element of a claim, "more advantageous" means better in money terms by any amount however small and "at least as advantageous" is to be construed accordingly—r.36.17(1)–(3).

r.36.21 applies. The provision does not apply to a Part 36 offer which has been withdrawn, which has been changed so that its terms are less advantageous to the offeree—where the offeree has beaten the less advantageous offer, or made less than 21 days before trial unless the court has abridged the relevant period.[34]

A defendant accepting a claimant's Part 36 offer outside the 21 day period but before the offer had been withdrawn was not entitled to an order under r.36.14 (r.36.17) as the issue of liability had been compromised and judgment had not been entered. The appropriate regime was under r.36.10 (r.36.13) and r.36.11 (r.36.14).[35]

Where judgment against the defendant is at least as advantageous to the claimant as the proposal contained in a claimant's Part 36 offer, the court must, unless it considers it unjust to do so, order that the claimant is entitled to:

(a) interest on the whole or part of any sum of money (excluding interest) awarded at a rate not exceeding 10 per cent above base rate for some or all of the periods, starting with the date on which the relevant period expired;

(b) costs (including any recoverable pre-action costs) on the indemnity basis from the date on which the relevant period expired;

(c) interest on those costs at a rate not exceeding 10 per cent above base rate; and

(d) provided that the case has been decided and that there has not been a previous order under the subparagraph, an additional amount not exceeding £75,000 calculated by applying the prescribed percentage to an amount which is the sum awarded to the claimant by a court, or where there is no monetary award, the sum awarded to the claimant by the court in respect of costs.

The prescribed percentage where the amount awarded by the court is up to £500,000 is 10 per cent of the amount awarded. Where the amount awarded by the court is above £500,000, the prescribed percentage is 10 per cent of the first £500,000 and (subject to the limit of £75,000) 5 per cent of any amount above that figure.[36] This provision does not apply to a Part 36 offer which has been withdrawn, or changed so that its terms are less advantageous to the offeree, or where the offeree has beaten the less advantageous offer made less than 21 days before trial unless the court has abridged the relevant period.[37]

5–12   The claimant's additional award under CPR r.36.17(4)(d) (previously CPR r.36.14(3)(d)) has come about as a result of Jackson LJ's recommendation in his Final Report that, where a defendant rejects a claimant's offer, but fails to do better at trial, the claimant's recovery should be enhanced by 10 per cent.

In considering whether it would be unjust to make the order described

---

[34] r.36.17(7) and (8).
[35] *Jolly v Harsco Infrastructure Services Ltd* [2012] EWHC 3086 (QB) Cranston J.
[36] r.36.17(4).
[37] r.36.17(7).

above, the court must take into account all the circumstances of the case including:

(a) the terms of any Part 36 offer;

(b) the stage in the proceedings when such an offer was made including, in particular, how long before the trial started the offer was made;

(c) the information available to the parties at the time when the offer was made;

(d) the conduct of the parties with regard to the giving of or refusal to give information for the purposes of enabling the offer to be made or evaluated; and

(e) whether the offer was a genuine attempt to settle the proceedings.

Where the court awards interest under these provisions and also awards interest on the same sum and for the same period under any other power, the total rate of interest must not exceed 10 per cent above base rate.[38]

The High Court has clarified that the additional amount which can be awarded under r.36.17(4)(d) should be calculated as a percentage of the basic monetary award but should not be applied to any award of interest. The Court awarded a Liquidator £360,000, plus statutory interest at 3 per cent above base rate. The defendant was also ordered to pay all the costs on the indemnity basis. The Court expressed the view that this was a case that should never have been defended. The Liquidator had beaten its own Part 36 offer of £325,000 inclusive of interest and the Judge also awarded an enhanced rate of interest of 10 per cent above base rate on the sum awarded from the end of the relevant period until the date of judgment, interest at 10 per cent above base rate on the costs and the additional amount allowed under r.36.17(4)(d).

This decision illustrates the potential advantages for claimants of making a Part 36 offer and also clarifies that where the claim includes a money claim, the additional amount is calculated as a percentage of the basic monetary award exclusive of interest.[39] The additional amount was not allowed in a case where, having made a Part 36 offer just before trial, the claimant beat her offer and sought payment of the additional amount under r.36.17(4)(d). The court declined to make such an order, because she had raised a matter of fundamental importance to her case only in the course of opening, and other important information was disclosed only on the eve of the trial.[40]

More advantageous

Sub-paragraph 72(vii) of the judgment in *Multiplex Construction (UK) Ltd v Cleveland Bridge UK Ltd*[41] (dealing with the effect of *Carver v BAA*) should be disregarded. *Carver* had effectively been reversed by the rule change in previous r.36.14(1A) (now r.36.17(2)—a change that was recommended by Lord Justice Jackson in his *Review of Civil Litigation Costs: Final Report*). The   **5–13**

---

[38]   r.36.17(5) and (6).

[39]   *Watchorn v Jupiter Industries Ltd* [2014] EWHC 3003 (Ch) HHJ Purle QC.

[40]   *Feltham v Bouskell* [2013] EWHC 3086 (Ch) Charles Hollander QC.

[41]   *Multiplex Construction (UK) Ltd v Cleveland Bridge UK Ltd* [2008] EWHC 2280 (TCC) Jackson J.

Judge making a Costs Order under r.44.2 was exercising a broad discretion, not just deciding who the winner on each issue was, but taking into account the conduct of the parties and all the circumstances of the case. The Judge was the best person to exercise that discretion having been immersed in the trial details.[42]

In a successful claim for dilapidations, it was common ground that there was no offer under CPR Pt 36 which had any automatic costs consequences. The defendant had however made a Part 36 offer by letter dated December 23, 2011 in the sum of £1,000,000. When interest was added to the sums awarded of £900,000 and £20,320.40 up to January 13, 2012, the last date of acceptance of the Part 36 offer, the sum awarded to the claimant exceeded the defendant's Part 36 offer by £3,637.90, which represented a very small percentage of the sum offered.

The court noted that previous Rule 36.14, had been amended on October 1, 2011, by the insertion of r.36.14(1)(A) (now r.36.17(2)). The claimant had not failed to obtain a judgment more advantageous than the defendant's Part 36 offer and therefore r.36.14 (r.36.17) did not apply. Ramsey J stated:

> *"The Part 36 offer made in this case could be said, in principle, to come within the wording of CPR 44.2(4)(c). It is an admissible offer to settle and is not an offer to which costs consequences under Part 36 apply. However I do not consider, even in a case such as this, where [the claimant] has only received a very small amount more than the sum which [the defendants] offered in its Part 36 offer, the court should approach CPR 44.2(4)(c) on the basis that this could lead to an order that a claimant should pay the defendants' costs. In my judgment, to do so would be to seek to use the provisions of CPR 44.2(4)(c) to give a similar effect to a Part 36 offer and thereby introduce the same uncertainty into Part 36 offers which are near to but below the sum awarded, as led to the criticism of Carver and the subsequent amendment introduced in CPR 36.14(1A) [now r.37.17].*
>
> *In my judgment the principle in sub-paragraph (vii) of [72] in Multiplex, derived as it was from Carver, is no longer a principle which applies to Part 36 and should not be applied as a special 'near miss' rule through CPR 44.2(4)(c). If there is an unreasonable refusal to negotiate then that is a matter which comes within the circumstances which the court can take into account under CPR 44.2(4) and sub-paragraph (a) in particular. I am doubtful that, on analysis, a 'near miss' offer can generally add anything to what otherwise would be conduct in the form of unreasonable refusal to negotiate . . . "[43]*

The court considered issues of conduct by both parties and the relative success and failure on various issues. In the light of those circumstances the court assessed costs by reference to the factors in CPR 44.2(4)(a) and (b). The claimant was awarded 80 per cent of its costs.[44]

---

[42]   *Dufoo v Tolaini* [2014] EWCA Civ 1536.
[43]   paras 26 and 36.
[44]   See *Hammersmatch Properties (Welwyn) Ltd v Saint-Cobain Ceramics & Plastics Ltd* [2013] EWHC 2227 (TCC).

At a trial on quantum, the claimant succeeded in beating the defendant's **5–14** Part 36 offer. The Judge when considering what order for costs to make, took into account, as a matter of discretion, the Part 36 offer which had been beaten. Eder J made it clear that he was not introducing a 'near miss' rule for Part 36 offers by the back door.[45] In the Judge's view the circumstances indicated that the claimant had insisted unreasonably on a higher figure than that offer, the claim had been much exaggerated and delays regarding disclosure and evidence had caused the defendant real difficulties in taking appropriate precautions to protect its position.[46]

There are numerous reported cases where offers which did not comply with r.36.5 have been held not to be Part 36 offers. In these circumstances however, the Court is not precluded from considering the fact that an offer has been made as part of the circumstances which it is required to take into account when considering what order for costs to make.[47] The Court has held that Part 36 should be construed as designed to protect defendants from claims being pursued, on the basis that a claimant might be able to persuade a defendant to pay more than the legal entitlement, or to pay the legal entitlement more quickly than would otherwise be the case, where the costs of contesting the entitlement would not be worth incurring. Part 36 is not intended to reward in costs, claimants who pursue their claims on such a basis.[48]

In a case where the claimant had achieved judgment against the defendant which was more advantageous than the proposal set out in its Part 36 offer, the defendants argued that it would be "unjust" to apply the previous r.36.14(3)(b) and (c) (now r.36.17(4)(b) and (c)). It was argued that the claimant had only succeeded as a result of material that had come to light since the Part 36 offer had been made. The argument was rejected by the Court of Appeal on the basis that the defendants were experienced litigators in the field and must have appreciated that there was a very serious risk that there would be a significant recovery above the interim payment which had already been made. The defendants had enough information to evaluate the Part 36 offer which they had rejected.[49]

It is for the offeree to satisfy the court that it is unjust for the court to make **5–15** the normal order. The court must take into account all the circumstances of the case including the matters set out in previous r36.14(4) (now r36.17(5)). They are not the only matters to be considered. Anything which is relevant must be considered as well, including uncertainty as to the developing condition and prognosis of a claimant under a disability.[50] There is no limit to the circumstances which could make it unjust that the ordinary consequences under r36.14 (now 3.17) should follow. Where an action had been about

---

[45]   See *Hammersmatch Properties (Welwyn) Ltd v Saint-Cobain Ceramics & Plastics Ltd* [2013] EWHC 2227 (TCC).
[46]   *Sugar Hut Group Ltd v A J Insurance* [2014] EWHC 3775 (Comm) Eder J.
[47]   For example, *Rowles–Davies v Call 24-7 Ltd* [2010] EWHC 1695 (Ch) Bernard Livesey QC; *Carillion J M Ltd v PHI Group Ltd* [2012] EWCA Civ 588; [2012] CP Rep 37.
[48]   *D Pride & Partners v Institute for Animal Health* [2009] EWHC 1617 (QB); [2009] 5 Costs LR 803, Tugendhat J.
[49]   *Bent v Highways and Utilities Construction & Allianz Insurance* [2011] EWCA Civ 1539.
[50]   *SG (a child) v Hewitt* [2012] EWCA Civ 1053.

restoration of reputation and the conduct of the defendant's disciplinary procedures the court ordered the costs to lie where they fell.[51]

Where a claimant obtained judgment materially in excess of the figure proposed by way of settlement in the claimant's Part 36 offer, which had been rejected by the defendant company, the claimant applied to add the husband and wife directors as defendants in order to obtain an order for costs against them under s.51 of the Senior Courts Act 1981. A third party costs order was made. The question then arose as to the appropriate rate of interest on the claimant's costs in respect of the Part 36 offer. The court held that previous r.36.14 (now r.36.17) dealt with the position which applied when judgment was entered. The relevant judgment was that against the defendant company and interest at 6 per cent above base rate was awarded from the date of the refused Part 36 offer until the date of judgment. In respect of the costs of the s.51 proceedings, which were governed by r.44.3(6)(g) the court awarded interest at one per cent above base rate.[52]

In personal injury proceedings, the court having found in favour of the claimant, ordered that the costs should be on the standard basis, save that the costs attributable to dealing with the evidence of the defendant's expert witnesses should be assessed on the indemnity basis.[53] The defendant contended that it had made a written offer on costs, with a better outcome than the claimant had obtained. The court held that it was not possible to conduct a preliminary assessment of costs to establish arithmetically whether the defendant's offer was better on a pound for pound basis than the outcome achieved by the claimant. The justice of the case required the defendant to pay the claimant's costs of the oral hearing, together with the costs of the subsequent dispute as to costs of that hearing on the standard basis.[54]

Costs in the case and Part 36

5–16   In a libel action brought by three claimants against three defendants in respect of emails sent in January and July 2012, the claimants each accepted offers of settlement which had been made by the third defendant. At the same time, the claimants gave notice of discontinuance of their claims against the first and second defendants.

The court had to determine the appropriate final orders in respect of damages and costs to give effect to the settlements and the discontinuance. The main issues were whether such costs orders as were made against the claimants should be on the standard or the indemnity basis, whether the claimants should be jointly and severally liable for costs ordered in favour of the third defendant, and whether—and if so to what extent—costs and damages due to the claimants should be set off against costs due to the third

---

[51] *Smith v Trafford Housing Trust* [2012] EWHC 3320 (Ch) Briggs J.
[52] *Chantrey Vellacott v The Convergence Group plc* [2007] EWHC 1774 (Ch) Rimer J.
[53] Such an order would be extremely difficult to assess, and would probably not result in any significant difference in the amount of costs awarded.
[54] *Williams v Jervis* [2009] EWHC 1838 (QB) Roderick Evans J.

defendant. There was also an issue in respect of the effect of an order for costs in the case in respect of the third defendant's strike out application.

The court explained:

> *"The 'general effect' of an order for costs in the case is that 'the party in whose favour the court makes an order for costs at the end of the proceedings is entitled to that party's costs of the part of the proceedings to which the order relates': PD44 paragraph 4.2. Here, that general rule cannot be very readily applied; at the end of the proceedings the court has made orders for costs in favour of each party, save for [one] . . .*
>
> *The action has concluded by settlement via Part 36 and without prejudice save as to costs offers. All the claimants have obtained judgment for damages. [Two of the claimants] have recovered substantial damages, sums which on [the third defendant's] case are the maximum they could possibly have obtained. Yet it is said that they are the losers because their recovery is but a fraction of what they claimed. Views could differ about that conclusion, in this case and in others. It is easy to see that if [that] criterion were adopted there could often be lengthy argument as to which party has in reality 'won'.*
>
> *A simpler and better criterion is to hand for a case like this, which is to have regard to when in the proceedings the relevant costs were incurred and which party has obtained an order for costs in relation to that phase of the proceedings. As a starting point I would suggest that acceptance of a Part 36 offer, which will ordinarily lead to an order for the costs up to the relevant date, should also carry with it any costs incurred within that period which are the subject of an order for costs in the case. Equally, if an offer is accepted 'out of time' and an order is made, in the ordinary way, for the offeree to pay costs since the expiry of the relevant period that order should carry with it any costs incurred in that period which are the subject of an order for costs in the case."*[55]

The court ordered the third defendant to pay the two claimants' costs of the strike out application.[56]

Cases in which the offeror's costs have been limited to court fees

Where, because of failure to file a costs budget on time or otherwise, 5–17
the offeror is limited to applicable court fees, "costs"[57] means, in respect of the costs subject to any such limitation, 50 per cent of the costs assessed without reference to the limitation together with any other recoverable costs.[58]

RTA Protocol and EL/PL Protocol offers to settle

Section II of Part 36 applies to an offer to settle where the parties have fol- 5–18
lowed the RTA Protocol or the EL/PL Protocol, and started proceedings under

---

[55] paras 89–91.
[56] *Ontulmusv Collett* [2014] EWHC 4117 (QB) Warby J.
[57] In rr.36.13(5)(b), 36.17(3)(a) and 36.17(4)(b).
[58] r.36.23. This provision is intended to mitigate the effect of the claimant being unable to recover more than the applicable court fees.

Part 8, in accordance with Practice Direction 8B (the Stage 3 procedure). Parties may make an offer to settle in whatever way they choose, but any offer which is not made in accordance with Section II will not have any costs consequences.[59]

A Protocol offer under Section II must be set out in the Court Proceedings Pack (Form B) Form, and contain the final total amount of the offer from both parties. The offer is deemed to be made on the first business day after the Court Proceedings Pack is sent to the defendant.[60]

A Protocol offer is treated as exclusive of all interest, and has costs consequences only in relation to the fixed costs of the Stage 3 procedure (as provided for in r.45.18), not in relation to the costs of any appeal from the final decision in those proceedings. The amount of a Protocol offer must not be communicated to the court until the claim is determined. Any other offer to settle must not be communicated to the court at all.[61]

Costs consequences following judgment

5–19   Where on any determination by the court, the claimant obtains judgment against the defendant for an amount of damages that is:

(a)   less than or equal to the amount of the defendant's Protocol offer;

(b)   more than the defendant's Protocol offer, but less than the claimant's Protocol offer; or

(c)   equal to or more than the claimant's Protocol offer.

Where (a) applies, the court must order the claimant to pay the fixed costs in r.45.26, and interest on those fixed costs from the first business day after the deemed date of the Protocol offer under r.36.26.

Where (b) applies, the court must order the defendant to pay the fixed costs in r.45.20.

Where (c) applies, the court must order the defendant to pay interest on the whole of the damages awarded at a rate not exceeding 10 per cent above base rate for some or all of the period, starting with the date specified in r.36.26, the fixed costs in r.45.20, interest on those fixed costs at a rate not exceeding 10 per cent above base rate, and an additional amount calculated in accordance with r.36.17(4)(d).[62]

Deduction of benefits

5–20   For the purposes of (a) above, the amount of the judgment is less than the Protocol offer where the judgment is less than the offer once deductible amounts identified in the judgment are deducted.[63]

---

[59]   CPR r.36.24.
[60]   CPR rr.36.25, 36.26.
[61]   CPR rr.36.27, 36.28.
[62]   r.36.29(1)–(4).
[63]   r.36.30.

Offers other than Part 36 offers

It is open to either party in litigation to make offers which do not comply   5–21
with the requirements of Part 36. These may be open offers or offers without
prejudice save as to costs. These are generally known as Calderbank offers,
which arose in the Family Division where there was no provision for payment
into Court, but the parties could be at risk as to costs, particularly in respect
of financial arrangements.

In deciding what order to make about costs the Court is required to have
regard to all the circumstances including the conduct of all the parties,
whether a party has succeeded on part of its case and if not wholly successful,
the extent to which that party has succeeded and any admissible offer to settle
which is drawn to the Court's attention and which is not an offer to which
the costs consequences of Part 36 apply.[64] The question of who was the successful party or the unsuccessful party to an action can be determined by who
ultimately wrote the cheque at the end.[65]

Costs of detailed assessment proceedings

Rule 47.20(4) clarifies that the provisions of Part 36 apply to the costs of   5–22
detailed assessment proceedings with certain modifications. Where an offer to
settle is made whether under Part 36 or otherwise, it should specify whether
or not it is intended to be inclusive of the costs of preparation of the bill,
interest and VAT. Unless the offer makes it clear that the position is otherwise,
it will be treated as being inclusive of all those matters.[66]

In proceedings for detailed assessment, the paying party wrote to the
receiving party, setting out what they described as Part 36 offers, which were
stated to be open for 21 days, and offered a proportion or fixed sum in respect
of the receiving party's costs. The offers were rejected, and the paying party
made a further offer in respect of a third receiving party, if the other receiving
parties were willing to accept the Part 36 offers. These offers were accepted,
but the costs hearing still took place because the paying party contended they
were entitled to costs in respect of the period from the expiry of the 21 days
referred to in the original offers, until the point when the offers had been
accepted. The court made no order for the costs in respect of that period. The
court held, on the facts, that the earlier offer was not a Part 36 offer, because
it specifically excluded the offerors from recovering all of their costs, and it
could not, by its very terms, comply with CPR 36.10(1) (now 36.13(1)).

The subsequent offer was indistinguishable from that in *C v D*,[67] and the
subsequent offer should be treated as a Part 36 offer, particularly since all the
parties treated the offers as having been made under Part 36. The overriding
objective, and common sense, suggested that an offer which was expressed to
be a Part 36 offer, and which otherwise appeared to comply with Part 36, had

---

[64]   r.44.2(4), Practice Direction 44, paras 4.1–4.2.
[65]   *Day v Day* (Costs) [2006] EWCA Civ 415; [2006] CP Rep 35.
[66]   Practice Direction 47 para.19.
[67]   *C v D* [2011] EWCA Civ 646.

to be given substantially the same effect as a Part 36 offer. The offer which was accepted was significantly better than the original offer, and the allocation of liability for costs for the period between the expiry of the 21 days and acceptance was a matter for the Judge's discretion, without the presumption in favour of the paying party inherent in r.36.10(4) and (5) (Rule 36.13(4) and (5)). The right order to make was that each party should bear its own costs from the expiry of the 21 days.[68]

Questions and answers
Q1. Where there has been a trial of preliminary issues, what is the position with regard to Part 36 offers which may have been made?

Acceptance of a Part 36 offer in a split-trial case

5–23   Where there has been a trial but all the issues in the case have not been determined,[69] any Part 36 offer which relates only to parts of the claim or issues that have already been decided can no longer be accepted. Subject to that proviso, and unless the parties agree, any other Part 36 offer cannot be accepted earlier than seven clear days after judgment is given or handed down in that trial.[70]

Where an offer, which relates to the whole of the claim, is accepted after the expiry of the relevant period, the court must, unless it considers it unjust to do so, order that the claimant be awarded costs up to the date on which the relevant period expired, and, that the offeree pay the offeror's costs for the period from the date of the expiry of the relevant period to the date of acceptance. In considering whether it would be unjust to make such orders the court must take into account all the circumstances of the case including the matters set out in r.36.17(5) (see **Costs consequences following judgment** above). The claimant's costs include any costs incurred in dealing with the defendant's counterclaim if the Part 36 offer states that it takes the counterclaim into account.[71] Rule 36.16 deals with restrictions on disclosure in such cases.

It is open to the Court to depart from the normal costs rule in previous r.36.10(5) (now r.36.13(5)). Where a young boy had suffered frontal lobe damage in a road traffic accident, it was material that the inherent uncertainty in prognosis would have resolved well before the limitation period expired so that the child did not need to commence proceedings before the position was clear. The defendant had made a pre-action Part 36 offer in full and final settlement; the claimant accepted the offer after the date of its expiry. The Court approved the settlement, but at first instance it was held that the defendant should be entitled to its costs from the date of acceptance. The Court of Appeal held that the Judge's conclusion did not give weight to the particular features

---

[68]   *Howellv Lees-Millais* [2011] EWCA Civ 786.
[69]   Within the meaning of r.36.3(e).
[70]   r.36.12 and also see r.36.3.
[71]   Rule 36.13(5)–(7). For cases which led to the revision of this rule, see *Fitzpatrick Contractors Ltd v Tyco Fire & Integrated Solutions (UK) Ltd* [2009] EWHC 274 (TCC) Coulson J; *Thompson v Bruce* [2011] EWHC 1730 (QB) John Leighton Williams QC; *Kunaka v Barclays Bank Plc* [2010] EWCA Civ 1035; *Sutherland v Turnball* [2010] EWHC 2699 (QB) Stadlen J.

of the claimant's case, the consequence of omitting to give weight to the matters that were in the claimant's favour was that the normal rule dominated when it should not have done. In the circumstances it was unjust to make the normal costs order, and the claimant was awarded his costs throughout.[72]

There was previously no general rule that in the case of a split trial the Court should ordinarily reserve the costs until the end of the case. Mr Justice Eder stated that there was an urgent need for the rule to be reviewed and possibly reformulated in order to address the question of split trials. In the particular case, due to the substantial level of costs, costs were reserved.[73]

Eder J eventually gave three main judgments. The first dealt with the outcome of the preliminary issues (Part 1); the one cited above he referred to as "Part 2"; and the third dealt with further issues concerning claims co-operation and also quantum (Part 3). The costs by this time had "spiralled out of all proportion" to the amount which was then in dispute.

5–24

During the course of the proceedings the defendants made various offers of settlement. Although the claimants had succeeded in relation to the preliminary issues (Part1), they had failed to obtain a money judgment more advantageous than any of the defendants' settlement offers. The claimants' success on Part 1 resulted in no ultimate financial benefit to them; they would have been enormously better off if they had accepted any of the offers.

Relying on previous r.36.14 (now r.36.17) the Court held that the rule meant that "the Court will make the order there specified 'unless it considers it unjust to do so'". The burden of showing such injustice is a "formidable obstacle".

Eder J stated:

> *"It follows that the real question, in my view, is whether the claimants can show any relevant 'injustice' so as to displace the general rule, bearing fully in mind that the burden of doing so is a 'formidable obstacle'. In this context and without seeking to lay down any hard and fast rules, it seems to me that where a claimant fails to 'beat' a Part 36 offer made by a defendant, the mere fact that such defendant may fail on certain issues would not necessarily of itself make it 'unjust' to displace the general rule under Part 36 and to require the claimant to pay the costs from the date on which the relevant period expired and interest on such costs under Part 36.14(2) (r.36.17(3)). However, on the other hand . . . it seems to me that the fact that a defendant may make a Part 36 offer does not give such defendant carte blanche to run any defence whatsoever so as to entitle such defendant necessarily to expect that the CPR Part 36 consequences will automatically to apply to those issues on which such defendant lost."*[74]

In the light of the above and bearing in mind that the claimants had succeeded on Part 1, The defendants were awarded 25 per cent of their costs on Part 1. They were awarded all their costs on Part 2.[75]

---

[72]   *SG v Hewitt* [2012] EWCA Civ 1053.
[73]   *Ted Baker Plc v Axa Insurance UK Plc* [2012] EWHC 1779 (Comm) Eder J.
[74]   para.17.
[75]   *Ted Baker Plc v AXA Insurance UK Plc* [2014] EWHC 4178 (Comm) Eder J.

This decision remained case-specific until the introduction of the new rules. In a different case, the judge decided that success on the preliminary issue did not mean that the claimant would ultimately establish any claim in contract at all, and the incidence of costs should therefore be the same as if it had been tried as part of that claim. The judge did not think that this was a reason for departing from the general rule. The defendants had asked for a preliminary issue. They did so because it was thought to be helpful to the parties, and to the Court, for the question of proper law to be determined as a discrete issue. The judge agreed, but the corollary of this was that the question did not arise as part and parcel of the trial but was tried separately. That necessarily involved a separate hearing with separate preparation and the incurring of separate costs on that issue. It is in general a salutary principle that those who lose discrete aspects of complex litigation should pay for the discrete applications or hearings which they lose, and should do so when they lose them rather than leaving the costs to be swept up at trial.[76]

Q2. Are costs recoverable if a claimant's Part 36 offer is accepted in circumstances where the claimant's costs budget has not been filed on time?

5–25   This question was originally raised after the decision in *Mitchell* but before the Court of Appeal decision in *Denton*. Given the more measured approach of the Court in *Denton*, it would seem that if the Part 36 offer has been accepted within the relevant period, the claimant will be entitled to the costs of the proceedings up to the date on which notice of acceptance was served on the offeror (r.36.13(1)). If the acceptance of the offer is after the expiry of the relevant period and the parties are unable to agree the liability for costs, liability for costs must be determined by the Court (r.36.13(4)). The outcome may, however, depend on how late the budget was—if, indeed, it has been filed—and all the circumstances because the canny defendant might argue that the offer was only made because it knew it had only a very limited costs liability after the date the budget fell due and r.3.14 applied. On the other hand the consequences of the Court requiring the claimant to apply for relief from sanction and then refusing such relief would merely be to generate further satellite litigation, an outcome which the Court in *Denton* was at pains to avoid. Rule 36.23 somewhat ameliorates the draconian effect of r.3.14.

Q3. What is the position where a Part 36 offer is withdrawn at the same time as the claimant purports to accept it?

5–26   The rules governing the withdrawal of offers are now rr.36.9 and 36.10. The following decision still holds good. An NHS Trust made a Part 36 offer to a claimant which stated that if it was accepted within 21 days, the Trust would be responsible for the claimant's costs. The offer pointed out that it could be withdrawn before the expiration of that period with permission of the

---

[76]   *Merck KGAA v Merck Sharp & Dohme Corp* [2014] EWHC 3920 (Ch) Nugee J.

Court. Before the expiration of the relevant period the Trust obtained permission to withdraw its offer but did so without serving any notice or evidence on the claimant who had accepted the offer on the day it was withdrawn. Leggatt J held that an application should not be made without notice unless that would enable the respondent to take steps to defeat the purpose of the application or there had been no time to give notice before the urgent assistance of the Court was required. It was wrong in principle for the Trust to make its application for permission without notice to the claimant and for the Court to entertain the application. It was all the more wrong to conceal from the claimant the grounds on which the order had been made. The making of orders which determined questions of substantive rights between the parties without notice could only be justified if that party had the right to apply to set aside the order. The tests would be applied when considering whether to grant a party permission to withdraw a Part 36 offer was whether there had been a sufficient change of circumstances to make it just to do so.[77] The only new circumstances which could make it just were circumstances which the Trust was able and willing to make known to the claimant at the time of serving notice of withdrawal.[78]

Under new CPR 36.10(3), where the offeree serves notice of acceptance of the offer before the expiry of the relevant period and the offeror applies to court for permission to withdraw or change its terms within seven days of the offeree's notice (or, if earlier, before the first day of trial), the court will only give permission if satisfied that there has been a change of circumstances and that it is in the interests of justice.

Q4. Are defendants who refuse Part 36 offers which are successful always going to be penalised in costs or does the Court have a discretion?

Not Always. Where a claimant's Part 36 offer which had been refused, but not bettered at trial, expired days before the trial commenced and the defendants had not received its witness statements until the final day of the expiry of the offer, the High Court ruled that making a defendant who rejected a Part 36 offer pay an additional 10 per cent of the sum awarded for costs, pursuant to previous r.36.14(3)(d) (now r.36.17(4)(d)), would introduce a 'penal' element and be unjust. The ruling was made after an injunction had been granted to the claimant restraining the defendant from joining another company before the end of his 12-month notice period.[79]

5–27

---

[77] *Cumper v Pothecary* [1941] 2 KB 58.
[78] *Evans v Royal Wolverhampton Hospitals NHS Foundation Trust* [2014] EWHC 3185 (QB) Leggatt J.
[79] *Elsevier Ltd v Munro* [2014] EWHC 2728 (QB) Warby J. See also *Feltham v Bouskell* [2013] EWHC 3086 (Ch) Charles Hollander QC.

Q5. Is the following case still good law—Hammersmatch Properties (Welwyn) Ltd v Saint Gobain Ceramics and Plastics Ltd[80]? Is Eder J's costs decision in Sugar Hut etc. v AJ Insurance[81] reintroducing Carver by the back door?

5–28   The general view is that *Hammersmatch* is still good law, but the decision in *Sugar Hut* may cause confusion. In the latter, Eder J found that he was entitled to take the defendant's Part 36 offer into account as a matter of conduct and in accordance with the wide discretion of the court, even though it was narrowly beaten by the claimant, when ordering the successful claimant to pay the defendant's costs from a certain date. It could be said that this runs counter to Ramsay J's warning against allowing CPR 44.2(4)(c) to be used as a basis for making an order for the claimant to pay the defendant's costs where there is a "near miss" Part 36 offer. Ramsay J was concerned that this would introduce the same degree of uncertainty as led to the criticism of *Carver* (CPR 44.2(4) requires the court, when making a costs order, to have regard to "all the circumstances"—this includes the conduct of all the parties (CPR 44.2(4)(a)) and any admissible offer to settle drawn to the court's attention which is not an offer to which the Part 36 costs consequences apply (CPR 44.2(4)(c)).)

On the other hand, Eder J made it clear that he was not introducing a "near miss" rule by the back door and went to significant lengths to emphasise that *Sugar Hut* could be distinguished from *Hammersmatch* as his conclusion was not based on a near-miss analysis, did not involve any speculation about what negotiations might have taken place and all the circumstances supported the view that the claimant had insisted unreasonably on a higher figure than that offered.

Q6. How important is mediation and refusal to mediate in relation to Part 36?

5–29   When the Court exercises its discretion under r.44.2, it has to have regard to all the circumstances including the conduct of the parties both before and during the proceedings. "Conduct" includes a refusal to agree to alternative dispute resolution (ADR). The factors to be taken into account include the nature of the dispute, the merits of the case, the extent to which other settlement methods have been attempted, whether the costs of ADR are disproportionately high, whether any delay in setting or attending the ADR would be prejudicial, and whether ADR has a reasonable prospect of success.[82] Where a party reasonably considered that it had a strong case and where a party was faced with an unfounded claim and wished to contest it rather than buy it off, the Court should be slow to characterise that as unreasonable conduct. The fact that a party reasonably believed that it had a watertight case might well be sufficient justification for refusal to mediate.[83] The Court has to look

---

[80]   *Hammersmatch Properties (Welwyn) Ltd v Saint Gobain Ceramics and Plastics Ltd* [2013] EWHC 2227 (TCC).
[81]   *Sugar Hut etc. v AJ Insurance* [2014] EWHC 3775 (Comm).
[82]   See *Halsey v Milton Keynes General NHS Trust* [2004] EWCA Civ 576; [2004] 1 WLR 3002.
[83]   See *Halsey* (above) and *Daniels v Commissioner of Police of the Metropolis* [2005] EWCA Civ 1312; [2006] CP Rep.9.

beyond the polarised positions of the parties. A skilled mediator might be able to find middle ground by analysing the parties' position and making each reflect on its own and the other's position. By bringing other commercial arrangements or disputes into the discussion or by finding future business opportunities, a mediator might find solutions that the parties had not considered. On the facts of the particular case, the defendant's refusal to mediate had deprived the parties of the opportunity of resolving the case without a hearing as had the claimant's failure to accept the defendant's offer. The fair and just outcome was that neither party's conduct should modify the general rule on costs. The claimant was accordingly ordered to pay the whole of the defendant's costs on the standard basis.[84]

In *Garritt-Critchley v Ronnan*[85] the defendants accepted the claimant's Part 36 offer just before judgment was about to be given following a four day trial. The judge did not criticise the late acceptance of the Part 36 offer but penalised the defendants in costs because he considered that they had been wrong in consistently refusing to mediate (the defendants had refused to mediate because they were confident of their position and believed that the parties were too far apart). The judge stated that the claim involved a question of fact which was a classic case for mediation and parties did not know whether they were too far apart until they sat down and explored settlement. Mediation also costs less than trial. If the defendants had accepted the claimant's last offer of mediation, the difference in costs might have been almost £100,000.

The judge applied *Halsey*, which held that in deciding whether a party had acted unreasonably in refusing ADR, the court should bear in mind the advantages of ADR over the court process and have regard to all the circumstances of the particular case.

In a building dispute the claimant made a Part 36 offer to settle, and also **5–30** suggested mediation. At trial the Judge awarded damages which were less than the claimant had claimed, and less than their Part 36 offer. The Judge ordered no order for costs up to the expiry of the period for acceptance of the Part 36 offer, and ordered the claimant to pay the defendant's costs thereafter. The Court of Appeal held that the Judge had erred fundamentally in his appreciation of the significance of the claimant's Part 36 offer. There was nothing in Part 36 which stated that an offeror was to be prejudiced as to costs because she expressed her willingness to accept less than her formal claim. An order for no order as to costs did substantial justice between the parties. The claimant was the winner but only just. On an issues-based approach she had failed on three issues, but succeeded on one issue which had taken a substantial amount of time. The defendants' rejection of offers to enter into settlement

---

[84] *Northrop Grumman Mission Systems Europe Limited v BAE Systems (AL Diriyah C41) Limited* [2014] EWHC 3148 (TCC); [2014] TCLR 8, Ramsey J.
[85] *Garritt-Critchley v Ronnan* [2014] EWHC 1774.

negotiations or mediation was unreasonable, and conduct which ought to be taken into account.[86]

While mediation is not compulsory, it is now well established that the courts may robustly encourage parties to embark on it and an unreasonable failure to do so places a party at risk of being penalised in costs. This decision is a reminder that refusing mediation is a high risk strategy, and lawyers and their clients should consider their position carefully.

In Chapter 36 of his Final Report Jackson LJ recommended:

> *"4.2 I recommend that:*
> *(i) There should be a serious campaign (a) to ensure that all litigation lawyers and judges are properly informed about the benefits which ADR can bring and (b) to alert the public and small businesses to the benefits of ADR.*
> *(ii) An authoritative handbook should be prepared, explaining clearly and concisely what ADR is and giving details of all reputable providers of mediation. This should be the standard handbook for use at all JSB seminars and CPD training sessions concerning mediation."*

There is growing pressure from the judiciary and court users for greater use of ADR. The Jackson ADR Handbook was published in January 2013, written by three distinguished authors under the banner of the Judicial College, The Civil Justice Council and The Civil Mediation Council.

Q7. Do you agree that it may be difficult to decide who has obtained the more advantageous result in a detailed assessment? Also, does the amendment to r.36.14(3) (now r.36.17(4)) in April 2013, to enhance claimants' recovery by 10 per cent apply in detailed assessments?

5–31   Where a Part 36 offer has been made in detailed assessment proceedings, it will be for a specified amount. When the bill is totalled at the end of the detailed assessment there should be no difficulty in ascertaining whether or not the offer has been beaten. The power of the Court under Rule 36.17(4) to award interest not exceeding 10 per cent above base rate on the sum awarded, to award indemnity costs, to award interest on those costs at a rate not exceeding 10 per cent above base rate, and an additional amount in accordance with r.36.17(4)(d) is certainly exercisable but will inevitably be fact sensitive, and the Court may consider it unjust to make any orders in these terms. It could be argued that where a detailed assessment has been carried out on the standard basis, the amount allowed will or should be reasonable and proportionate. To allow an additional amount of up to £75,000 would mean that the Court was awarding costs which were neither proportionate nor reasonable. This, however, assumes that the extra 10 per cent is costs. This does not appear to be correct. It may equally be argued that it is simply an "additional amount". In substantive claims the additional

---

[86]   *Rolf v De Guerin* [2011] EWCA Civ 78.

amount is not treated as damages but just a compensatory amount.[87] This means that the 10 per cent is not costs and so issues of proportionality do not arise.

Q8. If a defendant makes a Part 36 offer which does not take into account its counterclaim and the offer is then accepted, what happens to the counterclaim?
"Counterclaim" is defined by the CPR glossary as 'a claim brought by a defendant in response to the claimant's claim which is included in the same proceedings as the claimant's claim'. A counterclaim is treated for certain purposes as if it were a claim (r.20.3). Rule 36.2(3) provides that a Part 36 offer may be made in respect of the whole, or part of, any issue that arises in a claim, counterclaim or other additional claim, and state whether it takes into account any counterclaim (r.36.5(1)(e)). Rule 36.14(3) provides that if a Part 36 offer which relates to part only of the claim is accepted, the claim will be stayed as to that part upon the terms of the offer. The question which has to be decided is whether the counterclaim is 'part only of the claim' or is a claim in its own right. Whilst the rules provide for a Part 36 offer to take into account the existence of a counterclaim if so desired, there is no requirement to do so and it is accordingly arguable that a counterclaim is a claim in its own right and would continue notwithstanding any Part 36 offer accepted in respect of the claim. The options for a party making a Part 36 offer, where a counterclaim exists, appear to be: either to ensure that the offer takes into account the counterclaim or to make an offer without prejudice save as to costs, i.e. a Calderbank offer.

5–32

Q9. What is the requirement for open offers in detailed assessment proceedings meant to achieve and how they will co-exist with Part 36 offers?
Practice Direction 47 para.8.3 sets the matter out clearly:

5–33

> *"The paying party must state in an open letter accompanying the points of dispute what sum, if any, that party offers to pay in settlement of the total costs claimed. The paying party may also make an offer under Part 36."*

Lord Justice Jackson's objective in inserting this requirement was to ensure that the parties were not in fact arguing over an insignificant amount of money. It is clearly open to the paying party to make an open offer of 0 per cent. This would presumably only be done if there were an arguable point of principle which might well result in the receiving party recovering nothing. There is no requirement that the open offer and any Part 36 offer should be in the same terms.

If a paying party fails to make an open offer as required by the Practice Direction, it would clearly be within the power of the costs judge to strike out

---

[87]   See *OOO Abbott v Design & Display Ltd* [2014] EWHC 3234 (IPEC) HHJ Hacon.

the points of dispute or if that were felt to be too draconian, to rely only on the written points of dispute and not permit any further oral argument.

The Court of Appeal expressly considered provisions of the CPR which contain mandatory language, but where no sanction is provided for any failure to comply in *Altomart v Salford Estates (No.2) Ltd*.[88] The court accepted the proposition that there might be implied sanctions which were capable of engaging CPR 3.9 and equally there might be cases not analogous with CPR 3.9 and where it was a matter for the court to determine the consequence of non-compliance. It is clear that the open offer does not form part of the Points of Dispute (it merely accompanies that document) and therefore it is difficult to see how any argument suggesting that the Points of Dispute should be struck out would find favour (indeed there is a risk it would be seen as an attempt to turn the rules into 'tripwires' and invoke possible costs sanctions). Perhaps a more measured approach would be to identify the failure to comply to the paying party promptly, suggesting a short period for rectification, and, in default of compliance reserve the position to the question of costs of the assessment, if relevant, under 'conduct' within CPR 47.20(3)(a).

Q10. How are Calderbank offers treated in relation to costs?

5–34   The Court of Appeal has made it clear that the effect of a Calderbank offer is not to be assessed by analogy with the terms of r.36.17(2) which defines a 'more advantageous' judgment as one that is 'better in money terms by any amount, however small' than the relevant offer. Parts 36 and 44 of the CPR are separate regimes with separate purposes. Part 36 is a self-contained procedural code which specifies particular consequences in the event that such offers are not accepted. Those consequences include features which go far beyond that which might be ordered by way of costs under Part 44. Whilst Part 36 is highly prescriptive and highly restrictive of the exercise of any discretion by the Court, Part 44 confers on the Court a discretion in almost the widest possible terms. It contains no rules as to the way in which the Court has to have regard to offers and there is no equivalent to the 'more advantageous' test in Part 36.[89]

Q11. How does the cap on damages in the IPEC apply where there is also a claim for costs?

5–35   In the Intellectual Property Enterprise Court (IPEC) the cap on the maximum value permitted for a claim for damages on an account of profits is £500,000. A claimant in IPEC proceedings obtained judgment for an amount well in excess of its rejected Part 36 offer. The question was whether the 'additional amount' payable by the defendant under previous r.36.14(3)(d) (now r.36.17(4)) should be treated as further damages (subject to the £500,000 cap) or whether it was a separate payment unaffected by the cap. The Court held that it appeared to

---

[88] *Altomart v Salford Estates (No.2) Ltd* [2014] EWCA Civ 1408.
[89] *Coward v Phaestos Ltd* [2014] EWCA Civ 1256.

be clear from the note to r.36.14 in the White Book and the authorities there mentioned that the 'additional amount' had nothing to do with compensating a claimant for any wrong committed by the defendant in the substantive dispute. It was solely intended to serve as an incentive to encourage claimants to make and defendants to accept appropriate Part 36 offers.[90]

Q12. When the question of costs is being decided is it possible for a party to refer to without prejudice correspondence in order to establish that the other party did not respond to Part 36 offers?

A defendant who had been found liable for misusing the claimants' confi-   5–36
dential information made two Part 36 offers during the course of an inquiry as to damages. The claimants did not respond to either offer and made no counter-offer. When the court was dealing with the costs of the inquiry the defendant criticised the claimants' conduct and served a witness statement which referred to an exchange of without prejudice correspondence between solicitors attempting to settle the question of costs. The claimants sought an order to strike out those passages which referred to the without prejudice correspondence.

The court stated that there was a strong public policy justification for denying the ability to rely on without prejudice correspondence at any stage in the proceedings including costs assessment. Where a without prejudice offer was made the recipient was free to make a without prejudice response. The response might be to make a counter-offer, ask for more information, reject the offer or simply ignore it. All these responses were protected by privilege. The fact that the claimants were seeking costs on the indemnity basis did not amount to a waiver of privilege but was based on criticism of the defendant's conduct.[91]

---

[90]   *000 Abbott v Design and Display Ltd* [2014] EWHC 3234 (IPEC) HHJ Hacon.
[91]   *Vestergaard Frandsen v Bestnet Europe Ltd* [2014] EWHC 4047 (Ch) Iain Purvis QC.

CHAPTER 6

Qualified One-Way Costs Shifting

Introduction

The introduction of a system of one-way costs shifting (QOCS) in personal injury litigation was the subject of close and detailed scrutiny and debate during Lord Justice Jackson's review. Amongst its primary attractions was that it was seen to provide a possible solution to the problem and costs of the 'indefensible' regime of After the Event Insurance (ATE) in such cases,[1] particularly given that claimants were perceived as being successful in the majority of personal injury claims.   6–01

In clinical negligence claims where the success rate of claimants was lower, the relatively higher costs of ATE premiums in such cases provided a counterbalancing justification for the consideration of one way costs shifting.

Accordingly, the firm recommendation was made that a system of one-way costs shifting should be introduced in all such cases with the specific aim of reducing the costs of personal injury litigation, in particular by removing the need for ATE. One way costs shifting was part of a package, therefore, along with the restrictions in recoverability of ATE introduced by s.46 of LASPO.

Jackson LJ, however, was alive to the need to deter frivolous or fraudulent claims and to encourage acceptance of reasonable offers, aims which would be undermined by wholesale protection to claimants from the risk of adverse costs orders no matter what. Accordingly, the proposed system of one way costs shifting was to be qualified to address these requirements, hence QOCS.

To avoid undue complexity and impracticality, QOCS was to be introduced for all personal injury claims, rather than merely being restricted to low value claims or claims run on Conditional Fee Agreements. In fact, the definition in CPR 44.13(1) makes clear that QOCS applies (at least in part) not merely to a 'pure' personal injury claim, but to any proceedings which include such a claim. When introduced, the only absolute exception was for cases where a claimant had entered into a pre-commencement funding arrangement (considered below).

Jackson LJ's proposal was for a system which provided a "broadly similar degree of protection against adverse costs" to that which applied to publicly funded litigants through what was then s.11 of the Access to Justice Act 1999.[2]   6–02

The proposal involved a broad test, based on the test applicable in such cases, whereby the costs ordered against a claimant in such cases would not exceed:

---

[1]   Final Report, pp.184 and 188.
[2]   Now s.26 of LASPO—see Final Report, p.189.

" . . . *the amount, if any, which is a reasonable one for him to pay having regard to all the circumstances including (a) the financial resources of all parties to the proceedings; and (b) their conduct in connection with the dispute to which the proceedings relate.*"

The proposal would firstly have allowed the courts to address concerns in relation to frivolous and fraudulent claims. Secondly, it would have ensured that QOCS could be limited where the claimant's means were such that it would be unjust not to require the claimant to pay costs. It would also have allowed for the possibility of a 'football pools' type application, whereby a defendant who was not allowed to enforce a costs order might, in limited circumstances, reapply to do so where the claimant finances subsequently and substantially improved.

Whilst Jackson LJ's general proposal for a system of qualified one-way costs shifting was adopted, his proposed test was not and a more rigid approach, which does not include any limitation by reference to the claimant's financial resources, was introduced.

In order to address Jackson LJ's second concern, that of incentivising claimants to make Part 36 offers despite QOCS protection, Jackson LJ proposed the 10 per cent increase in general damages which did come into effect, in relation to cases where there was no pre-commencement funding arrangement,[3] as a result of the Court of Appeal's second bite of the cherry in *Simmons v Castle*.[4]

The new rules

6–03   The new rules are set out in CPR 44 Part II and CPR 44 PD 12.1.

The scope of the new rules

6–04   The rules apply to all proceedings which include a claim for damages for personal injuries or under the Fatal Accidents Act 1976 or claims under the Law Reform (Miscellaneous Provisions) Act 1934 (CPR 44.13(1)) (this includes claims arising out of clinical negligence (see the broad definition of 'claim for personal injuries' in CPR 2.3).

Pre action disclosure applications are excluded (CPR 44.13(1)).

QOCS does not apply to proceedings 'ancillary' to personal injury claims—that is to say claims such Civil Liability (Contribution) Act 1978 as claims by a defendant to a personal injury action against a third party alleging that that third party was responsible for the claimant's injuries, even where such claims are brought as Part 20 claims within the claimant's personal injury action. Proceedings, in CPR 44.13, is intended to refer to the claimant's claim for damages for personal injury.[5]

There is no exception for appeals (arising from claims within the scope of CPR 44.13) and therefore QOCS applies to such appeals.

---

[3]   As defined in CPR 48.2.
[4]   *Simmons v Castle* [2012] EWCA Civ 1288; [2013] 1 WLR 1239.
[5]   *Wagenaar v Weekend Travel Ltd* [2014] EWCA Civ 1105, at 34–46.

Importantly, there is no restriction on the application of QOCS by reference to the date on which proceedings were brought. Although the new rules only came into effect on April 1, 2013, they apply to all claims involving a claim for damages for personal injury (subject to one exception below) whether or not proceedings were issued prior to April 1, 2013.

This has the somewhat unexpected, but possibly intended, effect that not only did defendants who were involved in litigated personal injury claims which had been issued prior to April 1, 2013 find that the risks the claimant faced in the claim had shifted mid litigation, but that even in claims which had concluded prior to April 1, 2013 and where the defendant had obtained a costs order in its favour, its ability to enforce that costs order was now restricted by virtue of QOCS.

This effect was tolerably clear from the face of the rules, but has been affirmed by the Court of Appeal's decision in *Wagenaar*, where Vos LJ considered that the rules were clearly intended to operate 'retrospectively' in this way.[6]

There is a single operative transitional provision—CPR 44.17—which provides that QOCS does not apply where the claimant has entered into a pre-commencement funding arrangement as defined in CPR 48.2. **6–05**

That definition broadly covers Conditional Fee Agreements (but not any other kind of retainer) or ATE policies entered into before April 1, 2013 in relation to the matter that is the subject of the proceedings in which the cost order is made.[7]

Accordingly, where a claimant has entered into either a CFA or has taken out ATE in respect of the claim before April 1, 2013, QOCS is not available at all. There may be cases where the claimant has taken out one, but not the other (for example has entered into a CFA pre-April 2013 but did not take out ATE, perhaps because none could be found before the deadline). In such cases, it may seem harsh that the claimant is denied QOCS protection when QOCS was intended, primarily, to be a quid pro quo for not taking out ATE and the claimant has not taken ATE. However, such apparent injustices in individual cases are arguably an inevitable consequence of broad based procedural reform.

There may be scope for arguments as to what the position would be if the claimant had entered into a pre-April 2013 CFA, for example, but chose to 'abandon' that arrangement pre-issue (whether because of a change of solicitors or otherwise) and to enter into a new funding arrangement. CPR 44.17 provides that QOCS is unavailable 'where the claimant has entered into' such an arrangement and would, therefore, appear to exclude the ability to gain QOCS protection by later abandoning that arrangement. The factual question **6–06**

---

[6] *Wagenaar v Weekend Travel Ltd* [2014] EWCA Civ 1105, at 29–30.
[7] There are technical complexities to the definitions which are addressed in the section on funding arrangements. Note that the taking out of a post March 31, 2013 ATE policy does not affect the availability of QOCS, even where part of that ATE premium may remain recoverable in principle between the parties in a clinical negligence claim pursuant to the Recovery of Costs Insurance Premiums in Clinical Negligence Proceedings Regulations 2013.

upon which the availability of QOCS is predicated appears to be simply whether or not such an arrangement has ever been entered into in connection with the case, and not whether or not that is the operative arrangement at the time any application of QOCS is being considered.

This approach seems to have been adopted by Master Haworth in the SCCO in the case of *Landau v The Big Bus Company*[8] where, in a situation where the claimant (acting in person by this point) had entered into a pre-commencement funding arrangement in relation to matters at first instance, but not in relation to an appeal from the first instance judgment, the court held that QOCS was not available in respect of the costs of the appeal, firstly because the appeal related to the same 'matter' which was the subject of the proceedings (and therefore the first instance CFA was a pre-commencement funding arrangement per CPR 48.2(1)(i)(aa)) and secondly that, in any event, the appeal was part of the same 'proceedings' for the purposes of CPR 44.17. The latter issue is a point that seems arguable, not least in light of the Court of Appeal's decision in *Hawksford Trustees*[9] where the Court of Appeal treated an appeal as separate proceedings in relation to a different funding issue, namely the recoverability of ATE premiums—an argument considered, but dismissed, by the Master.

The effect of the new rules

6–07   QOCS does not prevent the making of a costs order against a personal injury claimant. Any question of whether to make such an order falls to be decided on 'usual' principles by reference to CPR 44.2.

By the same token, it is a mistake for claimants to regard QOCS as a guarantee of an award of costs in their favour. The court's discretion under CPR 44.2 remains untrammelled and regardless of the impact of QOCS, a claimant may still find their costs being disallowed or reduced in a case where they have won if their conduct or other circumstances warrant it.

The effect of QOCS is limited to the defendant's ability to enforce any costs order that has been made.

In practice, however, it can be anticipated that the presence of QOCS, as with the presence of adverse costs protection for publicly funded litigants, will, in certain circumstances, have an effect on the frequency with which defendants seek adverse costs orders where the option might be open to them to do so. This is particularly so given the absence of a 'football pools' or 'lottery win' provision allowing the defendant to return to seek enforcement of an order is an otherwise impecunious claimant's resources drastically improve. As noted, financial resources (present or future) are (probably) immaterial to any question of the application of QOCS.

Because the QOCS rules operate on enforcement of orders, where a claim comes within the scope of CPR 44 Part II any issue of the enforcement of any

---

[8]   *Landau v The Big Bus Company* Unreported October 31, 2014.
[9]   *Hawksford Trustees Jersey Ltd v Stella Global UK Ltd* [2013] EWCA Civ 987; [2012] 1 WLR 3581.

costs order (including interim orders) against a claimant is deferred until after the conclusion of the proceedings, including after any agreement or assessment of costs (CPR 44.14(2)). Note, this does not mean that the assessment or agreement itself is deferred. Quite the opposite. These still take place at the usual time and must be concluded before any issue of enforcement, and therefore whether QOCS prevents enforcement, falls to be considered. The wording of CPR 44.14(2) also supports the argument that the assessment of costs is not to be regarded as 'proceedings' within the meaning of that word for the purposes of QOCS.

The basic operation of the rules, where QOCS applies, may be summarised as follows: **6–08**

(i)   Any adverse costs order may be enforced in full to the extent that it does not exceed the damages and interest awarded to the claimant (CPR 44.14(1)).

(ii) Where the claimant's claim has been struck out on the basis that it: (i) discloses no reasonable grounds; or (ii) was an abuse of process; or (iii) the conduct of the claimant or someone acting on his behalf (and with the claimant's knowledge of their conduct) was likely to obstruct the just disposal of the proceedings, then the costs order may be enforced in full (CPR 44.15(1)). In such a situation, of course, the claimant will not have been awarded any damages, so this provision simply allows full enforcement of any costs orders made in the defendant's favour in the proceedings, as if QOCS did not exist.

(iii) Where the claimant's claim is found, on the balance of probabilities, to have been 'fundamentally dishonest', then the order for costs may be enforced to its full extent with the permission of the court (CPR 44.16(1)). This, of course, covers a number of possibilities. The claim may have failed, but not been struck out per CPR 44.15, in which case the defendant will need permission to enforce the costs order at all. The claim may have succeeded and some damages may have been awarded, but the claim may still be found to have been fundamentally dishonest, in which case the defendant can enforce without permission to the extent of the damages and interest awarded, but requires permission to enforce any further.

(iv) Where the claim is brought in whole or part for the benefit of a person other than the claimant or a dependant in a Fatal Accidents Act case, or where the claim is only in part a personal injury claim, the defendant may enforce the order up to the full extent with the permission of the court (CPR 44.16). Again, in such cases, the defendant will be entitled to enforce in part without permission if damages have been awarded, but needs permission to go beyond the level of damages and interest (if any).

Each of these provisions warrants a little further examination.

In relation to the basic operation of QOCS by restriction on enforcement (CPR 44.14), perhaps the single most interesting question is what is meant by 'enforcement'. The defendant's right to 'enforce' a costs order in its favour is restricted.

It is restricted to the limit of damages and interest awarded to the claimant. There is no mention of the claimant's costs.

However, the very section of the CPR which precedes QOCS deals with the ability of a party to 'set off' one costs order against another. Is a set off enforcement? If it is not, then it would appear that the QOCS rules do not prevent a defendant setting off its costs against any costs awarded to the claimant, in addition to enforcing the costs order to the extent of damages awarded (subject, of course, to the total limit of the costs awarded to the defendant).

If, however, a set off of costs against costs does amount to enforcement, then the defendant's rights are limited to those under CPR 44.14.

6–09   The issue is undecided, at least in the specific context of QOCS. In *Vava*,[10] Andrew Smith J declined to allow a set off of one costs order against another in circumstances where parties had entered into a QOCS like arrangement (but where QOCS did not in fact apply). He did so on the grounds that it would be 'unfair' in the circumstances to do so.

Existing authority in the not dissimilar area of costs protection for publicly funded litigants indicates that an order for set off of costs is not to be regarded as enforcement of the order because it does not place the claimant under any obligation to pay, but merely reduces the amount that they can recover.[11] This would appear to support an argument that a defendant can firstly seek to set off costs awarded to it against those awarded to a claimant and, if thereafter, there remains a net liability to the defendant, seek to set this against damages and interest under CPR 44.14, rather than being limited to the CPR 44.14 set off. The issue will no doubt be the subject of specific argument and authority in due course in the QOCS context.

CPR 44.15 requires little further discussion. The categories of strike out referred to therein mirror those in CPR 3.4(2)(a) and (b) and issues as to when such a strike out is appropriate are beyond the scope of this section. The only real gloss to note is that where the strike out is on the basis that the conduct of the proceedings was such as to be likely to obstruct the just disposal of the proceedings, in order to disapply QOCS it is necessary, in addition, that the court concludes that such conduct was that of the claimant himself or that he knew of the relevant conduct on the part of the person so acting on his behalf. A defendant seeking a strike out on this basis in a personal injury claim should take care to ensure that this additional aspect is specifically addressed in any judgment given on the strike out (and ideally recited in the order).

6–10   CPR 44.16 and the introduction of a test of 'fundamental dishonesty' had given rise to much debate.

That debate is likely to grow when s.57 of the Criminal Justice and Courts Act 2015 comes into effect whereby a finding, on the balance of probabilities,

---

[10]   *Vava v Anglo American South Africa Ltd* [2013] EWHC 2326 (QB); [2013] 5 Costs LR 805.
[11]   *R (Burkett) v London Borough of Hammersmith & Fulham* [2004] EWCA Civ 1342, at 50.

that the claimant in a personal injury claim has been fundamentally dishonest in relation to that claim ('the primary claim') or a 'related claim' will require the court (the term used in s.57(2) is 'must') to dismiss the primary claim in its entirety, including any part of that claim in respect of which the claimant has not been dishonest (s.57(3)), unless the claimant would suffer substantial injustice as a result. No commencement date has yet been set for s.57 at the time of going to press, though a date within the early part of 2015 seems likely.[12]

Whether a different approach will be taken to the issue of 'fundamentally dishonest' in that context will have to be seen in time. What appears more likely is that that provision will run in parallel with CPR 44.16 such that, where a claim is found to have been 'fundamentally dishonest', the court may dismiss the entire claim, but if it considers that substantial injustice would result, will instead allow the claim to proceed but may then allow the defendant to enforce any costs orders it obtains in full as, in effect, a lesser penalty.

What does 'fundamentally dishonest' mean? It is relatively early days, but some guidance is available. 'Dishonesty' is a concept the courts are extremely familiar with and there is clear judicial guidance as to the issues a court must consider in deciding in a personal injury context whether a claimant has been dishonest.[13] More contentious is the 'fundamentally' aspect, which has troubled parliamentarians in recent debates in relation to the use of the term in s.57 of the new Act.

There have been a number of first instance cases where the issue has arisen. **6–11** The most thoroughly argued and most authoritative at this stage appears to be that of *Gosling*,[14] which was a classic case of a successful, but dishonestly exaggerated, claim, though with an added complication that the claimant succeeded only against one defendant and discontinued against a second. In that case, the judge held that a claim was not fundamentally dishonest merely because he had been dishonest in respect of some collateral matter or some minor, self contained head of damage, but that where the dishonesty went to the root of a substantial part of the claim the test was made out.

The case appears to confirm, though only at first instance level, a number of propositions. Firstly, that CPR 44.16(1) may apply where the dishonesty does not infect the entire claim, but goes only to a substantial part of it—the classic exaggerated claim case. Secondly, where the test in CPR 44.16(1) is made out, the court is not bound to allow the defendant to enforce the costs order to its full extent, but is then given a discretion to decide to what extent to allow such enforcement.

Both propositions appear logical interpretations of the rule, though there will no doubt be further argument on these and related topics.

CPR 44 PD 12 contains clear guidance in relation to arguments under CPR

---

[12] A deliberate parliamentary intervention to strengthen the law in this area beyond the existing position as set out by the Supreme Court in *Summers v Fairclough Homes Ltd* [2012] UKSC 26; [2012] 1 WLR 2004.
[13] See, for example, *Brighton & Hove Bus v Brooks* [2011] EWHC 2504.
[14] *Gosling v Hailo & Screwfix Direct* Unreported April 29, 2014 CC (Cambridge).

44.16(1) and in particular that where parties settle proceedings the court will not, 'save in exceptional circumstances' order that issues relating to fundamental dishonesty be tried (12.4(b)) and that such issues will normally be determined at trial (12.4(a)). The logic is obvious and needs little explanation, but the point should not be overlooked by defendants. Settlement of a claim will usually be an effective bar to taking this point.

A claimant cannot, however, escape such scrutiny (at least in relation to fundamental dishonesty) by discontinuing the claim (CPR 44 PD 12.4(c)).

CPR 44.16(2) has attracted less debate. However, its impact should not be overlooked.

6–12   CPR 44.16 applies in two types of claims. The one which has received less attention is the second (CPR 44.16(2)(b)), namely where a claim is made "for the benefit of the claimant other than a claim to which this Section applies". This is intended to cover claims where the beneficiary of the claim is the claimant, but the claimant's claim is only partially a personal injury claim (the classic example being a housing disrepair claim where there may be a claim for personal injuries as part of a wider claim).

By virtue of CPR 44.16(2) the mere fact that procedurally, the claim as a whole is deemed a personal injury claim, because it includes a claim for damages for personal injury, does not prevent the court disapplying QOCS, to the extent just. Commonly, this is likely to be used so that the court can allow full enforcement of adverse costs orders in relation to that part of the claim which was not a personal injury claim, and is likely to be used in cases where the personal injury claim is viewed as being the more modest or less complex part of the claim. An example might be a professional negligence claim which included an ancillary claim for damages for personal injury.

More contentious is CPR 44.16(2)(a), which allows the court to disapply QOCS where the claim in whole or party is for the financial benefit of a third party.

The Rule itself gives only limited guidance as to the circumstances where it will apply. The Practice Direction is more specific and provides examples of where the claim is "made for the financial benefit of a person other than the claimant", including credit hire claims and subrogated claims (PD 12.2).

6–13   Whilst this seems to be the clear intention of the rulemakers, there is likely to be argument in the future as to whether or not claims, such as credit hire or subrogated claims are properly claims brought for the financial benefit of another party, a wording which appears to cut across the traditional and well established legal status of claims by such parties where the involvement of the third party is seen as being *res inter alios acta* (that is to say something which is considered not to be the court's business when considering the claim between the parties), particularly in the context of costs, save in particular and unusual circumstances.[15]

The fact that the 'examples' are given in the Practice Direction rather

---

[15]   See the classic case of *TGA Chapman v Christopher* [1998] 1 WLR 12 in the context of subrogated claims.

than forming part of the rule might be said to provide greater scope for such arguments.

The clear intention of CPR 44.16(2) is that where QOCS is disapplied in this situation, it is not the claimant that should suffer. CPR 44.16(3) contains a clear point to the making of a costs order directly against the third party in such a circumstance, subject to consideration of the usual rules for such orders under CPR 46.2. Whilst such a third party costs order would not remove the order against the claimant, it is to be anticipated that in such cases the court's likely approach would be to decline to allow enforcement (beyond damages and interest) against the claimant, but to make a third party costs order for the relevant sum or percentage or issues against the third party for whose benefit that part of the claim was brought, and CPR 44 PD 12.5 clearly points in this direction, indicating that it will be 'exceptional' that (further) enforcement will be allowed against the claimant.

Whether the working of CPR 44.16(3) (and CPR 44 PD 12.5) is intended to and does in any way relax the established common law as to the circumstances in which a third party costs order is available is a moot point and will no doubt be argued in due course.

A wider use of QOCS

The Ministry of Justice published detailed proposals for the extension of a   **6–14** version of QOCS to defamation and privacy claims, such proposals being put out to consultation which closed in November 2013. Although the original intention was for QOCS to be introduced in this area with effect from April 2014, no implementation date has yet been given and it is not clear if, when or if so in what final form QOCS will be introduced in this area.

Given the uncertainty, the proposals are not considered in any detail here, save to note that the proposals were for a rather different model of QOCS, whereby QOCS would be available to both claimants and defendants and organisations and parties with significant financial resources would be excluded from the scheme, with full costs protection only being available to those who would suffer 'severe financial hardship' if forced to pay adverse costs. Whether that model remains and is implemented in due course remains to be seen.

There have been calls for the wider extension of QOCS, most notably from Ramsey J,[16] including to actions against the police, but there are no firm proposals in this regard and the delays and difficulties with the defamation extension suggest that it will be some considerable time before any such extension might materialise.

---

[16] In his speech to the Compass Law Commercial Litigation Conference: *http://www.litigationfutures.com/news/extension-qocs-key-true-jackson-says-ramsey* [Accessed January 29, 2015].

Questions and answers

Q1. How will QOCS apply where a claim compromises both a personal injury and a non personal injury element?

6–15   This will have to be the subject of judicial guidance in due course. The rule expressly allows the court to disapply QOCS to the extent that it considers just where this situation arises (CPR 44.16) and the Practice Direction envisages that where this arises the court will normally order the claimant to pay costs notwithstanding that they exceed the level of damages and interest awarded (i.e. will allow enforcement beyond the limit in CPR 44.14, which is what CPR 44.16 expressly envisages).

In practice, it is likely that the court will seek to identify the true nature of the claim. Where the personal injury claim was dominant and the 'additional claim' a modest ancillary part which is unlikely to have significantly increased the costs then the court may decide not to allow any enforcement beyond CPR 44.14. Where the 'additional claim' was dominant, then the court may allow full enforcement. Perhaps more commonly, the court may seek to identify, by percentage, date or in some other way, the 'additional claim' and allow enforcement in that regard accordingly.

Given that the claimant in this scenario will already probably have suffered some costs deduction against damages (CPR 44.14) and given that the quantum of costs may have been assessed (CPR 44.13(3)) the court may simply make an order that enforcement of a certain sum above the level of damages is just. The Court of Appeal is unlikely to be keen to interfere with a broad exercise of discretion here unless the outcome is manifestly unjust.

Q2. Will QOCS be extended to other areas in due course?

6–16   This seems highly likely, with defamation and privacy claims being first in line. However, the process is slow and it seems highly likely that in that area at least any model of QOCS introduced will differ significantly from the model in CPR 44 Part III.

Q3. Do parties still have to costs budget where QOCS applies and, if so, is the agreeing of budgets in such cases likely to be more difficult?

6–17   In answer to the first part of the question, the answer it a simple 'yes', assuming the case is within CPR 3.12. QOCS relates to enforcement only. Until a case is concluded, a defendant will not know whether or not the case is one where there might be good grounds to seek a disapplication of QOCS. In any event, the defendant may be in a position to enforce a costs order against damages without needing to seek to disapply QOCS. There are a wide range of situations where the defendant may be entitled to, and able to enforce, some or all of its costs. In any and all of these situations, the defendant will need to be able to quantify its costs and, if it has failed to file a costs budget, is likely to find those costs (at least post the date on which a budget should have been supplied) limited to court fees only pursuant to CPR 3.18 or to suffer some other form of costs penalty or reduction.

As to agreeing budgets in such cases, there is no reason in principle why the budget should be more or less difficult to agree. QOCS also applies, for example, in publicly funded claims, where a not dissimilar form of costs protection exists. In both types of case, the budgeting rules apply without amendment. In practice, there will be concerns in such cases that defendants will be inclined to underestimate their own costs (because they are unlikely to be recovering them in many cases, or recovering them in full even in cases where some success is achieved), with a view to painting the claimant's budgeted costs as disproportionate by comparison. Also, that in such cases the perceived greater likelihood that the claimant will be recovering costs at the end of the case may make the defendant more inclined to take every opportunity to limit those costs, and therefore to take a more aggressive approach at the budgeting stage.

Anecdotally, it appears to be the case that the most regularly contested CCMCs relate to personal injury claims, including clinical negligence and there appears to be a greater willingness to agree budgets between the parties in commercial claims. Whether this has anything particularly to do with QOCS or is merely a reflection of the fact that personal injury has long been the hotbed of satellite costs litigation is a moot point.

Q4. Is QOCS excluded where the claimant has Before The Event Insurance?

No. Provided the claim is within CPR 44.14, and provided that the claimant has not entered into a CFA or ATE prior to April 1, 2013 in relation to the claim, then the method of funding is irrelevant. QOCS is available.

6–18

This applies even where the claim was commenced prior to April 1, 2013— and even where the costs order was made prior to April 1, 2013 but has not yet been enforce.

Q5. Does QOCS apply to costs incurred prior to April 1, 2013?

Yes. Provided the claim is within CPR 44.13 and provided the claimant has not entered into a pre-commencement funding arrangement (CPR 48.2), then QOCS applies and the defendant's ability to enforce a costs order is restricted accordingly. Although there is scope for argument beyond that raised in *Wagenaar*, the Court of Appeal's decision in that case disposed of the primary argument that COCS could not operate retrospectively in this way.

6–19

Q6. Is QOCS excluded where the claimant has entered into a pre-commencement funding arrangement, even if the claimant then is advised to not pursue the claim by the initially instructed solicitor but later does so under a post April 2013 funding arrangement with a different firm?

These issues need to be resolved. However, the wording of CPR 48.2 and CPR 44.17 suggest that the answer to this is 'yes'. The fact that there has been a pre-commencement funding arrangement in respect of that claim, even if

6–20

as a matter of fact that arrangement no longer operates and as a matter of fact there will not and could not have been any claim for additional liabilities if the claim succeeded, will mean that QOCS is not available. This may seem harsh, but is a consequence of seeking to introduce a simplified transitional provision which may seem to operate harshly on defendants in some instances (see the retrospectivity point) whilst also operating harshly on some claimants.

Q7. The claimant has incurred costs unnecessarily in an unmeritous claim. They have now served a notice of discontinuance and, as QOCS applies, they are not liable for the defendant's costs (unless an exception applies). In the above circumstances, is it possible for the defendant to apply for a wasted costs order even though a notice of discontinuance has been filed by the claimant?

6–21   This question covers a number of issues.

Firstly, the assumption that the claimant is not liable, in principle, for the defendant's costs is wrong. CPR 38.6 is not disapplied merely because QOCS applies. As discussed above, the defendant is entitled in principle to the same costs order whether QOCS applies or not. QOCS only addresses the enforcement of that order. Of course, as with publicly funded claims, it may be the case that the difficulties with enforcement mean that, save where the costs order is automatic (which, of course, it is under CPR 38.6(1) unless the court orders otherwise), there will be cases where the defendant chooses not to spend money arguing for a costs order which serves little practical benefit. However, in the example given, the defendant will by default have a costs order in its favour.

As to exceptions, CPR 44 PD 12.4(c) must not be overlooked. A claimant cannot (automatically) escape the risk of a finding of fundamental dishonesty by discontinuing the claim.

An interesting issue arises where the claim is one which was arguably abusive or in relation to which it could be argued that there were no reasonable grounds for bringing the claim, but the claimant has beaten the defendant to the point by discontinuing the claim before an application could be heard to have the proceedings struck out. CPR 44 PD 12.4(c) does not address this. Under CPR 38.4 it would be possible to apply to have the notice of discontinuance set aside in order for the court to hear an application to strike out which, if successful, would allow for full enforcement of the costs order without permission. It is likely that the court will only permit this in exceptional circumstances—perhaps where a claimant has been repeatedly warned as to the abusive nature of the claim, but has persisted, but then responds to a formal application to strike out by discontinuing. However, it remains to be seen in practice how the court approaches such issues.

Accordingly, the defendant is not left entirely without remedy in this situation (though in practice, whether even an enforceable costs order is of any value against an impecunious claimant is a question which must be considered).

As to the possibility of seeking a wasted costs order, the ability to make such an application is not ousted by the fact of the discontinuance. However, as is the case with publicly funded claimants (see the guidance in *Symphony Group PLC v Hodgson*[17]) the court will be very astute to guard against the risk that the wasted costs application is motivated by an inability to recover costs against the claimant, rather than being a properly founded application for wasted costs against a solicitor. Wasted costs orders will not be made against a solicitor merely because they acted for a claimant in respect of a claim which is doomed to fail. The courts will assume, unless it can be established to the contrary, that the solicitor will have properly advised the client and will have been acting on instructions.

Q8. I need to discontinue proceedings against a number of defendants in an action. Obviously, when I file a notice of discontinuance, there will be a deemed order for costs against the claimant. According to Practical Law's guidance "Discontinuance: an overview" the court may vary such an order only in some circumstances. However, my understandings of QOCS (from CPR 44.14, 44.15 and 44.16) is that an order for costs may only be enforced if the claim has been struck out (no court permission needed) or if it is fundamentally dishonest (court permission needed). We do not have sufficient time to obtain written consent from each and every defendant in a consent order but in any event consider that we would be QOCS protected even by serving a Notice of Discontinuance.

This is largely answered in the previous answer. A costs order will be deemed to be made against the claimant unless the court orders otherwise, pursuant to CPR 38.6. Assuming the claim is within CPR 44.13 and no other exception applies, then QOCS protection will be available. However, if the claim is one which might be said to have been brought in a 'fundamentally dishonest' fashion, the defendants will still be able to ask the court to grant permission to enforce some or all of the costs order.

6–22

There is also a risk that the defendants might be able to persuade the court to set aside the notice of discontinuance and ask the court instead to strike the claim out, to avail themselves of the exceptions under CPR 44.15. The circumstances in which this will be allowed remain to be seen, but it is likely to require an exceptional case.

---

[17] *Symphony Group PLC v Hodgson* [1993] 3 WLR 830, 842.

CHAPTER 7

Fixed Costs, Indemnity Costs, Litigants in Person

Background

With regard to the Jackson reforms it is still too early to say what effect they have had on either the topics covered in this chapter or those covered in **Chapter 8.**

Part 45 of the Civil Procedure Rules deals with fixed costs and is divided   **7–01** into sections. The topics dealt with are as follows:

- Section I—Fixed Costs in the normally accepted sense, i.e. costs which are payable in a given set of circumstances.
- Section II—Road Traffic Accidents—fixed recoverable costs.
- Section III—Pre-Action Protocol for Low Value Personal Injury Claims in Road Traffic Accidents and Low Value Personal Injury (Employers' Liability and Public Liability) Claims.
- Section IIIA—Claims Which No Longer Continue Under the RTA and EL/PL Pre-Action Protocols—Fixed Recoverable Costs.
- Section IV—Scale Costs for Claims in the IPEC.
- Section V—Fixed Costs: HM Revenue & Customs.
- Section VI—Fast Track Trial Costs.
- Section VII—Costs Limits in Aarhus Convention claims.

Section I of Pt 45 sets out the amounts which are to be allowed in respect of solicitors charges in cases to which it applies unless the court otherwise orders.[1] The fixed costs provisions apply where the only claim is a claim for a specified sum of money exceeding £25 and certain circumstances apply.[2]

Section II of Pt 45 sets out the costs allowable in proceedings relating to certain road traffic accidents. The provisions apply to road traffic accident disputes,[3] where the accident giving rise to the dispute occurred on or after October 6, 2003. The fixed costs provisions are intended to meet the case where the parties have been able to agree damages within certain limits but have been unable to agree the amount of costs. The agreed damages, include damages in respect of personal injury, damage to property or both. The total value of the agreed damages must not exceed £10,000 or be within the small claims limit.[4] The provisions of this section do not apply where the claimant is a litigant in person, or where Section III or IIIA of Part 45 applies.[5]

---

[1] CPR 45.1(1) and see PD 45, paras 1.1–1.3.

[2] The provisions apply where: (i) judgment in default is obtained under r.12.4(1); (ii) judgment on admission is obtained under r.14.4(3); (iii) judgment on admission on part of the claim is obtained under r.14.5(6); (iv) summary judgment is given under Pt 24; (v) the court has made an order to strike out a defence under r.3.4(2)(a) as disclosing no reasonable grounds for defending the claim; or (vi) r.45.4 applies (defendant only liable for fixed commencement costs).

[3] "Road traffic accident", "motor vehicle" and "road" are defined in r.45.9(4).

[4] CPR r.45.9(2), CPR r.26.8(2) sets out how the financial value of a claim is assessed for the purposes of allocation to track.

[5] CPR r.45.9(3).

Section III: Pre-Action Protocols for Low Value Personal Injury Claims in Road Traffic Accidents and Low Value Personal Injury (Employers' Liability and Public Liability) Claims is in two distinct parts.

The RTA Protocol Scheme

7–02 The provisions of the RTA Protocol apply to a claim for damages exceeding £1,000, but not exceeding £10,000, arising from a road traffic accident occurring on or after April 30, 2010, and before July 31, 2013, or a claim for damages not exceeding £25,000 arising from a road traffic accident occurring on or after July 31, 2013. Claims which fall within the scope of the scheme must follow the process, although a claimant is entitled to settle directly with an insurer/defendant without using the process. The process may be adopted by agreement for claims arising from an accident prior to the implementation date, but the claimant's solicitor will only be allowed the fixed recoverable costs applicable to the new process.

The rules and practice directions are unusual, in that they relate to work done in accordance with the RTA and EL/PL Protocols, rather than (except in relation to Stage 3) to proceedings in court. The case will no longer continue under the Protocol if there is fraud at any stage, and under Stage 1 if there is no admission of liability or there is an allegation of contributory negligence; under Stage 2 if damages cannot be agreed. Stage 3 applies where quantum cannot be agreed; application is then made to the court to determine the quantum.

The Pre-action Protocol for Low Value Personal Injury (Employers' Liability and Public Liability) Claims

7–03 This protocol deals with low value personal injury employers' liability and public liability claims. An employers' liability claim is a claim by an employee against the employer for damages arising from a bodily injury sustained by the employee in the course of employment, or a disease that the claimant is alleged to have contracted as a consequence of the employer's breach of its duty of care in the course of the employee's employment, other than a physical or psychological injury caused by an accident or other single event. A public liability claim is a claim for damages for personal injuries arising out of a breach of duty of care made against a person other than the claimant's employer, or the claimant's employer in respect of matters arising other than in the course of the claimant's employment, but it does not include a claim for damages arising from a disease that the claimant is alleged to have contracted as a consequence of breach of a duty of care, other than a physical or psychological injury caused by an accident or other single event.[6] The protocol sets out the behaviour which the court expects of the parties prior to the start of proceedings where a claimant claims damages not exceeding £25,000 in an EL or PL claim.[7] The EL/PL Protocol applies where either the claim arises from an accident occurring on

---

[6] EL/PL Protocol 1.1.
[7] EL/PL Protocol 2.1.

or after July 31, 2013, or in a disease claim no letter of claim has been sent to the defendant before that date. The claim must include damages in respect of personal injury and must not exceed the upper limit of £25,000 on a full liability basis, including pecuniary losses but excluding interest. The claim must not be one in which the small claims track would be the normal track (i.e. the claim must be for more than £1,000). The protocol ceases to apply to a claim where at any stage the claimant notifies the defendant that the claim has now been re-valued at more than the upper limit.[8] The protocol does not apply to a claim:

(i) where the claimant or defendant acts as personal representative of a deceased person;
(ii) where the claimant or defendant is a protected party[9];
(iii) in a public liability claim—the defendant is an individual;
(iv) where the claimant is bankrupt;
(v) where the defendant is insolvent and there is no identifiable insurer;
(vi) in the case of a disease claim, where there is more than one employer defendant;
(vii) for personal injury arising from an accident or alleged breach of duty occurring outside England and Wales;
(viii) for damages in relation to harm, abuse or neglect of or by children or vulnerable adults;
(ix) which includes a claim for clinical negligence;
(x) for mesothelioma; or
(xi) for damages arising out of a road traffic accident.

The fixed costs in r.45.18 apply in relation to a claimant only where a claimant has a legal representative.[10]

With effect from July 31, 2013, Section IIIA applies where a claim is started **7–04** under either the RTA or EL/PL Protocol, but no longer continues under the relevant protocol or the stage 3 procedure. This section does not apply to a disease claim which is started under the EL/PL Protocol.[11]

Section IV of Pt 45 sets out the scale costs for claims in the IPEC. The provisions do not apply where the court considers that a party has behaved in a manner which amounts to an abuse of the court's process or the claim concerns the infringement or revocation of a patent or registered design, the validity of which has been certified by a court in earlier proceedings.[12]

The court will make a summary assessment of the costs of the party in whose favour any order for costs is made. Rules 44.2(8), 44.6(b) and Pt 47 do not apply to s.IV.[13] The court will reserve the costs of an application to the conclusion of the trial when they will be subject to summary assessment. Where a party has behaved unreasonably the court may make an order for

---

[8] EL/PL Protocol 4.1–4.2.
[9] As defined in CPR r.21.1(2).
[10] EL/PL Protocol 4.3, 4.4.
[11] CPR r.45.29A. Nothing in Section IIIA prevents the court from making an order under r.45.24.
[12] r.45.30(1) and (2).
[13] r.45.30(3).

costs at the conclusion of the hearing. Where the court makes a summary assessment of costs it will do so in accordance with Section IV of Pt 45.[14]

Section V of Pt 45 sets out the amounts which are to be allowed in respect of HMRC charges in specified cases, unless the court orders otherwise.[15] Part 8 applies where the only claim is a claim conducted by an HMRC officer in the County Court for recovery of a debt, and the Commissioners obtain judgment on the claim. Any appropriate court fee will be allowed in addition to the costs set out in Tables 9 and 10 and the claim may include a claim for fixed commencement costs.[16]

Table 9 sets out the fixed costs on commencement of the County Court claim conducted by an HMRC officer, the amount claimed in the claim form is used to determine which band in Table 9 apples. Table 10 sets out fixed costs on entry of judgment in a County Court claim conducted by an HMRC officer. The total to be included in the judgment for HMRC charges is the total of the fixed commencement costs, and the amount in Table 10 relevant to the value of the claim. In cases where the only claim is for a specified sum of money, and the defendant pays the money claimed within 14 days after service of the particulars of claim, together with the fixed commencement costs stated in the claim form, the defendant will not be liable for any further costs unless the court orders otherwise.[17]

7–05   Section VI of Part 45 governs the amount of fast track trial costs and their application. "Fast track trial costs" means the cost of a party's advocate for preparing for and appearing at the trial. It does not include any other disbursements, or any VAT payable on the advocate's fees. The "trial" includes a hearing where the court decides an amount of money or the value of goods. 'Trial" does not include the hearing of an application for summary judgment, or the court's approval of a settlement or other compromise by, or on behalf of, a child or protected party.[18]

Section VII of Part 45 limits the amount of costs recoverable in Aarhus Convention claims.[19] The provisions of Section VII do not apply where the claimant has not stated in the claim form that the claim is an Aarhus Convention claim, or has stated that it is not an Aarhus Convention claim, or, although it is such a claim, the claimant does not wish those rules to apply.[20] If the claimant has stated in the claim form that the claim is an Aarhus Convention claim, the limits on costs apply unless the defendant has in the acknowledgment of service denied that the claim is an Aarhus Convention claim and has set out

---

[14]   r.63.26.
[15]   CPR r.45.33. "HMRC charges" are claimed as "legal representative's costs" on relevant court forms and means the fixed costs set out in Tables 9 and 10 of Section V.
[16]   CPR r.45.33(3)–(6).
[17]   CPR r.45.34, 35 and 36 and Tables 9 and 10.
[18]   Under CPR r.21.10; CPR r.45.37(1) and (2) and Practice Direction 45, paras 4.1–4.3.
[19]   An Aarhus Convention claim means a claim for judicial review of a decision, act or omission all or part of which is subject to the provisions of the UNECE Convention on Access to Information Public Participation in Decision Making and Access to Justice in Environmental Matters done at Aarhus, Denmark on June 25, 1998, including a claim which proceeds on the basis that the decision, act or omission or part of it is so subject—CPR r.45.41(2).
[20]   r.45.42.

the grounds for that denial and the court has determined that the claim is not an Aarhus Convention claim. In such a case, the court is required to determine the issue at the earliest opportunity. If the court holds that the claim is not an Aarhus Convention claim it will normally make no order for costs in relation to those proceedings. If it holds that the claim is an Aarhus Convention claim, it will normally order the defendant to pay the claimant's costs of those proceedings on the indemnity basis and the order may be enforced notwithstanding that this would increase the costs payable by the defendant beyond the amount to which such Convention claims are limited.[21] Subject to the above, a party to an Aarhus Convention claim may not be ordered to pay costs exceeding £5,000 where the claimant is claiming only as an individual and not as or on behalf of a business or other legal person, or £10,000 in all other cases.[22] Where a defendant is ordered to pay costs the amount recoverable is limited to £35,000.[23]

The availability of protective costs orders for environmental cases falling within the Aarhus Convention had been deliberately limited to judicial review claims and did not extend to statutory appeals or applications. Accordingly, it was not appropriate for the Court to exercise its discretion to grant cross-protection in respect of an application to quash planning permission under the Town & Country Planning Act 1990 s.288, as this would side-step the limitation deliberately enacted in the CPR to give effect to a convention which had not been directly incorporated into domestic law. Legislative action was necessary to remedy r.45.41's non-compliance with the Convention (it applies only in relation to judicial review proceedings).[24]

The basis of assessment

Where the court assesses costs, whether by summary or detailed assessment, it   **7–06**
will (subject to any statutory provisions relating to, e.g. legal aid costs) assess those costs on either the standard basis or the indemnity basis. In either case the court will not allow costs which have been unreasonably incurred or which are unreasonable in amount. Where the court is assessing costs on the standard basis it will in addition only allow costs which are proportionate to the matters in issue and will resolve any doubt which it may have as to whether costs were reasonably incurred or reasonable and proportionate in amount in favour of the paying party. Where the amount of costs is to be assessed on the indemnity basis there is no proportionality requirement but the court will resolve any doubt which it may have as to whether the costs were reasonably incurred or were reasonable in amount in favour of the receiving party.[25] Where the court makes an order about costs without indicating the basis upon which costs are to be assessed or purports to make an order on a basis other than the standard or indemnity basis the costs will be assessed on the standard basis.[26]

---

[21]   r.45.44.
[22]   r.45.43, PD 45, para.5.1.
[23]   r.45.43, PD 45, para.5.2.
[24]   *Secretary of State for Communities & Local Government v Venn* [2014] EWCA Civ 1539.
[25]   CPR r.44.3(1)–(3).
[26]   CPR r.44.3(4).

Costs on the indemnity basis

7–07   The court awarding costs on the indemnity basis should be satisfied that there is something in the conduct of the action or the circumstances of the case which takes the case out of the norm in a way which justifies an order for indemnity costs.[27] Following *Excelsior Commercial & Industrial Holdings*[28] it is appropriate to award costs on the indemnity basis where the conduct of a party has taken the situation away from the norm. It is not always necessary to show deliberate misconduct, in some cases unreasonable conduct to a high degree would suffice. The claimant's refusal of two reasonable offers to settle would have been enough in itself to warrant an order on the indemnity basis.[29]

The power to award costs on the indemnity basis may extend to the manner in which a party's expert had prepared and given evidence. In the particular case the defendant was ordered to pay the claimant's costs of having to recall its own expert on the indemnity basis.[30] In another case involving an expert who was "inexperienced and overenthusiastic" the claimants, having put forward a figure at which they were prepared to settle, refused to settle at that figure when the defendants offered it. No explanation for the refusal was given. Akenhead J awarded costs on the indemnity basis against the claimants. Because of the claimants' unwillingness to accept the amount offered by the defendants in settlement, an enormous amount of time, costs and Court resources had been wasted, and the defendants were entitled to costs on the indemnity basis.[31]

The Court of Appeal has held that there should be no general principle applicable to all applications under r.31.22 (concerning subsequent use of disclosed documents) to the effect that indemnity costs would be awarded against the applicant. There are many different kinds of such applications and the general rules as to costs ought to be applicable to them as to any other application before the Courts. On the facts of the case the Judge at first instance had ample grounds for awarding indemnity costs in the circumstances. The applicant's application was one which was extraneous to the existing proceedings. It required a huge amount of effort from the respondent in terms of liaison, checking and legal consideration. The respondent had been fully entitled to resist the application in the public interest. These factors took the case outside the norm. An order for costs on the indemnity basis was justified.[32]

Litigants in person

7–08   Prior to 1975, litigants in person who were successful in proceedings could recover only their out of pocket expenses.[33] The Litigants in Person Fees and Expenses Act 1975 and the Rules of Court made subsequently, enable litigants

---

27   *Excelsior Commercial & Industrial Holdings Ltd v Salisbury Hammer Aspden & Johnson* [2002] EWCA Civ 879; [2002] C.P. Rep. 67.
28   *Excelsior Commercial & Industrial Holdings Ltd v Salisbury Hammer Aspden & Johnson* [2002] EWCA Civ 879; [2002] C.P. Rep. 67.
29   *Franks v Sinclair (Costs)* [2006] EWHC 3656 (Ch); [2007] W.T.L.R. 785, David Richards J.
30   *Siegel v Pummell* [2015] EWHC 195, Wilkie J.
31   *Igloo Regeneration (General Partner) Ltd v Powell Williams Partnership (Costs)* [2013] EWHC 1859 (TCC), Akenhead J.
32   *Tchenguiz v Serious Fraud Office* [2014] EWCA Civ 1471.
33   *Buckland v Watts* [1970] 1 QB 27 CA.

in person to recover some payment for the time which they expend in conducting litigation. CPR 46.5 is so worded that it is possible for a litigant in person to recover payment for legal advice as well as payment for time spent in conducting the litigation. There is an absolute cap on the amount recoverable by the litigant in person, namely two-thirds of the amount which would have been allowed if he had been legally represented, plus disbursements reasonably expended. The Court of Appeal has decided that in principle a litigant in person is entitled to his time for researching his case at the rate fixed by statute subject to a cap of two thirds of what he would have recovered if he had been legally represented.[34]

In certain specified proceedings, where any costs of a litigant in person are ordered to be paid by another party to the proceedings or in any other way, there may be allowed on the assessment or other determination of the costs sums in respect of any work done and any expenses and losses incurred by the litigant in or in connection with the proceedings to which the order relates.[35] This provision applies to civil proceedings as follows:

(a)   in the county court, in the Senior Courts or in the Supreme Court on appeal from the High Court or the Court of Appeal;
(b)   before the Lands Tribunal for Northern Ireland;
(ba)   before the First-tier Tribunal or the Upper Tribunal; or
(c)   in or before any other court or tribunal specified in an order made under section 1 of the Litigants in Person (Costs and Expenses) Act 1975 by the Lord Chancellor.[36]

A litigant in person who does not fall within the provisions of the 1975 Act   **7–09**
may claim only out of pocket expenses, although these may include fees and expenses charged by a solicitor to a litigant to equip him to argue a case in person.[37] There is no provision for the costs of litigants in person in criminal proceedings. Proceedings before the VAT Tribunal are also excluded. The Court of Appeal has held that the power to award costs for tribunal hearings is confined to sums recoverable at common law.[38]

The official receiver, acting without a solicitor in disqualification proceedings, is a litigant in person, and is not limited to disbursements merely because he is salaried. Where costs over and above disbursements have been incurred these are pecuniary in nature and amount to pecuniary loss. The costs will be assessed in accordance with CPR r.46.5.[39]

The court has no power to award costs to a litigant in person in respect of

---

[34]   *R v Legal Services Commission Ex p. Wulfshon* [2002] EWCA Civ.
[35]   Litigants in Person (Costs and Expenses) Act 1975 s.1(1).
[36]   The scope of the Act has been extended to the Employment Appeal Tribunal by the Litigants in Person (Costs and Expenses) Order 1980 (SI 1980/1159) and to Magistrates' Courts in England and Wales in relation to civil proceedings before these courts by the litigants in person (Magistrates' Courts) Order 2000 (SI 2001/3438).
[37]   *Buckland v Watts* [1970] 1 Q.B. 27; [1969] 3 W.L.R. 92; (1969) 113 S.J. 384; *Malloch v Aberdeen Corp* [1973] 1 W.L.R. 71; [1973] 1 All E.R. 304; 1973 S.L.T. (Notes) 5. See also *Commissioners of Customs and Excise v Ross* [1992] All E.R. 65; [1990] S.T.C. 353.
[38]   *Nader (t/a Tryus) v Customs and Excise Commissioners* [1998] S.T.C. 806, CA, and see *Customs and Excise Commissioners v Ross* (1990) 2 All E.R. 65; [1990] S.T.C. 353, Simon Brown J.
[39]   *Re Minotaur Data Systems Ltd* [1999] 1 W.L.R. 1129; [1999] 3 All E.R. 122; [1999] B.C.C. 571, CA. (Magistrates' Courts) Order 2001 (SI 2001/3438).

assistance given by a non-legally qualified acquaintance. "Legal services" refer to services that are legal and provided by or under the supervision of a lawyer. Any payment made by the litigant to the assistant is not recoverable because it is not a disbursement which would have been made by a legal representative. The assistance being given was not expert assistance within CPR r.46.5(3)(c).[40]

McKenzie Friends

7–10   On July 12, 2010 the Master of the Rolls and President of the Family Division handed down a Practice Note,[41] which applies to civil and family proceedings in the Court of Appeal (Civil Division), the High Court, County Courts and the Family Proceedings Court in the Magistrates' Courts. The Note is issued as guidance, not as a Practice Direction, and sets out to remind courts and litigants of the principles set out in the authorities.

Litigants have the right to have reasonable assistance from a lay person (McKenzie Friends), but McKenzie Friends have no independent right to provide assistance. They have no right to act as advocates or to carry out the conduct of litigation.

McKenzie Friends may: (i) provide morale support for litigants; (ii) take notes; (iii) help with case papers; and (iv) quietly give advice on any aspect of the conduct of the case. A McKenzie Friend may not: (a) act as a litigant's agent in relation to the proceedings; (b) manage litigants' cases outside court, for example by signing court documents; or (c) address the court, make oral submissions or examine witnesses. The Practice Note points out that while litigants ordinarily have a right to receive reasonable assistance from McKenzie Friends, the court retains the power to refuse to permit such assistance. It may do so where it is satisfied that, in that case, the interests of justice and fairness do not require the litigant to receive such assistance.

The following factors should not be taken to justify the court refusing to permit a litigant receiving such assistance: (i) the case or application is simple or straightforward, or is for instance a directions or case management hearing; (ii) the litigant appears capable of conducting the case without assistance; (iii) the litigant is unrepresented through choice; (iv) the other party is not represented; (v) the proposed McKenzie Friend belongs to an organisation that promotes a particular cause; and (vi) the proceedings are confidential and the court papers contain sensitive information relating to a family's affairs.

7–11   A litigant may be denied assistance of a McKenzie Friend because its provision might undermine or has undermined the efficient administration of justice. Such circumstances might include: (i) the assistance is being provided for an improper purpose; (ii) the assistance is unreasonable in nature or degree; (iii) the McKenzie Friend is subject to a civil proceedings orders or a civil restraint order; (iv) the McKenzie Friend is using the litigant as a puppet;

---

[40]   *Uhbi (t/a United Building and Plumbing Contractors) v Kajla* [2002] All E.R. (D) 265, CA.
[41]   Practice Note (Sen Cts: McKenzie Friends: Civil and Family Courts) [2010] 1 W.L.R. 1881; [2010] 4 All E.R. 272; [2010] 2 F.L.R. 962.

(v) the McKenzie Friend is directly or indirectly conducting the litigation; and (vi) the court is not satisfied that the McKenzie Friend fully understands the duty of confidentiality.

The Note points out that McKenzie Friends do not have a right of audience or a right to conduct litigation, and it is a criminal offence to exercise rights of audience or to conduct litigation unless properly qualified and authorised to do so. The court may grant such rights to a McKenzie Friend on a case by case basis, but the courts should be slow to grant any application from a litigant for a right of audience or a right to conduct litigation to any lay person, including a McKenzie Friend. The court should only be prepared to grant such rights where there is good reason to do so, taking into account all the circumstances of the case. Such grants should not be extended to lay persons automatically or without due consideration. They should not be granted for mere convenience.

Litigants may enter into lawful agreements to pay fees to McKenzie Friends for the provision of reasonable assistance in court, or out of court by, e.g. carrying out clerical or mechanical activities such as photocopying documents, preparing bundles, delivering documents to opposing parties or the court, or the provision of legal advice in connection with court proceedings. Such fees cannot lawfully be recovered from the opposing party. Even where the court has granted a McKenzie Friend the right to conduct litigation, fees said to be incurred by a McKenzie Friend are, in principle, recoverable from the litigant for whom the work was carried out, but cannot lawfully be recovered from the opposing party. Where a McKenzie Friend is granted a right of audience, the fees incurred by the McKenzie Friend are, in principle, recoverable from the litigant on whose behalf the right is exercised, and are also recoverable, in principle, from the opposing party as a recoverable disbursement.

Questions and answers
Q1. Is it not unfortunate that there will not be fixed costs across the entire fast track as Jackson recommended [yet] but merely some more fixed costs for certain lower value claims?

Professor Paul Fenn carried out a great deal of work during the course of the   **7–12**
Jackson Review and produced a matrix for fixed costs across the fast track based on a considerable amount of data which had been made available to him by the ABI and others. The matrix was published in the final report and was accepted both by Jackson LJ and his assessors. The fixed costs in relation to Low Value Personal Injury Claims in Road Traffic Accidents ("the RTA protocol") or for Low Value Personal Injury (Employers' Liability and Public Liability) Claims ("the EL/PL protocol") have been reduced significantly below the earlier figures which had been the result of industry-wide agreement. The new figures appear to have been arrived at following the prohibition of referral fees by reducing the previous figures by the perceived amount of referral fees. This has done nothing to reduce arguments about hourly rates since solicitors now argue that instead of paying referral fees, they have to pay the same or larger amounts in marketing costs.

Q2. What guidance can be given about retainer arrangements to emphasise the importance of the advice to a client about these and ensuring that retainer arrangements are still clear and enforceable where a legal representative is asked to represent a client in litigation which will inevitably involve the application of fixed costs?

7–13   The situation must be clearly explained to the client. A solicitor may agree that any charges will be limited to the amount recoverable from a paying party (i.e. the limit of fixed costs). If the legal representative intends to charge the client an amount which is likely to exceed the fixed recoverable costs, this must be explained to the client in clear terms. In respect of client care, r.2 of the 2007 Code of Conduct set out a detailed and prescriptive list of the type of information that solicitors were required to give to clients. Under the 2011 Code, Chapter 1 sets out the general outcomes including that clients are in a position to make informed decisions about their matter. "Indicative behaviour" sets out how solicitors might go about this by, for example, agreeing an appropriate level of service with the client. The Solicitors Regulation Authority states that the new code allows greater flexibility according to the needs of the client and the type of work that the solicitor undertakes, but there is also greater emphasis on the needs of the individual client, particularly those who are vulnerable.

Chapter 1 of the Code does not specify the information that must be given to clients or the form it should take. This is because solicitors are required to focus on the principles and achieving the right outcomes for clients. The SRA Handbook points out:

> *"Providing clear information at the outset and as the matter progresses is a benefit not only to clients but also to [the solicitor's firm]. Some of the most common causes of complaints are lack of clear information about costs, failure to follow instructions, delay and failure to keep clients informed. It is important to monitor complaints to [the solicitor's firm] as these can indicate failure to provide good client care as well as other problems within the firm."*

Solicitors should only enter into fee agreements with their clients that are legal and which the solicitor considers are suitable for the client's needs and take account of the client's best interest. Clients must receive the best possible information both at the time of engagement and, when appropriate, as their matter progresses about the likely overall cost of their matter and must be informed of their right to challenge or complain about a bill and the circumstances in which they may be likely to pay interest on an unpaid bill.

Retainer is the name given to the contract which exists between a solicitor and the client. Where there is no retainer the relationship of solicitor and client does not exist and the solicitor is not entitled to render a bill. The contract between the solicitor and the client may be on any terms which are mutually agreeable provided that the terms do not infringe the restrictions laid down in Part III of the Solicitors Act 1974 or the statutory requirements relating to conditional fee agreements or damages-based agreements.

Q3. Is the indemnity basis applicable in cases where there is an abuse of process or where a party has been guilty of unreasonable conduct?

The Companies Court, in applying the decision in *Excelsior Commercial and Industrial Holdings Ltd*[42] ordered the claimant to pay the costs of an unfair prejudice petition on the indemnity basis where the petition had been an abuse of process and should never have been brought, and where the claimant had no basis for defending the company's claim for breach of duty as a director and employee. The costs of both actions had been increased significantly by virtue of the claimant's highly aggressive tactics in the conduct of the litigation. Overall the case constituted a departure from the norm, which made it just to order costs to be paid on the indemnity basis.[43]

7–14

The court ordered an unsuccessful claimant to pay costs on the indemnity basis and to pay interest on the costs from one year before the commencement date of the trial because of the claimants' unreasonable conduct in that the case had changed constantly throughout the course of the proceedings and the claimant had produced wholly unacceptable volumes of documentation.[44]

In another example, where claimants had sued their former financial advisor, the defendant, before serving its defence, applied for summary judgment. Four months later the application was withdrawn. The Court had to decide the question of costs. There was nothing sufficiently unusual about the case to justify departing from the general rule that the unsuccessful party should be ordered to pay the successful party's costs. The Court went on to make an order on the indemnity basis because the defendant was not justified in seeking summary judgment before filing the defence. The application constituted conduct which was sufficiently 'out of the norm' within the meaning in *Excelsior* and other authorities.[45]

Q4. What is the position of litigation funders in relation to orders for costs, particularly orders for costs on the indemnity basis?

Where claimants funded by third party litigation funders lost the claim, the litigation funders were ordered to pay the costs of the defendant on the indemnity basis up to the limit of their investment. Christopher Clarke LJ stated:

7–15

> *"Justice requires that when the case fails so comprehensively, not merely on the facts but because it was wholly bad in law, the funder should, subject to the Arkin cap, bear the costs order to be paid by the person whom or which he has unsuccessfully supported, assessed on the scale which the Court thinks it just for that person to pay in the light of all the circumstances, including but not limited to that person's behaviour and that of those whom that person engaged."*

---

[42] *Excelsior Commercial & Industrial Holdings Ltd v Salisbury Hammer Aspden & Johnson* [2002] EWCA Civ 879; [2002] C.P. Rep. 67.
[43] *Re Flex Associates Ltd* [2010] EWHC 3690 (Ch) David Donaldson QC.
[44] *ABCI (formerly Arab Business Consortium International Finance & Investment Co) v Banque Franco-Tunisienne (Costs)* [2002] EWHC 567 (Comm) HH Judge Chambers QC.
[45] *The Libyan Investment Authority v Goldman Sachs International* [2014] EWHC 3364 (Ch) Rose J.

The Judge stated that the funder should, absent special circumstances, follow the fortunes of those from whom he himself hoped to derive a small fortune. To do otherwise would be unfair to the defendants and their personnel. To make an order for indemnity costs would not be to penalise but to recompense. Christopher Clarke LJ further stated:

> *"If it serves to cause funders and their advisors to take rigorous steps short of champerty, i.e. behaviour likely to interfere with the due administration of justice—particularly in the form of rigorous analysis of law, facts and witnesses, consideration of proportionality and review at appropriate intervals—to reduce the occurrence of the sort of circumstances that cause me to order indemnity costs in this case, that is an advantage and in the public interest".*[46]

Q5. The rules suggest that costs management does not affect indemnity costs. However there is now a confusion about this since Coulson J's decision in Elvanite Full Circle Ltd v Amec Earth and Environmental UK Ltd[47] suggests otherwise.

7–16   On the facts of the case the Judge decided not to make an order on the indemnity basis but went on to consider whether, if the defendant had been entitled to indemnity costs, the costs management order was irrelevant and was it possible for the defendant to recover more than the sums in the costs management order. Having acknowledged that a costs management order is expressed to be relevant only to an assessment of costs on the standard basis, he continued:

> *"However as a matter of logical analysis, it seems to me that the costs management order should also be the starting point of an assessment of costs on an indemnity basis even if the 'good reasons' to depart from it are likely to be more numerous and extensive if the indemnity basis is applied . . .*
> *If [the budget] is an accurate estimate of all the costs that will be incurred then it seems to me that it should be the relevant starting point for an assessment of costs on an indemnity basis as well as for an assessment on the standard basis . . .*
> *There is concern that, if an order for indemnity costs allows the receiving party to ignore the costs management order, then that will encourage successful parties to argue for indemnity costs every time . . . A paying party will have fought the trial assuming that, even if it loses, its opponent will be unlikely to recover more than the amount recorded in the costs management order, unless there is good reason for any departure. That is the certainty that the new regime provides. Even if the paying party has to pay costs on an indemnity basis that does not seem to me automatically to justify an abandonment of that certainty and the encouragement of a costs free for all . . .*
> *In any given case it might be said that an award of indemnity costs—which does not require any assessment of proportionality—might be a 'good reason' to depart*

---

[46]   *Excalibur Ventures LLC v Texas Keystone Inc (Defendants and Costs Claimants) and Psari Holdings Ltd (Costs Defendants)* [2014] EWHC 3436 (Comm) Christopher Clarke LJ.
[47]   *Elvanite Full Circle Ltd v Amec Earth and Environmental UK Ltd* [2013] EWHC 1643 (TCC).

from the costs budget approved by the Court . . . I can well see that, in particular factual circumstances, an award of indemnity costs might be a good reason to permit such a departure. But that would be fact specific and it would not detract from the principle of at least starting the costs assessment by reference to the approved budget."[48]

It is probable that the Court of Appeal in *Denton* has overtaken this decision which was a decision under a pilot scheme which did not require the Form H to assert that it was in any way an attempt at proportionate costs.

Q6. What is the position of a solicitor or barrister acting on his or her own behalf?

It is a question of fact whether a solicitor in sole practice is acting for himself as a true litigant in person or, instead, represented by himself in the firm name. It was relevant that the underlying litigation concerned a claim for professional fees with allegations of negligence and breach of duty since those were matters arising out of the solicitor's practice as a solicitor and not out of the course of his private life.[49]

7–17

In proceedings where the claimant was a solicitor who had, at the same time, practised as a costs draftsman until July 1999, the court had to decide whether or not she was a litigant in person before April 26, 1999 and also whether she was a litigant in person after that date under the CPR. The question depended upon the criteria used to define the term "practising solicitor". Prior to April 26, 1999, the court found that the claimant was undoubtedly a practising solicitor from a regulatory point of view under the Solicitors Act and the Rules of Practice, but she was not a practising solicitor who was able to charge for her time for the purposes of RSC Ord.62 r.18(6) and the rule in *London Scottish Benefits Society v Chorley*.[50] The court therefore held that she was only entitled to recover costs for that period as a litigant in person. With regard to the period after April 26, 1999, it was accepted by the claimant that if a court found that she was not a practising solicitor for the purposes of RSC Ord.62 r.18 then she was unable to take advantage of PD 46, para.3.2. The court held that this provision was designed to do no more than preserve the rule in *London Scottish Benefits Society*. The criteria remained the same.[51]

Where the Bar Standards Board brought proceedings against a non-practising barrister before the Disciplinary Tribunal of the Council of the Inns of Court, the barrister successfully defended the proceedings in person. The Administrative Court expressed the view that the principle in *London Scottish Benefit Society* that a solicitor litigant acting in person was entitled to costs incurred in the expenditure of his own professional skill had been overturned by r.46.5(6) (formerly r.48.6(6)). Neither a solicitor nor a barrister acting in person could

48 paras 28–31.
49 *Hatton v Kendrick* [2002] EWCA Civ 1783; [2003] C.P. Rep. 32, CA.
50 *London Scottish Benefits Society v Chorley* [1884] 13 Q.B.D. 872.
51 *Joseph v Boyd & Hutchinson* [2003] EWHC 413 (Ch); [2003] 3 Costs L.R. 358, Patten J.

include in his proof of financial loss under r.46.5(4)(a) the cost of the provision of his own professional skill. Since a barrister was not a solicitor coming within the exception in PD 46(3) there was no means by which a barrister could avoid that conclusion and claim costs unless she employed someone else on her behalf. The Civil Procedure Rules did not apply however and were not even persuasive authority. If the Bar Standards Board wished to avoid having to pay the costs of a barrister's time and that barrister had successfully defended proceedings it was open to it to provide in its rules that the CPR should apply but it had not done so. The correct basis of assessing the cost was in accordance with the Board's own rules, namely to award such costs as the Tribunal thought fit. There was no basis for saying that the expenditure of a barrister's own time and skills should not be compensated where that barrister was successful.[52]

Q7. If a litigant in person instructs a barrister under the Direct Access scheme can the litigant recover any costs?

7–18   The Direct Access Scheme is a useful device for reducing costs, particularly in cases of a technical nature where a solicitor would otherwise be no more than a conduit between, e.g. a specialist tax practitioner and a specialist tax barrister. The scheme has however produced a difficulty in that a tax payer being advised by members of the Institute of Taxation and by counsel under the Direct Access Scheme appealed from a decision of the Commissioners and thence to the Court of Appeal where the tax payer was successful. Although it was conceded that the tax payer was entitled to his costs, there was considerable argument as to the extent of those costs. The Court of Appeal found that the tax payer had been acting as a litigant in person (although he had in fact taken no active part in the proceedings), that counsel's fee was recoverable since it was a disbursement which would have been made had solicitors been instructed but that the fees of the tax advisers were not recoverable save to the extent that they may have been acting in an expert capacity.[53]

Q8. In proceedings in the Intellectual Property Enterprise Court where costs are awarded against a party for unreasonable behaviour does the stage costs cap in Part 45 apply?

A claimant had behaved unreasonably in the course of an interlocutory application and costs were awarded under CPR 63.26(2). The court decided that those costs were themselves subject to the stage costs cap. Furthermore where there was more than one receiving party the stage costs had to be shared between them and did not apply to them individually.[54]

---

[52]   *R (Bar Standards Board) v Disciplinary Tribunal of the Council of the Inns of Court and Sivanandan (Interested Party)* [2014] EWHC 1570 (Admin).
[53]   *Agassi v Robinson (Inspector of Taxes)* [2005] EWCA Civ 1507; [2006] 1 W.L.R. 2126; [2006] 1 All E.R. 900; [2006] S.T.C. 580, CA.
[54]   *Akhtar v Bhopal Productions (UK) Ltd* [2015] EWHC 154 (IPEC), HHJ Hacon.

CHAPTER 8

The Court's Power in relation to Wasted Costs and Misconduct, Non-Party Costs

Wasted Costs: Introduction

In any proceedings in the Court of Appeal, the High Court and the County   8–01
Court the court may disallow, or order the legal or other representative concerned to meet the whole of any wasted costs, i.e. costs incurred by a party:

(a)   as a result of any improper, unreasonable or negligent act or omission on
        the party of any legal representative, or any employee of such a repre-
        sentative; or

(b)   which in the light of any such act or omission occurring after they were
        incurred the court considers it unreasonable to expect that party to pay.[1]

CPR r.46.8 sets out the procedure when the court is considering whether to
make an order for wasted costs under s.51(6) of the Senior Courts Act 1981
against a legal representative.

The Court of Appeal considered in detail the wasted costs jurisdiction introduced by the Courts and Legal Services Act 1990 in a judgment delivered on
January 26, 1994.[2] The court held that while litigants should not be financially prejudiced by the unjustifiable conduct of litigation by their or their
opponent's lawyers, the courts in the exercise of the wasted costs jurisdiction
should be astute to control the threat of a new and costly form of satellite
litigation. The Master of the Rolls reviewed the court's long-standing jurisdiction against solicitors[3] and noted that the jurisdiction was for the first time
extended to barristers. There could be no room for doubt about the mischief
against which the new provisions were aimed: the causing of loss and expense
to litigants by the unjustifiable conduct of litigation by their or the other
side's lawyers. Where such conduct was shown, Parliament clearly intended
to arm the courts with an effective remedy for the protection of those injured.

The Master of the Rolls affirmed the statement of principle in *Re A Barrister*   8–02
(Wasted Costs Order) (No.1 of 1999)[4] that when a wasted costs order was contemplated, a three-stage test should be applied:

---

[1]   Senior Courts Act 1981 s.51(6) and (7).

[2]   *Ridehalgh v Horsefield ; Allen v Unigate Dairies Ltd; Roberts v Coverite (Asphalters) Ltd; Philex Plc v Golban; Watson v Watson; Antonelli v Wade Gery Farr (A Firm)* [1994] Ch. 205; [1994] 3 W.L.R. 462; [1994] B.C.C. 390, CA.

[3]   He referred to *Myers v Elman* [1940] A.C. 282; [1939] 4 All E.R. 484; *Edwards v Edwards* [1958] P. 235; [1958] 2 W.L.R. 956; [1958] 2 All E.R. 179; (1958) 102 S.J. 402; *Wilkinson v Wilkinson* [1963] P. 1; *Mauroux v Soc Com Abel Periera Da Fonseca Sarl* [1972] 1W.L.R. 962; [1972] 2 All E.R. 1085; (1972) 116 S.J. 392; *Currie & Co v Law Society* [1977] Q.B. 990; [1976] 3 W.L.R. 785; (1976) 120 S.J. 819; *R&T Thew Ltd v Reeves (No.2) (Note)* [1982] Q.B. 1283; [1982] 3 W.L.R. 869; (1982) 126 S.J. 674; *Davy-Chiesman v Davy-Chiesman* [1984] Fam. 48; [1984] 2 W.L.R. 291; (1984) 81 L.S.G. 44; *Orchard v South Eastern Electricity Board* [1987] Q.B. 565; [1987] 2 W.L.R. 102; [1987] 1 All E.R. 95; (1986) 130 S.J. 956; *Sinclair-Jones v Kay* [1989] 1 W.L.R. 114; [1988] 2 All E.R. 611; (1988) 138 N.L.J. Rep. 99; *Holden v CPS* [1990] Q.B. 261 and *Gupta v Comer* [1991] 1 Q.B. 6290.

[4]   *Re A Barrister (Wasted Costs Order) (No.1 of 1999)*[1993] Q.B. 293.

(a) Had the legal representative of whom complaint was made acted improperly, unreasonably or negligently?

(b) If so, did such conduct cause the applicant to incur unnecessary costs?

(c) If so, was it, in all the circumstances, just to order the legal representative to compensate the applicant for the whole or part of the relevant costs?

Since the decision in *Ridehalgh v Horsefield* the House of Lords considered the immunity of advocates.[5] In each of the three cases the judge at first instance had concluded that solicitors enjoyed an advocate's immunity and struck out the claims as an abuse of process. The Court of Appeal decided that in none of the cases were the solicitors immune and restored the client's claim. The House of Lords decided that it was appropriate to reconsider the issue of advocate's immunity and went on to find that none of the reasons said to justify immunity had sufficient weight to sustain immunity in relation to civil proceedings. The House of Lords found that the powers of the courts and the CPR were such as to restrict the ability of clients to bring unmeritorious and vexatious claims against advocates, and accordingly public interest in the administration of justice no longer required that advocates should enjoy immunity from suit for alleged negligence in the conduct of civil proceedings. There was a similar finding in respect of criminal proceedings.

In finding that the appropriate court to deal with a wasted costs order was the court that had dealt with the proceedings to which the costs related, the Court of Appeal gave further guidance:

(1) The making of an order as to who should bear the costs and on what basis, in respect of proceedings which go to trial are, in principle, part of the overriding order made by the court at the conclusion of the trial.

(2) In the absence of at least a good reason to the contrary, the costs of proceedings should be dealt with by the tribunal, which determines the issue which disposes of the case immediately after the judgment in disposing of the case.

(3) In principle there is no difference between a costs order against a party and a costs order against a non-party; they are all part of the judicial function involved in disposing of a case.

(4) Where a wasted costs order is sought in respect of an interlocutory matter before trial it is often better for the application for wasted costs, only to be made after the trial.

(5) It is not mandatory that the application for wasted costs be made at the end of the trial. In many cases a party considering an application for a wasted costs order will ask the judge for time to consider whether to make such an application, and even if such an application is made, the normal course is for the court to give directions in relation to the disposal of the application rather than to deal with it straightaway.

(6) The application for a wasted costs order can be made after the order, in relation to the proceedings, has been drawn up, although the court

---

[5] *Arthur JS Hall & Co v Simons; Barratt v Woolf Seddon; Harris v Schofield, Roberts & Hill* [2000] 3 W.L.R. 543, HL.

hearing the application late will not necessarily grant it if there is no good reason for the delay.[6]

It is incumbent on a party seeking a wasted costs order to provide the court with **8–03** proper evidence as to what costs have been incurred as a result of the conduct complained of. Putting in a costs schedule covering all the costs claimed and then claiming a percentage of it as wasted costs was not acceptable.[7]

It is open to a litigant to seek a wasted costs order against the legal representatives of any party including his own representatives.[8]

The court does not have jurisdiction to make a wasted costs order against a legal representative who is not within the definition of "persons exercising a right to conduct litigation", e.g. because the representative has not issued proceedings.[9]

Delay in the conduct of proceedings can give rise to a wasted costs order. When considering making a wasted costs order the judge is obliged to carry out some enquiry into the costs incurred, although not a detailed enquiry. Provided that a reasoned assessment of the costs wasted is made, the judge may make an order in broad terms.[10]

The court cannot act as an appellate court in respect of its own order for costs except where fraud has been shown in the original application for the order.[11] This decision was distinguished in a case where the defendant was successful and an order was made for costs as between the parties. Prior to the detailed assessment the defendant sought a wasted costs order against the claimants' legal representative. On appeal it was held that the court did have jurisdiction to make a wasted costs order. The case was not concerned with revisiting costs with a view to a wasted costs order under s.51(6) of the 1981 Act but with revisiting a decision on costs as between the parties under s.51(1). This involved the exercise of two separate discretions and the discretion in relation to a possible wasted costs order could be exercised at any time until detailed assessment.[12]

At the time of writing the Criminal Justice Bill is going through Parliament and will come into force in 2015. It contains provision requiring the court to inform approved regulators of a wasted costs order when such an order has been made against one of the regulators' members.

Solicitor/Client

Project management and client care is a solicitor's primary obligation—costs **8–04** are part of this. Between the parties costs budgeting is part of this but separate. It's very important to understand that you need to do both.

---

[6]   *Gray v Going Places Leisure Travel Ltd* [2005] EWCA Civ 189; [2005] C.P. Rep. 21.
[7]   *Nwoko (Ned) v Oyo State Government of Nigeria* [2014] EWHC 4538 (QB) Eder J.
[8]   *Brown v Bennett* [2002] 1 W.L.R. 713; [2002] 2 All E.R. 273; [2002] Lloyd's Rep. P.N. 155, Neuberger J.
[9]   *Byrne v South Sefton HA* [2001] EWCA Civ 1904; [2002] 1 W.L.R. 775; (2002) 99(1) L.S.G. 19.
[10] *Kilroy v Kilroy* [1997] P.N.L.R. 66, CA.
[11] *Customs and Excise Commissioners v Anchor Foods* [1999] EWHC (Ch) Neuberger J.
[12] *Melchior v Vettivel* [2002] C.P. Rep. 24, Patten J.

Misconduct and the powers of the court on assessment

8–05   In assessment proceedings[13] the court has power to disallow all or part of the costs which are being assessed, or to order a party at fault, or his legal representative, to pay the costs which he has caused any other party to incur where there has been misconduct.[14] This power is in addition to the Wasted Costs jurisdiction under CPR r.46.8. Misconduct may arise where a party or his legal representative fails to conduct the detailed assessment proceeding in accordance with Part 47, or any direction of the court, or it appears to the court that the conduct of the party or the legal representative before or during the proceedings which gave rise to the assessment proceedings was unreasonable or improper.[15] The court is given power to penalise either the party or the legal representative depending upon the circumstances of the case. In this context it is suggested that behaving unreasonably or improperly means failing to comply with the overriding objective or failing to assist the court to further the overriding objective. Unreasonable or improper behaviour includes steps which are calculated to prevent or inhibit the court from furthering the overriding objective.[16] Where the court makes an order under this rule against a legally represented party and that party is not present when the order is made, the party's solicitor must notify the client in writing of the order no later than seven days after the solicitor received notice of the order (this will usually be at the time of the hearing). The court may require the solicitor to produce evidence that reasonable steps have been taken to notify the client.[17]

Before making an order under this rule the court must give the party or the legal representative a reasonable opportunity to attend the hearing to explain why such an order should not be made.

Inherent jurisdiction

8–06   The Court of Appeal has held that the inherent jurisdiction of the court should only be invoked to avoid a clear injustice. But where the legislature has stepped in with particular legislation in a particular area, then within that particular area the existing (inherent) jurisdiction is ousted or curtailed, at any rate insofar as the particular legislation is negative in character.

Given the extent of the statutory wasted costs provisions, it is unlikely that the inherent jurisdiction of the court will be relied upon save in the rarest of circumstances.

Where the court was persuaded that a solicitor had not acted negligently in continuing to act for a company which had been struck off the register, nonetheless the court was able to make an award of costs against the solicitor under its inherent jurisdiction on the basis that the solicitor had been acting without authority. The award was however reduced on the basis

---

[13]   This chapter covers misconduct in detailed assessment. For misconduct in proceedings generally see Chapter 4 and Chapter 7.
[14]   CPR r.44.11(2).
[15]   CPR r.44.11(1).
[16]   PD 46, paras 5.1–5.9.
[17]   CPR r.44.11(3).

that the defendants were clearly in a position to know the status of the company.[18]

Non-party costs orders

Section 51 of the Senior Courts Act 1981 gives the court full powers to deter- **8–07**
mine by whom and to what extent costs are to be paid. This means that the
court may make an order in favour of or against a person who was not previously a party to the proceedings. If the court decides to make such an order,
the person in favour of whom, or against whom, the order is contemplated
must be added as a party to the proceedings, for the purposes of costs only,
and must be given a reasonable opportunity to attend a hearing at which the
court will consider the matter further.[19]

An application for an order to join a party would normally be expected to
explain the nature of the claim against the intended party and the purpose to
be served by joining that party. If it became clear that the joinder was an abuse
of process the court would normally dismiss the application. At the stage of
joinder it is not appropriate to attempt a preliminary assessment of the merits
in order to see whether an application for a non-party costs order had any real
prospect of success.[20]

The Court of Appeal has laid down guidelines for the exercise of this
power.[21] The following are material considerations:

(a) An order for the payment of costs by a non-party is always exceptional[22];
     the judge should treat any application for such an order with consider-
     able caution.

(b) It is even more exceptional for an order for the payment of costs to be
     made against a non-party where the applicant has a cause of action
     against the non-party and could have joined him as a party to the origi-
     nal proceedings. Joinder as a party to the proceedings gives the persons
     concerned all the protection conferred by the rules.

(c) [No longer relevant].

(d) An application for payment of costs by a non-party will normally be
     determined by the trial judge.[23]

(e) The fact that the trial judge in the course of his judgment has expressed
     views on the conduct of the non-party neither constitutes bias, nor the
     appearance of bias.[24]

(f) The procedure for the determination of costs is a summary procedure

---

[18] *Padhiar v Patel* [2001] Lloyd's Rep. P.N. 328, Miss H Heilbron QC.
[19] CPR r.46.2(1). This rule does not apply where the court is considering whether to: (i) make an order against the Lord
Chancellor in proceedings in which the Lord Chancellor has provided legal aid to a party to the proceedings; (ii) make a
wasted costs order (as defined in r.46.8), and in proceedings to which r.46.1 applies (pre-commencement disclosure and
orders for disclosure against a person who is not a party) (CPR r.46.1; CPR r.46.2(2)).
[20] *PR Records Ltd v Vinyl 2000 Ltd* [2007] EWHC 1721 (Ch); [2008] 1 Costs L.R. 19, Morgan J.
[21] See *Symphony Group Plc v Hodgson* [1994] Q.B. 179; [1993] 3 W.L.R. 830; [1997] Costs L.R. (Core Vol.) 319, CA.
[22] Per Lord Goff, *Aiden Shipping Co Ltd v Interbulk Ltd (The Vimeira) (No.2)* [1986] A.C. 965; [1986] 2 W.L.R. 1051; [1986]
2 Lloyd's Rep. 117 at 980F.
[23] *Bahai v Rashidian* [1985] 1 W.L.R. 1337; [1985] 3 All E.R. 385; (1985) 82 L.S.G. 2162.
[24] *Bahai v Rashidian*, above at 1342H–1346F.

not necessarily subject to all the rules which would apply in an action. Thus, subject to any relevant statutory exceptions, judicial findings are inadmissible as evidence of the facts upon which they are based in proceedings between one of the parties to the original proceedings and the stranger.[25] Yet in the summary procedure for the determination of the liability of a solicitor to pay the costs of an action to which he was not a party, the judge's findings of fact may be admissible.[26] This departure from basic principles can only be justified if the connection of the non-party with the original proceedings was so close that he will not suffer any injustice by allowing the exception to the general rule.

(g) The normal rule is that witnesses in either civil or criminal proceedings enjoy immunity from any form of civil action in respect of evidence given during those proceedings. One reason for that immunity is so that witnesses might give their evidence fearlessly.[27] In so far as the evidence of a witness in proceedings might lead to an application for the costs of those proceedings against him or his company, it introduces another exception to the general principle.

(h) The fact that an employee, or even a director of a company gives evidence in an action does not normally mean that the company is taking part in that action in so far as that is an allegation relied upon by the party who applies for an order for costs against a non-party.[28]

(i) The judge should be alert to the possibility that an application for costs against a non-party is motivated by resentment or an inability to obtain an effective order for costs against a legally aided litigant. The court will be very reluctant to infer that solicitors to a legally aided party have failed to discharge their duty under the regulations.[29] The principle extends to a reluctance to infer that any maintenance by a non-party has occurred.[30] Exceptional circumstances are not a pre-condition to the power. Ultimately, the test is whether in all the circumstances it is just to exercise the power.[31]

8–08 The Privy Council (Lord Brown of Eaton-Under-Heywood) has set out the principles to be derived from the English and Commonwealth authorities:

> *"25(1). Although costs orders against non-parties are to be regarded as 'exceptional', exceptional in this context means no more than outside the ordinary run of cases where parties pursue or defend claims for their own benefit and at their own expense. The ultimate question in any such 'exceptional' case is whether in all the circumstances it is just to make the order . . .*

---

[25] *Hollington v Hewthorn & Co Ltd* [1943] K.B. 587. See also *National Justice Compania Naviera SA v Prudential Assurance Co Ltd ("The Ikarian Reefer" (No.2))* [2000] 1 All E.R. 3, CA; and *Robertson Research International Ltd v ABG Exploration BV, The Times*, November 3, 1999, Laddie J.

[26] *Brendon v Spiro* [1938] K.B. 176 at 192 per Scott LJ; *Bahai v Rashidian*, above at 1343D, 1345H.

[27] *Palmer v Durnford Ford* [1992] Q.B. 483; [1992] 2 W.L.R. 407; (1991) 141 N.L.J. 591 at 487.

[28] *Gleeson v J Wippel & Co Ltd* [1977] 1 W.L.R. 510; [1977] 3 All E.R. 54; [1977] F.S.R. 301 at 513.

[29] *Orchard v South Eastern Electricity Board* [1987] Q.B. 565; [1987] 2 W.L.R. 102; (1986) 130 S.J. 956.

[30] Per Balcombe LJ in *Symphony Group Plc v Hodgson* [1994] Q.B. 179; [1993] 3 W.L.R. 830; [1997] Costs L.R. (Core Vol.) 319.

[31] *Globe Equities Ltd v Globe Legal Services Ltd* [2000] C.P.L.R. 233; [1999] B.L.R. 232, CA.

(2). Generally speaking the discretion will not be exercised against 'pure funders' described in paragraph 40 of Hamilton v Al-Fayed as:
'those with no personal interest in the litigation, who do not stand to benefit from it, are not funding it as a matter of business, and in no way seek to control its course.'[32]
In that case the courts' usual approach is to give priority to the public interest in the funded party getting access to justice over that of the successful unfunded party recovering his costs and so not having to bear the expense of vindicating his rights.
(3). Where, however, the non party not merely funds the proceedings but substantially also controls or at any rate is to benefit from them, justice will ordinarily require that, if the proceedings fail, he will pay the successful party's costs. The non-party in these cases is not so much facilitating access to justice by the party funded as himself gaining access to justice for his own purposes. He himself is the 'real party' to the litigation, a concept repeatedly invoked throughout the jurisprudence—see, for example . . . Millett LJ's judgment in Metalloy Supplies Ltd (In Liquidation) v MA (UK) Ltd.[33]
Consistently with this approach, Phillips LJ described the non party underwriters in TGA Chapman Ltd v Christopher[34] as 'the defendants in all but name'. Nor, indeed, is it necessary that the non party be 'the only real party' to the litigation . . . provided that he is 'a real party in . . . very important and critical aspects'—see Arundel Chiropractic Centre Pty Ltd v Deputy Commissioner of Taxation[35] . . .
Some reflection of this concept of 'the real party' is to be found in CPR 25.13(2) (f) which allows a security for costs order to be made where 'the claimant is acting as a nominal claimant'.
(4). Perhaps the most difficult cases are those in which non-parties, receivers or liquidators (or, indeed, financially insecure companies generally) in litigation designed to advance the funders own financial interests . . . '[36]

Questions and answers

Q1. To what extent can advocates be held liable for loss or damages resulting from their conduct or advice?

Although the House of Lords held that public interest does not require advocates to be held immune from suit for the consequences of their negligence, that interest does require that the application of the principle should not stifle advocates' independence of mind and action in the manner in which they conduct litigation and advise their clients. In a case where it was alleged that counsel had been negligent in failing to give the claimant sufficiently detailed advice in deciding whether to accept a payment into court or proceed with the claim, it was held that the advice given fell within the range of

8–09

---

[32] But see now: *Excalibur Ventures LLC v Texas Keystone Inc* [2014] EWHC 3436 (Comm) Christopher Clarke LJ.
[33] *Metalloy Supplies Ltd (In Liquidation) v MA (UK) Ltd* [1997] 1 W.L.R. 1613; [1997] 1 All E.R. 418; [1997] B.C.C. 165.
[34] *TGA Chapman Ltd v Christopher* [1998] 1 W.L.R. 12; [1998] 2 All E.R. 873; [1997] C.L.C. 1306. 170.
[35] *Arundel Chiropractic Centre Pty Ltd v Deputy Commissioner of Taxation* [2001] 179 A.L.R. 406.
[36] *Dymocks Franchise Systems (NSW) Pty Ltd v Todd* [2004] UKPC 39; [2004] 1 W.L.R. 2807; [2005] 1 Costs L.R. 52.

that to be expected of reasonably competent counsel of that seniority and experience. It was possible in hindsight that the advice to the claimant to proceed was a wrong decision but it was not as mistaken a decision as had been represented.[37]

Q2. Can you give some examples of situations in which non-party costs orders may be made?

8–10   There are countless examples of orders being made applying those principles against directors or shareholders of companies, insurers, experts, solicitors and other parties.

In respect of non-party costs orders, the question arising is not one of rights and obligations since no such rights and obligations exist unless and until the Court exercises its discretion to make an order. If such an order is made against a non-party, it underlines the proposition that the non-party had no substantive liability in respect of the cause of action in question. The Court is not fettered by the legal realities and is entitled to look at the economic realities. In the instant case the non-party was a director of the company, the sole shareholder and entitled to all of the company's economic benefits and as sole director, made all decisions on the company's behalf. The company was under the director's absolute control and he ran it without regarding himself as accountable to anyone. Unlike most cases on non-party costs orders, the director was in fact a party and as such, entitled to participate in the trial to the fullest extent possible. The director had caused the company to advance a false defence which he must have known to be false. Those factors taken cumulatively made it just to order the director to pay the claimant's costs.[38]

In another case, Akenhead J held that it was clear from the authorities that the categories of case involving costs orders against non-parties were neither rigid nor closed. They were very much fact-sensitive. In a case where a non-party company director was at all material times the major shareholder in two defendant companies and had exercised full control of both of them throughout, he had stood to benefit from the litigation. He had funded at least half the costs and without such funding one of the companies was otherwise insolvent. The defendant's counterclaims were speculative and it had been unreasonable to pursue them. The decision to do so had been the director's. It was positively unlikely that even if he had been warned in advance that costs would be sought against him personally, he would not have continued to defend the claim and to pursue the counterclaims to judgment having regard to his character including his conviction that he was always right and everyone else was always wrong. The absence of any warning was more than cancelled out by the other factors. The director was ordered personally to pay the costs of and occasioned by the counterclaims.[39]

---

[37]   *Moy v Petman Smith (A Firm)* [2005] UKHL 7; [2005] 1 W.L.R. 581; [2005] Lloyd's Rep. Med. 293.

[38]   *Threlfall v ECD Insight Ltd* (Costs) [2013] EWCA Civ 1444; [2014] 2 Costs Law Reports 129.

[39]   *Weatherford Global Products Ltd v Hydropath Holdings Ltd and Clearwell International Ltd* [2014] EWHC 3243 (TCC) Akenhead J.

Q3. Is it possible to obtain a non-party costs order where the successful party already has an order in its favour?

A claimant bank obtained judgment against the first defendant in proceedings and was awarded 85 per cent of its costs on the indemnity basis. When the defendant failed to pay, the claimant obtained permission to serve a non-party costs application on the second defendant, out of the jurisdiction. Having decided various other issues against the second defendant, the Court found that it was entirely just that a non-party costs order be made against him so that he was liable for all sums owned by the first defendant to the claimant in respect of the costs awarded. The second defendant had transferred assets out of the first defendant with a view to depleting those assets and making it more difficult for the claimant to recover sums from the first defendant. There was a strong element of impropriety in making those transfers. The second defendant had control of the conduct of the first defendant's case in the litigation. He was the sole director and shareholder and was responsible for the first defendant's case which contained claims based on his own dishonest evidence. His motivation was the advancement of the first defendant's case against the claimant and the desire to protect its assets. The conduct of extensive parts of the defence and counterclaim was reprehensible and involved impropriety and dishonesty on the second defendant's part. He had caused the claimant to incur costs because of the first defendant's pursuit of its defence and counterclaim. The second defendant was the embodiment of the first defendant and conducted the proceedings with impropriety which resulted in huge elements of additional costs. It was the second defendant who stood to gain or lose in the event of the first defendant's success or failure in the action. He was therefore the 'real party' to the dispute and to the action. He could also be taken to have funded the litigation.[40]

8–11

Q4. How "controlling" does a non-party have to be to be the subject of a non-party costs order?

A hugely experienced Litigant in Person was found to be 'inextricably bound up' with the fortunes of the defendant companies. There was no effective distinction between him and the companies. He had represented the first and second defendants throughout. He was their sole director and he and a Mauritius company were the shareholders in the first defendant. The Court held that he must have known from past experience that his prospects of success in bringing the defendant's application (which was unsuccessful) were virtually non-existent. The defendant companies never had any intention of paying the claimant's costs when they lost. The non-party had irresponsibly caused the companies to defend the claim and the claimant to incur irrecoverable costs as a result.[41]

8–12

---

40   *Deutsche Bank AG v Sebastian Holdings Inc* [2014] EWHC 2073 (Comm); [2014] 4 Costs LR 711 Cooke J.
41   *Dunfermline Building Society v Ghana Commercial Finance Ltd* [2014] EWHC 3397 (QB) HH Judge Mackie.

Q5. What is the position where the successful party needs to obtain more information before applying for a non-party costs order? Does the court have power to order disclosure?

8–13   A company incorporated in Romania issued proceedings against a broking company and also applied for insolvency proceedings to be opened in Romania. The claimant company failed to comply with an order for security for costs by payment into court and its claim was struck out and judgment entered in favour of the defendant with an order for costs. The claimant company failed to have the judgment set aside or varied and failed to make any payment in respect of costs. The defendant company applied for an order that the claim-ant's solicitors should answer questions about who had financed their client's litigation. The Court held that the case had not yet reached the stage where a non-party would be added for the purpose of costs only. The Court had an ancillary power to order solicitors on record to disclose who had financed the litigation. The power under s.51 of the Senior Courts Act 1981 was ineffective unless there was an inherent power to discover who those persons might be (see *Abraham v Thompson*[42]).[43]

Q6. What is the potential liability of solicitors who fund litigation for their clients by acting without ATE or funding disbursements?

8–14   Following the decision of the Court of Appeal in *Myatt v National Coal Board*[44] the respondent Coal Board sought its costs from the appellants' solicitors personally. Although the court found that the appellants had themselves a financial interest in the outcome of the appeal, the question to be decided was whether there was jurisdiction to order the solicitors to pay some or all of the respondents' costs and if so how that jurisdiction should be exer-cised. Having referred to *Symphony Group Plc v Hodgson* and *Dymocks v Todd* the court held that a solicitor who is "a real party . . . in very important and critical respects" and who "not merely funds the proceedings but sub-stantially also contributes, or at any rate, is to benefit from them" may be potentially liable. The court did not accept that the mere fact that a solicitor was on the record prosecuting proceedings for his or her client was fatal to an application by the successful opposing party under s.51(1) and (3) of the Senior Courts Act 1981, that the solicitor should pay some or all of the costs. Had the appellants had no financial interest at all, the other party with an interest in the appeal would be the solicitors. In the judgment of the court they would undoubtedly be acting outside the role of solicitor. The court had no doubt that there was jurisdiction to make an order under s.51 (3) of the 1981 Act against a solicitor where litigation was pursued by the client for the benefit or to a substantial degree for the benefit of the solicitor. Taking into account the fact that the respondents had not warned the solicitors that they

---

[42]   *Abraham v Thompson* [1997] 4 All E.R. 362.
[43]   *SC DG Petrol SRL v Vitol Broking Ltd* [2014] EWHC 3900 (Comm) Walker J.
[44]   *Garrett v Halton BC* [2006] EWCA Civ 1017; [2007] 1 All E.R. 147, CA.

might apply for an order for costs against them so that they had not had a reasonable opportunity for deciding whether or not to continue with the proceedings, the solicitors were ordered to pay 50 per cent of the respondent's costs of the appeal.[45]

The Court of Appeal has dealt with two unrelated cases which raised the question as to the extent to which the solicitors acting on behalf of claimants could fund or "prime pump" litigation, for those of limited means when proceeding pursuant to a conditional fee agreement with no after the event insurance cover, without thereby exposing themselves to adverse costs orders in the event of the claims failing. In each case the Judge at first instance had dismissed the defendant's application for the claimant's solicitors to be joined as a party and for an order revealing how the claim had been funded. Each claim was appealed to Eady J, who allowed each appeal and required the solicitors to disclose how the claim had been funded. In the event the litigation threw up circumstances which, in the words of the Court of Appeal, "clearly justified the order that Eady J made". Thus, although both appeals were dismissed, the court expressed the view that payment of disbursements without more does not incur any potential liability for an adverse costs order. The order under appeal was an order for disclosure and the Court of Appeal found that by funding disbursements the solicitors had not stepped outside the normal role of a solicitor. It had come to light that the solicitors had pressed on with the case, regardless of specific instructions from their client not to do so without ATE. This was sufficient to require disclosure in each case.[46]

A successful defendant employer sought a non-party costs order against the unsuccessful employee's solicitors alleging that the solicitor's failure to obtain ATE meant that there was an undeclared conflict of interest between the solicitor and their client which had motivated the solicitors to continue with the case to ensure that the client would not have liability for the defendant's costs. At first instance the Judge found that the allegation that the solicitors had been aware of a conflict of interest was not made out, and there was no evidence to suggest conscious impropriety on the part of the solicitors. The Court of Appeal decided that a solicitor is entitled to act on a CFA for an impecunious client who was known or suspected to be unable to pay costs if unsuccessful. So far as the other side was concerned, whether the solicitor had negligently failed to obtain ATE did not impact on the costs they would incur unless it was demonstrably provable that the costs would not have been incurred.[47]

---

[45] *Myatt v National Coal Board* [2007] EWCA Civ 307; [2007] 1 W.L.R. 554; [2006] 5 Costs L.R. 798.
[46] *Flatman v Germany* [2013] EWCA Civ 278.
[47] *Heron v TNT UK Ltd* [2013] EWCA Civ 469.

CHAPTER 9

Assessments of Costs and Payments on Account of Costs

Introduction

The overall intentions of the 2013 reforms in respect of the process for deter- **9–01** mination of 'between the parties' costs are to reduce the issues and lessen the time, and therefore the cost, expended upon this stage of a claim, recognising that in many cases the 'costs of the costs' had become unreasonable and disproportionate. This aim is achieved by a combination of changes—some introducing entirely new concepts and procedures and some being simply variations of what already existed. They are:

- Costs management designed, in part, to reduce the costs in dispute at the conclusion of a claim and reduce for the need for/the scope of assessments. This has been considered in **Chapter 4**.
- The introduction of the further fixed costs schemes considered in **Chapter 7**, removing any need for assessments.
- Improvements to the summary assessment regime.
- A more efficient detailed assessment hearing process.
- The introduction of provisional assessments.
- A change of approach to payments on account of costs.

It is the last four of these upon which we shall concentrate in this chapter.

Summary assessment

One of the options outlined by Jackson LJ in his preliminary report[1] was **9–02** to abolish summary assessments altogether. He rejected this, describing the procedure as:

> *"a valuable tool which has made a substantial contribution to civil procedure, not least by deterring frivolous applications and reducing the need for detailed assessment proceedings."*

Instead, the process has been altered, but only slightly, and the emphasis on proportionality is likely to lead to more summary assessments in place of detailed assessments. The procedure for assessing costs by summary assessment is now found at CPR 44.6 and 44 PD 9. It remains familiar.

The court is charged with considering a summary assessment whenever it makes an order about costs that does not provide for fixed costs. The general rule is that a court will undertake a summary assessment at the end of a fast track trial and at the conclusion of any other hearing which has lasted not

---

[1] Review of Civil Litigation Costs: Preliminary Report, May 2009.

more than a day, unless there is good reason not to do so. There is a further steer to a summary assessment when appropriate at the end of a multi track trial in CPR 29 PD 10.5. Only the judge who has conducted the trial/hearing and made the relevant award of costs order may undertake the summary assessment. The parties must file and serve statements of costs not less than two days before a fast track trial and 24 hours before the time fixed for any other hearing.

The slight changes to the process are:

i)   there is a new N260—statement of costs; and
ii) the requirement to serve a statement of costs in advance now applies to Detailed Assessment hearings and the summary assessment of the costs of those proceedings.

i. The new N260—statement of costs

9–03   One of the major criticisms of the previous version of the N260, particularly where the summary assessment was of the entire costs of a claim, as distinct from a discrete application, was the lack of information that it contained. The new N260 ensures that the assessing judge has more detail by introducing a breakdown of the time spent on documents. CPR 44 PD 9.5(3) is no more prescriptive than its predecessor and only requires that "the statement of costs should follow as closely as possible Form N260". However, given the increased emphasis on enforcing practice direction compliance in the overriding objective at CPR 1.2(f), it will be a bold practitioner who uses a 'home-made' variation, as there is likely to be little sympathy, rather the prospect of some sanction, if the form used does not provide the information necessary in clear terms.

ii. The requirement to serve a statement of costs in advance of detailed assessment hearings

9–04   Rule changes made by omission of previous provisions are often overlooked as they are harder to spot. The provision previously found at s.45.3 of the Costs Practice Direction is no more. Parties seeking the costs of a detailed assessment must comply with the provisions of CPR 44 PD 9.5(4) and file and serve an N260 24 hours before the assessment.

The change of emphasis

9–05   A decision as to whether to undertake a summary assessment or to order a detailed assessment is a case management decision. The amended overriding objective applies to all case management decisions and requires the court to consider the proportionality of its decision. Notwithstanding the 'costs cap' in the provisional assessment regime (see below), there can be little argument that a summary assessment requires significantly less resource, both in costs and in court time, than a detailed assessment. Accordingly, there should be an increased number of summary assessments. The likelihood of this is enhanced by the fact that many of the multi track cases that might previously have gone to a detailed assessment will have been subject to costs management orders and, absent 'good reason', the court will only be troubled by the non budgeted costs—reducing the scope of, and the time needed for, a summary assessment.

Parties wishing to seek summary assessment at the end of trials/hearing that exceed one day should ensure that Forms N260 are available to the court and have been served so that this is a realistic option for the court if time permits (even if summary assessment does not take place, the N260 can, in appropriate cases then be referred to as the basis for a payment on account). Whilst there is sometimes resistance to a summary assessment where the costs are substantial, it is interesting that para.F14.2 of the Admiralty and Commercial Courts Guide envisages summary assessments of the costs of interim applications where the statement of costs of the receiving party is no more than £100,000, but requires parties to be prepared for the court to undertake such an assessment even where the costs exceed this sum.

Detailed assessment hearing process

In Ch.45 of his Final Report, Jackson LJ set out a number of recommenda-   **9–06**
tions designed to produce a more efficient and proportionate detailed assessment process. One, provisional assessment, is considered separately below. The others were:

- A new format of user-friendly bill that is inexpensive to prepare and ultimately can be linked to the same time capturing system that can prepare client costs estimates and Forms H for costs budgeting.
- Shorter and more focused Points of Dispute and Replies.
- Compulsory offers.
- The cross application of CPR 36 to detailed assessment proceedings generally and the requirement upon the paying party to make an open offer.
- Clarity on the date from which time runs to appeal decisions made in the detailed assessment.

Save in respect of the first of these recommendations, upon which work continues and completion approaches, the remainder were introduced in April 2013 by the following provisions:

- CPR 47 PD 8.2 requires Points of Dispute to be 'short and to the point'. If a Reply is served (and it remains optional) it must be limited to points of principle and concessions (CPR 47 PD 12.1).
- Under CPR 47 PD 8.3 the paying party must make an open offer to accompany the Points of Dispute.
- CPR 47.20 expressly applies the provisions of CPR 36 to detailed assessment proceedings (it is worth noting that any CPR 47.20 offer does not need to be the same as the open offer). The paying party must make an open offer to accompany the Points of Dispute (CPR 47 PD 8.3).
- CPR 47.14(7) makes it plain that where the assessment takes place at more than one hearing, the time for appealing does not run until the conclusion of the final hearing (presumably this also means that where there is

only one hearing, but over many days, the time for appealing any decision, regardless of which day it was made upon, does not run until the conclusion of the assessment).

Apart from the implementation of the recommendations above, the introduction of provisional assessment and the requirement to file and serve a Form N260 24 hours before the assessment hearing (see above), the procedure for detailed assessments remains as it was prior to April 2013. Initially the transitional provisions caused some concern, although these were set out in The Civil Procedure (Amendment Rules) 2013 SI 2013/262 at r.22. However, the passage of time ought to have resolved any problems by now.

Provisional assessment

9–07   In his final report, Jackson LJ recommended the introduction of provisional assessment under a pilot scheme. The pilot took place in certain courts in respect of bills for £25,000 and under. In the April 2013 amendments, the scheme was extended to all courts and applies to any 'between the parties' bill where the costs claimed are £75,000 or less.

A provisional assessment is one undertaken by the court on the basis of papers filed, without an oral hearing and any attendance by the parties. There is a limited opt-out provision found at CPR 47.15(6), under which the court may at any time consider the bill unsuitable for provisional assessment and may list for hearing with the procedure for a detailed assessment hearing then applying.

The procedure is set out at CPR 47.15 and 47 PD 14. It can be divided into four stages as follows:

i)   Pre-assessment.
ii)   The assessment.
iii) After the assessment excluding an oral hearing.
iv)   Oral hearings.

i) Pre-assessment

9–08   The title given to CPR 47 relates exclusively to detailed assessment. There can be no doubt that a provisional assessment is a form of detailed assessment. As such it is not surprising that many of the procedural provisions relating to the request for an assessment borrow heavily from those for detailed assessment hearings. However, at the pre-assessment stage there is a fundamental difference in respect of documents required. Other than the documents that must be filed with the request itself under CPR 47 PD.13.2 and 14.3(b)–(e) there is no requirement to file further documents in support of the bill between 14 and 7 days before the assessment—although the Senior Court Costs Office ("SCCO") Guide 2013 makes provision for a specific order to comply with the CPR 47 PD 13.2 filing obligation if the request has not been accompanied by these documents. Significantly, CPR 47 PD 13.11 does apply to provisional assessments, but the court retains the power to direct the filing of any further documents which the court considers that it needs to reach a decision. At the moment there appear to be conflicting practices around the country with some courts requiring all documents in support as if this were a normal detailed assessment hearing, some simply making requests for specific documents when needed and some requesting no documents at all. This is entirely a matter of judicial discretion. Note that unlike the position for detailed assessment hearings, the receiving party must file any CPR 36 offers (in a sealed envelope marked "Part 36 or similar offers", but which does not reveal which party/ies have made the offers). The rationale is obvious—parties are not present to draw the attention of the court to any relevant offers as they would be at the end of a detailed assessment.

ii) The assessment

Strictly there is no requirement either for the court to fix a date for a provisional assessment or to give notice of it as CPR 47 PD 13.4 and 13.6 do not apply and the parties are not permitted to attend the assessment. The only obligation on the court is to use its best endeavours to undertake the assessment within 6 weeks of receipt of the request. In practice in the SCCO and the County Court, non attended hearing dates are being allocated—in other words the judge has time specifically allocated in the list to deal with a provisional assessment even though no parties attend. Some come with a further order that should the court be able to undertake the assessment at an earlier date it will do so without notice to the parties. The rationale behind these orders is understandable. The Costs Judges and the District Bench simply cannot accommodate these assessments in addition to other work requirements and so discrete time is made available within lists. However, should lists go short and there not be other work, then the further order enables the court to undertake these assessments earlier than listed.

9–09

CPR 47.15(4) is clear that the assessment is based on the information in the bill, the supporting papers and the contentions in Form G (the Points of Dispute and any Reply to it). Documents filed beyond those required by the rules or by specific requests from the court may be ignored by the assessing judge and met with a request to arrange collection of them from the court staff. The rules are clear as to what documents must be considered and there is no obligation on the assessing judge to look at further documents filed unbidden (particularly when the time set aside for the assessment will not have been based on consideration of unrequested paperwork).

iii) After the assessment

After the assessment the court will return the bill provisionally assessed and the Form G. Whilst CPR 47 PD 14.4(2) suggests that the court's decisions will be on the Form G, the decisions may be on that, may be on the bill or on a separate document (for example where the court is giving a written judgment on a substantive point and there is insufficient room to do this on the bill or Form G).

9–10

The parties must agree the amount at which the court has assessed the bill within 14 days and any party wishing to challenge any aspect of the provisional assessment must file and serve a written request for an oral hearing within 21 days. If no request for an oral hearing is filed and served within that period then, save in exceptional circumstances, the provisional assessment is binding.

Practice varies on how costs of the provisional assessment itself are assessed where there is no challenge to the assessment. Some courts make costs orders when conducting the provisional assessment on alternative bases depending on whether or not any offers prove to be relevant. Others ask the parties to notify the court of the figure assessed, once calculated, and only then does the court open the envelope containing privileged offers and determine the costs. It may be that the latter approach will become more prevalent once the bills being assessed are subject to the proportionality cross check under CPR 44.3(2) as the likelihood is that the court will not wish to undertake that exercise until it knows what sum it has assessed as reasonably incurred and reasonable in amount.

The costs of the assessment are subject to the provisions of CPR 47.20 and the general rule is that the receiving party is entitled to the costs. CPR 47.15(5) caps the maximum costs the court will award to either party (other than the costs of drafting the bill and excluding court fees and VAT) at £1,500.

iv) Oral hearings

9–11   Any written request for an oral hearing must identify the item(s) challenged and provide a time estimate for the hearing of the challenge(s). On receipt of the notice the court will then fix a date for the hearing, giving at least 14 days notice to the parties.

The party requesting the oral hearing will pay the costs of that hearing unless it achieves an adjustment in its favour of 20 per cent or more of the sum provisionally assessed or the court orders otherwise. This potential costs penalty clearly is designed to preclude minor challenges. On a bill where the costs are limited to £75,000 anything other than a challenge to an item of substance is unlikely to result in a 20 per cent adjustment. There is limited guidance in CPR 47 PD 14.5 as to when the court may order otherwise, indicating that conduct and offers will be taken into account. As yet no authorities have emerged to supplement this guidance.

It is worth reiterating that a request for an oral hearing, as opposed to an application for permission to appeal, is the correct procedure to challenge any decision made on a provisional assessment.

A final word

9–12   Those keen to ensure that they comply with all relevant rules in the light of the more robust compliance regime now in place may find it a relief that CPR 47 PD 14.2(2) does not require compliance with CPR 47 PD 13.9 as this provision does not seem to exist.

Payment on account

Prior to April 2013 where the court made an order that a party was to pay costs   **9–13**
it could order a payment on account of those costs pending an assessment.
There was no presumption that it would do so, as was made clear in *Blackmore
v Cummins*.[2] The April 2013 reforms reversed this by the introduction of CPR
44.2(8), which provides that where the court makes a costs order and provides
for a detailed assessment of those costs, then it <u>will</u> order a reasonable sum on
account of those costs, unless there is good reason not to do so. This provision has also changed, seeming to make a temporal link between the order
for costs to be assessed and the payment on account. Many courts interpret
this to mean that there can only be one payment on account, with this being
ordered at the time of the costs order and that any further interim sums can
only be obtained under the procedure for an interim costs certificate *after* the
receiving party has filed a request for a detailed assessment hearing.

Questions and answers

Summary and detailed assessment

**Q1. What is the position when form N260 is either served/filed late or not
at all?**

CPR 44 PD .9.6 maintains the previous position—namely that a failure to file   **9–14**
and serve form N260 without reasonable excuse will be taken into account
when the court determines what order to make about costs of the claim or
hearing (as appropriate) and about the costs of any further hearings/assess-
ments which the failure may necessitate (so the failure is relevant both to the
award, as well as the amount, of assessed costs).

   The leading pre-April 2013 authority on this provision is *MacDonald v
Taree Holdings Ltd*.[3] The appellate court held that despite the use of the word
'must', the provision is not mandatory and the judge had been wrong to refuse
the successful party's application for summary assessment of his costs on the
grounds that he had not served a statement of costs upon the respondent 24
hours in advance. The court made a distinction between cases where there
had and had not been factors aggravating the failure to serve a statement.
If there were no aggravating features then a party should not be deprived of
all his costs. The court should take the matter into account but its reaction
should be proportionate. In these cases the court was presented with three
options as follows:

* Whether it would be appropriate to have a brief adjournment for the
  paying party to consider the statement and then to proceed to a summary
  assessment of the costs. In such a case the 'sanction' was that the judge
  should err in favour of awarding a lighter figure.
* Whether the matter should be stood over for a detailed assessment.

---

[2]   *Blackmore v Cummins* [2009] EWCA Civ 1276.
[3]   *MacDonald v Taree Holdings Ltd* [2001] C.P.L.R.439; [2001] 1 Costs L.R.147, Neuberger J.

- Whether the matter should be adjourned for summary assessment at a later date or for summary assessment to be dealt with in writing.

9–15 Does this approach survive the April 2013 reforms? In *Webb v E-Serv*,[4] albeit in an entirely different context of considering the time period to renew a request for permission to appeal, Turner J held that the word 'must' did convey a mandatory requirement. If this applied to a failure to comply with the provisions of CPR 44 PD 9.5 a party otherwise entitled to a costs order may not secure it as that provision makes the preparation, lodging and serving of a statement of costs a condition precedent to applying for costs (CPR 44 PD 9.5 refers to the fact that a party intending to seek costs <u>must</u> prepare a written statement and CPR 44 PD 9.5(4) states that this <u>must</u> be filed and served the prescribed amount of time before the hearing).

However, the outcome of two cases, one where no statement of costs had been filed or served and the other where the statement had been filed and served late, suggests that the court is still resisting complete disallowance of costs.

In *Wheeler v The Chief Constable of Gloucestershire Constabulary*,[5] neither party had filed a statement of costs in advance of an appeal. The upshot for the successful party was an order for costs to be the subject of a detailed assessment, but with the receiving party to pay the costs of those proceedings.

In contrast, in *Kingsley v Orban*,[6] where the successful party had filed and served a statement late and the first instance court had pressed on and assessed those costs without any concession to the late service, the appellate court looked at whether there were aggravating factors, determined there were not, but that the first instance court ought to have adjourned for a short period to allow the paying party time to consider the statement before proceeding to assess, and allowed the paying party to raise further points on appeal (all of which failed). However, it is worth mentioning that the judgment makes no reference to the decision in *Wheeler*, instead determining that there was no reason not to apply *MacDonald*

9–16 A halfway house was adopted by Akenhead J in *Group M UK Ltd v Cabinet Office*,[7] where a statement of costs was served only three hours before the handing down of a judgment when costs would be considered and, even then, that N260 did not contain the breakdown of time spent on documents. Akenhead J applied the *Denton v T H White*[8] three stage test to the breaches, concluding that the breaches were serious, that there was good reason for them and that it would wholly disproportionate to allow no costs and, instead, imposed a 'delay discount' of £2,240 as a sanction for what he described as a breach "at the lower end of serious".

Inevitably decisions will be case-specific. For example, whilst it may be

---

4 *Webb v E-Serv* [2014] EWHC 49 (QB) Turner J.
5 *Wheeler v The Chief Constable of Gloucestershire Constabulary* [2013] EWCA Civ 1791.
6 *Kingsley v Orban* [2014] EWHC 2991 (Ch) Nugee J.
7 *Group M UK Ltd v Cabinet Office* [2014] EWHC 3863 (TCC) Akenhead J.
8 *Denton v T H White* [2014] EWCA Civ 906.

appropriate to adjourn some cases for a detailed assessment where there is failure to file and serve a statement, if this failure were to occur in respect of a discrete application where the costs would be minimal, the court may take the view that an adjournment for a subsequent summary or detailed assessment in such a case would, applying the overriding objective, be disproportionate (even if the receiving party had to pay the costs of the assessment, as court time would have to be allocated to this). In such a case the court may determine that the successful party forfeits the right to a costs order on the application.

Avoid the uncertainty and the risk—comply!

Q2. Does the introduction of the breakdown of time spent on documents on the Form N260 mean that the court will deal with challenges to this on an item by item basis or will the court make one overall assessment of time spent on documents?

Notwithstanding the additional information provided in the documents schedule to the costs statement, the process remains a summary assessment. As such it would be inappropriate to expect the court to resort to micro management. The schedule was not introduced to turn summary assessments into quasi detailed assessments. Indeed, in his Final Report Jackson LJ indicated that he thought the 'old' N260 was adequate in respect of interim applications. His concern was that:

9–17

> "*in respect of summary assessments at the end of a trial or appeal, I consider that Form N260 provides insufficient information. The court is assessing not only costs related to the trial or appeal, but also the costs of the whole pre-trial process. In the short term, I recommend that a revised and more informative version of Form N260 be prepared for use in connection with summary assessments at the end of trial*".

Whilst we would expect the court to entertain submissions that the document time is unreasonable by reference to some examples from the schedule, the court is extremely unlikely to determine disputes over individual items in the schedule—rather it will use the schedule to inform the decision over the total document time that is reasonable or the total time for a particular task, e.g. drafting statements.

Q3. How does the proportionality cross check at CPR 44.3(2) work in the summary assessment process that is already one undertaken with a broad brush?

In *Morgan v Spirit Group Ltd*,[9] when overturning the decision of a recorder, the Court of Appeal made the obvious point that the court must undertake either a summary or detailed assessment of the costs. The recorder had not done so. Instead, in a paragraph, the recorder had simply determined a proportionate

9–18

---

[9]   *Morgan v Spirit Group Ltd* [2011] EWCA Civ 6.

figure and added something to that to allow for the existence of what he had, erroneously, described as 'a contingent fee agreement'. Summary though the assessment is intended to be, the court concluded that what had taken place here was not a summary assessment. So, summary though the procedure may be, it must still recognisably be an assessment.

These comments resonate loudly under the new regime, where the court is required to undertake an assessment of what is reasonably incurred and reasonable in amount for those items reasonably incurred <u>and then</u> step back and apply the proportionality cross check under CPR 44.4(2). If the summary assessment is too summary, then the court will struggle to draw a distinction between the determination of what is reasonable and the determination of what is proportionate. The court must undertake the determinations of reasonableness and proportionality separately as to do otherwise makes the flawed assumption that the conclusions always elide. They do not. Whilst they will in some cases, there will be cases where the reasonable costs fall within what is proportionate (in which case the court need do no more than articulate that the reasonably assessed costs are also proportionate), there will also be cases where the reasonable costs are not proportionate (in which case the court then determines the figure that is proportionate and assesses the recoverable costs in that sum—see **Chapter 3** on proportionality for more detail as to how the court will undertake this exercise).

Q4. How can the court use the costs budgets at assessment of the costs of the claim when neither the N260 nor the bill is divided into the same phases as the Form H to enable easy comparison?

9–19   It is certainly the case that the N260 does not match the budget phases, making ready comparison impossible. However, at this stage the same point is just as easily directed at the format of the bill for detailed assessment. In his Final Report, Jackson LJ looked forward to the day when time capture recording systems would lead to "a new software system should be developed, which will be capable of generating bills of costs at different levels of generality". In the meantime, the 'broad brush' of summary assessment will make it difficult to challenge the sums budgeted for phases that the court has costs managed. As a practical exercise, the budgeted sums will have to be deducted from the total sum claimed in the N260 or the bill to calculate what sum must relate to the non budgeted costs and only that sum is, unless there is a 'good reason' to depart from the budget for a specific phase/phases, 'live' at the assessment.

If there is a successful argument that there is a 'good reason' under CPR 3.18 to depart from the budgeted sum for a phase, then the court will have to assess the sum for that phase, deduct the budgeted sum for that phase from the overall sum and add back what it has assessed.

A more challenging exercise, particularly in a summary assessment, will be to argue that the receiving party has overspent on a particular budgeted phase (and compensated for this by an equivalent under spend on another budgeted phase), where the overall sum in the N260/the bill does not exceed the budgeted sums and the costs set out as incurred in the Form H at the time of the budget.

Similarly, at a detailed assessment of a claim which has settled and it is found or accepted that not all budgeted work under a particular phase has been completed at the time of settlement (and this is surely a 'good reason' to depart from the budget), it will be difficult to determine what deduction should be made to the bill. This is because the phase budget has been set by reference to what is a reasonable and proportionate sum for that phase and not by an assessment of hourly rate multiplied by time (see CPR 3 PD E.7.3 and see **Chapter 4** on case and costs management above). Accordingly, as the budget figure has not been set by overall time multiplied by hourly rates, it is inappropriate to work out what work has been done on that phase by reference to such a calculation and to deduct it from the total for that phase. Instead, the court may have to adopt a broad brush and determine what is reasonable and proportionate as a lump sum for the work done on the phase up to settlement and deduct that from the total phase figure.

The preceding paragraphs have concentrated on problems linking budgets   **9–20** to the documents required for assessments. It would be wrong not to balance the scales by pointing to a couple of positives. One is considered below under payments on account. The other is the simplicity of the assessment where there is no 'good reason' to depart from the budget. A useful illustration of this is the case of *Slick Seating Systems v Adams*.[10] In this case the trial judge had also case and costs managed the case throughout. In fact he concluded that an award of indemnity costs was appropriate (and duly assessed those summarily), but his approach amply illustrates the benefits of costs management as he was able to avoid a detailed assessment (as would probably have been the outcome prior to the costs management regime) and undertake the simplest of summary assessments as follows:

> "By running this case with a costs budget, I approved a budget of a grand total of £359,710.35 pence for doing this case through to trial. In my judgment that budget was proportionate to what was at stake: the £4.4million sum that I have just awarded. The claimants have laudably kept within that budget and have exercised due control over their activities and expenditure in an exemplary fashion. The statement of costs on 13.5.13 (which is today) is favourably compared with the costs estimate of 22.5.12. The form is signed by the partner of the solicitors and a member of the client company as well, Mr Beasley; the grand total is £351,267.35 pence. In my judgment that is a sum which is, looking at each of the phases, within the budget that was set and the claimants are to be commended with controlling the budget throughout this particular period.
> That will be the sum that I would award to be paid within 14 days without the need for detailed assessment, detailed assessment becoming otiose . . . "

---

[10]   *Slick Seating Systems v Adams* [2013] EWHC 1642 (QB); [2013] 4 Costs LR 576, HH Judge Simon Brown QC.

Q5. Albeit in a family context, does not the case of SB v MB (Costs)11 suggest that summary assessment is confined to fast track trials and other hearings lasting a day or less?

9–21 It is a curiosity of Pt 28 of the Family Procedure Rules 2010 ("FPR"), which deals with costs by importing large sections of the CPR, that the rule itself has been updated to take account of the 2013 reforms (see CPR 28.3), but that the practice direction accompanying it has not (all the references are to the pre 2013 CPR and, directly relevant to answering this question, the FPR refer to 'the costs practice direction').

In *SB v MB (Costs)* Hayden J declined to undertake a summary assessment as to do was "likely to fall foul" of what was para.13.2 of the Costs Practice Direction. In fact, the relevant provisions he identified of what was 13.2 (namely that this was not a fast track trial and that the hearing had exceeded one day) are in the same terms as what now appears at CPR 44 PD 9.2(a) and (b)). However, it is clear that the possibility of 'falling foul' of the Practice Direction was not determinative. Hayden J had already identified that there were elements of costs which would require consideration beyond the time and information available to the court that day. As such there was no need for the court to consider the application of the 'general rule' at what is CPR 44 PD 9.1 and was Costs PD 13.1 and the other steers referred to above illustrating that CPR 44 PD 9.2 is not an inflexible strait jacket (e.g. CPR 29 PD 10.5).

Q6. Does qualified one-way costs shifting ("QOCS") apply to the detailed assessment procedure?

9–22 To date there has been very little authority on QOCS.

The question of what constituted proceedings for the purpose of CPR 44.13 was considered in *Wagenaar v Weekend Travel Ltd (T/A Ski Weekend and Nawelle Serradj.*[12] There was no doubt that the claim between claimant and defendant was a personal injury claim, but the court construed "proceedings which include a claim for damages for personal injuries narrowly" and determined that an additional claim by the defendant for an indemnity from the third party was not 'proceedings' for the purpose of CPR 44.13. However, the court was clear that where there is a single claim against one or more defendants which includes a claim specified in CPR 44.13(1) (even if there are other components to the claim such as property damage), QOCS applies to the entire claim.

Applying *Wagenaar*, it might seem that if the detailed assessment is in respect of costs in a single claim against one or more defendants for one of the types of claim specified in CPR 44.13(1), then QOCS protection applies to the costs of the assessment process. However, *Wagenaar* was not considering this situation and the judgment is confined to consideration of the substantive litigation between the parties. The wording of CPR 44.14(2) appears to support the alternative view:

---

[11]   *SB v MB (Costs)* [2014] EWHC 3721 (Fam).
[12]   *Wagenaar v Weekend Travel Ltd (T/A Ski Weekend and Nawelle Serradj* [2014] EWCA Civ 110.

"44.14(2) Orders for costs made against a claimant may only be enforced after the proceedings have been concluded and the costs have been assessed or agreed."

The use of the word 'and' suggests that the process of assessment or agreement of costs is in addition to the proceedings, which conclude at the end of the substantive dispute involving one of the types of claim in CPR 44.13(1). On that basis we lean to the conclusion that QOCS protection does not apply to the costs of the detailed assessment process. This conclusion gains further support from CPR 47.20(7) which, albeit in the context of consideration of CPR Part 36, expressly provides that detailed assessment proceedings "are to be regarded as an independent claim".

This may be a moot point where it matters not by what route the claimant has to pay any costs of the detailed assessment (namely where the damages are such that QOCS protection would not prevent off-setting in full anyway against damages and it is only the route by which the court reaches this outcome that turns on the construction of 'proceedings'), but, where there is insufficient to off-set, this argument is pertinent. A definition of 'proceedings' for the purpose of CPR 44.13–44.17 would provide welcome certainty.

Q7. Is there any sanction if a paying party fails to make an open offer under CPR 47 PD 8.3?
On the face of it no sanction applies to this provision. However, the Court   **9–23**
of Appeal expressly considered provisions of the CPR which contain mandatory language, but where no sanction is provided for any failure to comply in *Altomart v Salford Estates (No.2) Ltd*.[13] The court accepted the proposition that there might be implied sanctions which were capable of engaging CPR 3.9 and equally there might be cases not analogous with CPR 3.9 and where it was a matter for the court to determine the consequence of non compliance.

Accordingly, it seems that if a paying party wishes to rely on an open offer made after the service of the Points of Dispute, where no such offer accompanied that document, then, by implication the court should approach this as analogous to an application for relief from sanction. The outcome of any applications made by 'receiving parties' for some sort of sanction are far less predictable. It is clear that the open offer does not form part of the Points of Dispute (it merely accompanies that document) and therefore it is difficult to see how any argument suggesting that the Points of Dispute should be struck out will find favour (indeed there is a risk it will be seen as an attempt to turn the rules into 'tripwires' and invoke possible costs sanctions). Perhaps a more measured approach is to identify the failure to comply to the paying party promptly, suggesting a short period for rectification, and, in default of compliance reserve the position to the question of costs of the assessment, if relevant, under 'conduct' within CPR 47.20(3)(a).

---

[13]   *Altomart v Salford Estates (No.2) Ltd* [2014] EWCA Civ 1408.

Provisional Assessment

Q8. Does the £75,000 limit for provisional assessment include or exclude VAT?

9–24   This is a purely procedural point. CPR 47.15 and its PD provisions describe the limit of £75,000 as being in respect of costs. The definition of 'costs' in CPR 44.1 <u>does not</u> include a reference to VAT—in fact, VAT is defined separately in the same rule. Accordingly, it seems that the £75,000 limit does not include VAT and refers to the total profit costs and disbursement sum. Notwithstanding this, many practitioners are not completing the provisional assessment part of form N258 and are requesting detailed assessment hearings where the total sum only exceeds £75,000 because of the VAT.

Q9. There seems to be a feeling that a paying party who does not serve Replies to the Points of Dispute is at a disadvantage at a provisional assessment. Should receiving parties serve Replies in this situation as a matter of course?

9–25   CPR 47.13, which makes Replies optional, and CPR 47 PD 12, which requires Replies to be limited to points of principle and concessions, both apply to provisional assessment by virtue of the provisions of CPR 47 PD 14.2. Accordingly, the court ought not to be penalising a party who complies with these provisions. Indeed the reverse is true and the court ought to be astute not to entertain Replies that contain 'general denials, specific denials or standard form responses'. Replies should not be filed as a matter of routine and there should be no disadvantage to the receiving party as a result.

    By the same token, paying parties should not serve 'extended' Points of Dispute in an attempt to make up for the fact that there will be no opportunity for oral submissions. CPR 47 PD 8.2 is unambiguous—Points of Dispute must be 'short and to the point'.

Q10. Does the costs cap include or exclude success fees (where the transitional provisions still permit recovery of success fees between the parties)?

9–26   The costs cap may include both base costs and success fees. The qualification is that combined they cannot exceed £1,500. So, by way of examples:

- If the base costs are assessed at £750 and the success uplift is allowed at 100 per cent, then both base costs and success fees are recoverable in full, as together they do not exceed the cap.
- If the base costs are assessed at £1,000 and the success uplift is allowed at 100 per cent, then the base costs are recoverable in full, but only £500 of the success fee is recoverable.
- If the base costs are assessed at £1,500 and the success uplift is allowed at 100 per cent, then the base costs are recoverable in full, but none of the success fee is recoverable.

Q11. Does the costs cap include the additional amount under CPR 36.14(3) (d) (from April 6, 2015 CPR 36.17(4)(d)) as applied by CPR 47.20?

The 'additional amount' is not defined in CPR 36.14 (to be 36.17 from April 6, 2015), CPR 47.20 or elsewhere in the rules. Perhaps of more significance is that the phrase does not appear in the definition of costs in CPR 44.1. In these circumstances it is certainly arguable that it is a sum outside the cap. This interpretation would make sense of the word 'additional' and also give effect to the purpose of CPR 47.20, namely to encourage settlement by the threat to the paying party of a heightened liability if a reasonable proposal is not accepted. This view is supported by the decision in *OOO Abbott v Design and Display Ltd*,[14] where it was argued that the 'additional amount' counted towards the £500,000 cap in the Intellectual Property Enterprise Court. HHJ Hacon held that the 'additional amount' had nothing to do with compensation, but was solely to do with a procedure to serve as an incentive to encourage claimants to make appropriate offers.

9–27

Q12. How does the £1,500 cap operate in respect of cases that are dealt with under the provisional assessment provisions, but where there are interim applications, e.g. to set aside a default costs certificate, for an interim costs certificate or for relief from sanction?

It is important to stress that the costs cap of £1,500 at CPR 47.15(5) is the maximum amount that the court will award to any party as the <u>costs of the assessment</u>.

9–28

If there is an application to set aside a default costs certificate, then it seems that cannot be an application made within the assessment, as by definition, at that time, there is a default costs certificate with the costs of the assessment proceedings dealt with under CPR 47.11. As such, any application to set aside a default costs certificate appears to be a free standing application and the costs under any award of costs fall to be assessed (one would expect summarily) there and then as costs of that discrete application.

Similarly, an application for relief from sanction—presumably in connection with the late service of a Reply to the Points of Dispute—seems to be a free standing application. It is not part of the assessment process set out in CPR 47. As such it follows that any costs awarded on such an application would not be costs of the assessment and would be entirely separate from the cap. Indeed, in both this scenario and that relating to default costs certificates, it is conceivable that the costs of these applications will be awarded to a different party than the one which is awarded the costs of the assessment.

It is arguable that there is no jurisdiction for the court to issue an interim costs certificate in a provisional assessment. This is because CPR 47.16(1), which enables the court to issue such a certificate, relates to cases where the receiving party has filed a request for a detailed assessment hearing. The very nature of the provisional assessment regime dispenses with hearings save

---

[14]   *OOO Abbott v Design and Display Ltd* [2014] EWHC 3234 (IPEC) HHJ Hacon.

where the court determines that the matter is unsuitable for the regime and lists a hearing or, after the assessment on paper, when a party requests an oral hearing. Having said this, CPR 47 PD 14.2 applies CPR 47.14(1) to the provisional assessment regime and the wording of that provision refers to a 'request for a detailed assessment hearing'. In reality, the point is unlikely to arise as CPR 47 PD 14.4(1) provides that the court will use its best endeavours to undertake the provisional assessment within six weeks of receipt of the request. This is reinforced in para.10.2(e) of the SCCO Guide 2013, which states that any application for an interim costs certificate in a case proceeding to a provisional assessment will not be listed for hearing before the date fixed for the provisional assessment unless there is some good reason for an early listing,

Q13. Is the amount of the bill or the sum in which it is assessed in a provisional assessment likely to inform how much of the capped fee is awarded, e.g. does a bill of £70,000 justify an award of a higher proportion of the £1,500 than a bill of £20,000?

9–29   There is no straightforward answer to this. The cap is not set as a sliding scale. It will depend entirely upon what the court determines is the reasonable and proportionate sum in any given case. Value alone <u>does not</u> determine this. There may be complex points of principle raised for determination within the assessment of a £20,000 bill that do not arise in a bill of £70,000. This links to the factors defining proportionality at CPR 44.3(5) and factors relevant to the assessment of costs at CPR 44.4(3).

Q14. Can the court make more than one award of costs for the provisional assessment and, if so, is the total amount apportioned between the parties limited to £1,500 or may there be separate awards to each party, each with a cap of £1,500?

9–30   CPR Pt 47.20 applies to the principle of the award of costs of the assessment proceedings. As such there is a general rule (47.20(1)(a)) that the receiving party will recover the costs of the assessment. However, this is immediately qualified to permit the court to make some other order in respect of all <u>or part</u> of the costs of the assessment (47.20(1)(b)). CPR 47.20(3) then lists specific considerations, amongst all the circumstances, that the court must take into account and CPR 47.20(4) applies CPR 36. It is clear from this that the court may decide to make more than one costs award in the assessment (perhaps taking into account when a CPR 36 offer was made). However, when considering this the court must consider the terms of CPR 44.2(6) and (7). This may lead to two awards of costs for separate and specific periods or one award, but of a specified percentage only.

   If the court does make awards of costs to more than one party to the assessment, the wording of CPR 47.15(5) seems clear—the maximum it will award to 'any party' is £1,500. So, if there are two parties who both receive costs awards for certain specified periods of the assessment, it appears that each may recover up to £1,500. However, given the amount of work required in the provisional assessment process, it seems unlikely that a reasonable and proportionate amount would see the combined costs exceed £1,500 by much (save if it was a case where there is still a success fee recoverable between the parties).

Q15. Does the £1,500 cap on costs under CPR 47.14 include costs incurred in 'Costs Only Proceedings' under CPR 46.14?

It would seem not. The argument that the costs of the CPR 46.14 process   **9–31** are not costs of the substantive claim and so, by definition, must be costs of the provisional assessment (relying on the judgment of Brooke LJ in *Crosbie v Munroe*[15]) and included within the £1,500 limit, was dealt a fatal blow by the Court of Appeal in *Tasleem v Beverley: Bartkauskaute v BartKauskiene*.[16] As Sharp LJ concluded:

> "*The bringing of Part 8 costs-only proceedings is not the commencement of, or part of, the detailed assessment proceedings, albeit it is a necessary preliminary to that process if there are no underlying proceedings in existence. This is because detailed assessment proceedings are distinct from the proceedings whether under Part 7 or Part 8 which have given rise to the costs order (see CPR rule 47.6(1)).*"[17]

Accordingly, any costs awarded under CPR 46.14 are entirely separate from the costs cap in CPR 47.14. Of course, the outcome of the provisional assessment may inform what award of costs the court makes on the CPR 46.14 proceedings—for example, the paying party may have made an offer before those proceedings in a sum that exceeds the receiving party's subsequent recovery on the assessment. For this reason it may be inappropriate for the court to decide who is entitled to the costs of the CPR 46.14 proceedings until after the assessment of the costs of the substantive proceedings has taken place. An appropriate order may defer the award of costs until the conclusion of the detailed assessment (whether by provisional assessment or not) and, if that is by settlement, give liberty to either party to restore for this purpose. The court will then deal with the award and any consequent summary assessment.

This may seem an obvious conclusion as the simple fact is that Pt 47.15   **9–32** states that it only applies to certain "detailed assessment proceedings" and Pt 46.14 proceedings are not detailed assessment proceedings (as is clearly apparent from the title 'Costs only Proceedings'). If further support was needed, it can be found in CPR 44.1 where 'detailed assessment' is defined as a procedure for determining the amount of costs under Pt 47. 'Costs only Proceedings' may enable a party to start detailed assessment proceedings, but they do not determine the amount of costs—obvious until one remembers that in *Crosbie*, Brooke LJ had concluded that:

---

[15] *Crosbie v Munroe* [2003] EWCA Civ 350.
[16] *Tasleem v Beverley: Bartkauskaute v BartKauskiene* [2013] EWCA Civ 1805.
[17] para.18.

> " . . . assessment proceedings cover the whole period of negotiations about the amount of costs payable through the Part 8 proceedings to the ultimate disposal of those proceedings, whether by agreement or court order."[18]

However, the Court of Appeal in *Tasleem* specifically considered *Crosbie* and took the view that it served only to support its conclusions.

Q16. How does the court deal with the proportionality cross check after a provisional assessment where the assessed bill is returned to the parties to do the arithmetic?

9–33   As time passes and cases fall within the new proportionality provisions of CPR 44.3(2) rather than the old '*Lownds*' provisions (see **Chapter 3— Proportionality**), this will become a pertinent issue. It is unlikely that the court will calculate the total of the bill immediately after assessing what is reasonably incurred and reasonable in amount (not only because CPR 47 PD 14.4(2) places the responsibility for agreeing the total sum at the door of the parties, but also because of the time it may take to do this and in case it makes an arithmetical mistake).

As some cases with the new proportionality test have already started to work their way through the provisional assessment process it seems clear that there are already two schools of thought. They are that:

i)   The court returns the bill, the Form G and any separate rulings to the parties to add up, but adds an order as follows (or in similar terms):

> "*The proportionate sum pursuant to CPR 44.3(5) factors is £x. If the reasonably incurred and reasonable in amount costs exceed £x when the bill is recalculated then anything over £x is disproportionate and the bill is provisionally assessed at £x. If the reasonably incurred and reasonable in amount costs are less than £x when the bill is recalculated then those costs are proportionate and the bill is provisionally assessed in the recalculated sum.*"

This completes the provisional assessment and time for requesting an oral hearing is triggered by this order.

ii)   The court requires the parties to confirm the recalculated sum after assessing what is reasonably incurred and reasonable in amount, together with any submissions on proportionality, and this is then referred back to the assessing judge to determine proportionality. Having done so the bill is then returned to the parties provisionally assessed in the recalculated sum, if it was proportionate, or, provisionally assessed in a lower figure (being the sum determined proportionate) if the recalculated sum was disproportionate. The provisional assessment is only completed for the purpose of the time for requesting an oral hearing at this stage.

9–34   There are attractions to both procedures. The advantages of the former are that it concludes the provisional assessment earlier, leads to quicker payment

---

[18]   para.34.

and involves less time and costs commitment by the parties and the court. It is also prevents problems if the assessment was undertaken by a part-time member of the judiciary who may not be available to do the subsequent proportionality element of the assessment if it is deferred.

The advantages of the latter approach are that the parties have the yardstick of the reasonably incurred and reasonable in amount sum when considering and making submissions on proportionality and the assessing judge has the same yardstick when assessing proportionality.

As the assessment of proportionality under CPR 44.3(5) is an entirely free standing one, the time, costs and judicial continuity arguments seem the more compelling at first blush. However, this approach seems to overlook the wording of CPR 44.3(2), which only refers to the fact that the court *may* disallow or reduce reasonably incurred costs if they are disproportionate. Surely until the costs reasonably incurred and reasonable in amount have been calculated the parties are not in a position to make specific submissions and, therefore, the court is not in a position to reach a decision? An illustration of this is where the receiving party wishes to rely upon CPR 44.3(5)(d) to argue that the conduct of the paying party generated specific additional work. Until it is clear what the court has allowed in respect of the reasonably incurred and reasonable in amount costs for that additional work, it is impossible to determine whether the argument is purposeful—for if the court allowed none of that work anyway, then it cannot sound in the proportionality argument.

Q17. What happens in respect of the costs where at an oral hearing a party does not achieve an adjustment in its favour of 20 per cent or more, but the adjustment made does make a CPR 47.20 offer relevant?

This question is best answered by reference to a specific example. In the example the paying party makes a Part 36 offer to pay the receiving party £10,000. The bill is provisionally assessed at £10,500. The paying party seeks an oral hearing at which the bill is reduced to £9,900. On the face of it the receiving party has not obtained an outcome (under CPR 47.20(4)(e)) more advantageous than the Part 36 offer. However, the oral hearing has only seen an adjustment in favour of the paying party of 5.7 per cent (£600 divided by £10,500).

9–35

It is important to note that the question raises the costs of the provisional assessment generally and not just the costs of the oral hearing. They raise separate issues and need to be considered individually.

The costs of the oral hearing

CPR 47.15(10) provides a general rule that the party requesting the oral hearing pays the costs of and incidental to that hearing. There are two qualifications to this general rule. The first is that the party requesting the oral hearing sees an adjustment in its favour of 20 per cent or more. In our example that has not been achieved. The second is if the court orders otherwise.

9–36

Which CPR provision prevails—47.15 or 47.20 (and by implication 36.14

(to be 36.17))? The simple answer seems to be that a specific rule trumps a general rule (see for example *Solomon v Cromwell Group Plc*[19] in support of this proposition) and as CPR 47.15 relates specifically to oral hearings as part of the provisional assessment process, that provision prevails. So, in our example, the starting point is that the paying party still pays the costs of the oral hearing. However, as stated this is the 'starting point' as the second qualification to the general rule in CPR 47.15 permits the court to order otherwise. There is some guidance as to when it might do otherwise in CPR 47 PD 14.5. This requires the court to take into account the conduct of the parties and any offers made when considering whether to depart from the general rule. Whilst it is a matter of discretion, this suggests that the CPR Part 36 offer will still be relevant to the oral hearing, but not as a CPR Part 36 offer, with the consequences attached to that, but simply as an offer under CPR 47 PD 14.5. The court must then determine what, if any, departure from the general rule in CPR 47.15(10) is appropriate.

The costs of the provisional assessment (excluding the oral hearing)

9–37 CPR 47.15(10) relates only to the costs of the oral hearing. Accordingly, CPR 47.20 applies and when determining the costs of the provisional assessment (excluding the costs of the oral hearing) the court looks at the end result. In our example the receiving party has failed to obtain an outcome more advantageous than the paying party's CPR Part 36 offer and so, by cross application, CPR 36.14 (to be 36.17) applies.

A final word

9–38 Suppose in our example it had been the receiving party who had made the relevant CPR Part 36 offer, which it had not exceeded under the initial assessment, but which it had after the oral hearing (although again not achieving an adjustment of 20 per cent or more at the oral hearing). If, after considering whether to depart from the general rule, the court had determined that the receiving party should be awarded the costs of the oral hearing, would the additional sum under CPR 36.14(3)(d) (to be 36.17(4)(d) from April 6, 2015) be payable on that sum? There is certainly a compelling argument (based on the specific rule trumping the general rule) that it would not be payable, as costs relating to the oral hearing have been awarded under CPR 47.15(10)(b) and not under CPR 47.20 and by application CPR 36.14 (to be 36.17). Of, course, for those costs excluding the oral hearing, the additional sum would be payable as those costs would be awarded under CPR 47.20 specifically applying CPR 36.14(3)(d) (36.17(4)(d) from April 6, 2015).

---

[19] *Solomon v Cromwell Group Plc* [2011] EWCA Civ 1584.

Payments on account

Q18. Is there any rule of thumb as to what proportion of the costs claimed the court will order as a reasonable sum by way of payment on account?
There never has been any genuine 'rule of thumb'. *Mars UK Ltd v Teknowledge*   **9–39**
Ltd (Costs)[20] is often cited as authority for the proposition that two-thirds of
the sum claimed is an appropriate amount. In fact, the route by which the
payment on account was reached in that case is far from straightforward and
does not endorse any specific percentage as a general rule.

The decision is fact specific in each case. However, the advent of costs
budgets may assist and simply the process. In *Elvanite Full Circle Ltd v AMEC
Earth & Environmental (UK) Ltd,*[21] Coulson J used the budget set as the basis
for a determination of the reasonable sum to be paid on account stating, "the
costs management order is likely to be the benchmark for the costs to be
recovered", and based the payment on account on the conclusion that the
receiving party's costs were unlikely to be much under the budgeted sum. Of
course, the budgeted sums cannot include costs that had been incurred at the
time the budget was set. Accordingly, it may be that in the absence of an indication that the budget is to be subject to some fundamental challenge under
'good reason to depart from the budget' under CPR 3.18, a starting point
will be the budgeted sum. Indeed, in *Thomas Pink Limited v Victoria's Secret
UK Limited,*[22] Birss J concluded that the advent of costs budgets had altered
the position. The budget was £678,000. The claimant sought £644,000 as a
payment on account and the defendant proposed £350,000 (which the court
accepted was 'the sort of figure one would have expected to have awarded').
However, having posed the question whether the costs budgeting rules have a
significant impact on orders for payments on account, Birss J concluded that:

> "The sum sought by the claimants is essentially the budgeted sum at the time they
> asked for it. It seems to me that the impact of costs budgeting on the determina-
> tion of a sum for a payment on account of costs is very significant although I am
> not persuaded that it is so significant that I should simply award the budgeted
> sum. Bearing in mind that unless there is good reason to depart from the budget,
> the budget will not be departed from, but also taking into account the vagaries of
> litigation and things that might occur and the fact that it is, at least, possible that
> the assessed costs will be less, although no good reason why that is so has been
> advanced before me, I will make an award of 90% of the sum in the claimant's
> budget (£644,829.10) rounded up to the nearest thousand."[23]

---

[20] *Mars UK Ltd v Teknowledge Ltd (Costs)* [1999] 2 Costs L.R. 44 Jacob J.
[21] *Elvanite Full Circle Ltd v AMEC Earth & Environmental (UK) Ltd* [2013] EWHC 1643 (TCC) Coulson J.
[22] *Thomas Pink Limited v Victoria's Secret UK Limited* [2014] EWHC 3258(Ch) Birss J.
[23] para.60.

CHAPTER 10

The Effect of the Jackson Civil Justice Reforms on Solicitor-Client Costs

Introduction

The Legal Aid, Sentencing & Punishment of Offenders Act 2012 and associated secondary legislation, together with the reforms to the Civil Procedure Rules introduced in April 2013, have had a significant effect on the conduct of litigation and on the scope of costs recovery between the parties. **10–01**

Apart from the imposition of a number of statutory caps on the levels of success fees (in personal injury claims) and on the levels of the 'payments' under Damages Based Agreements, and some relatively minor procedural amendments aside, those changes do not directly address the question of solicitor-client costs.

It is important to note that the fundamental legal principles underpinning the ability of a solicitor to charge a client and the ability of a client to dispute those charges are unaffected. The law in this regard emanates from a combination of statutory provision (primarily ss.56–75 of the Solicitors Act 1974) and common law and it is doubtful that amendments to the CPR alone would have the standing to alter those principles.

However, a number of the key changes undoubtedly have an indirect impact on the question of costs as between the solicitor and the client, and the solicitor therefore needs to be alert to this in order to avoid negative consequences. In some areas of reform, such as costs budgeting, it appears that the attempt to control solicitors charging by the back door was intentional. In others, for example in relation to proportionality, the effect was perhaps less intentional, and the precise impact less obvious to see at this stage.

Those key changes will be considered in turn. It is beyond the scope of this section to consider in detail the established legal principles relating to assessment of solicitor client costs, beyond by way of brief overview and consideration of how those principles have been, or may be, affected by those changes. Risk management and law firm management are also outside the scope of this book. However, by pointing out where issues arise as a result of the Jackson reforms, this chapter aims to give readers a clear steer that they should consider carefully and, if appropriate, seek further guidance. It is also a plea for detailed guidance to be given by those who can.

A brief overview

There is a fundamental distinction between costs on a solicitor-client basis **10–02**
and costs between the parties. The latter are payable as a result of any costs order or agreement between the parties and are subject to the very broad

discretion conferred on the court by s.51 of the Senior Courts Act 1981 and any rules of procedure made thereunder.

However, costs on a solicitor-client basis are payable as a result of the contract between the solicitor and the client. Subject to specific statutory and procedural restrictions, the key determining factor therefore is the terms of the contract between the solicitor and client.

As with any other form of costs payable under a contract where the liability is a contractual one, the costs are payable on the indemnity basis, unless the contract otherwise provides (see CPR 44.5 for the position in relation to costs payable under contracts generally).[1]

Accordingly, the starting point is that a solicitor-client costs dispute is a contractual dispute and is subject to any limitations within that contract.

However, as noted, there are numerous statutory, common law and procedural restrictions imposed which fundamentally change the character of the claim as between solicitor and client. These exist primarily as a combination of a recognition of the peculiar position of solicitors and the court's supervisory jurisdiction over them and a form of what would, in modern parlance, be termed 'consumer protection'.

These provisions may be analysed in three main categories.

Retainers

10–03 Firstly, provisions which govern the nature of the contract that a solicitor may enter into with a client are primarily restrictive—that is to say they limit the nature of the arrangements beyond what would be permitted in an ordinary commercial context.

These arrangements, in turn, fall primarily into two main categories, namely those relating to what is termed 'non-contentious business' and those relating to contentious business. As to what is and is not contentious business, there is a very circuitous definition of both at s.87 of the Solicitors Act 1974, whereby contentious business is defined as business done "in or for the purposes of proceedings begun before a court or before an arbitrator . . . not being business which falls within the definition of non-contentious business" and non-contentious business is defined as 'any business done by a solicitor which is not contentious business'. The key point to note is that work which would have been classed as non-contentious business will be classed as contentious business provided that that work was done with a view to proceedings being begun and proceedings were in fact begun.[2]

If further guidance on this issue is required, the most comprehensive recent consideration of the issues is to be found in Chief Master Hurst's judgment in *Tel-Ka Talk Ltd*.[3]

The primary statutory provisions in this regard are s.57 of the Solicitors Act

---

[1] The introduction of the concept of indemnity basis assessment of costs between the parties only came much later, with the introduction of the concepts of "standard' and 'indemnity' basis in 1986.

[2] See *Re Simpkin Marshall Ltd* [1959] Ch 229.

[3] *Tel-Ka Talk Ltd v HMRC* [2010] EWHC 90175 (Costs).

1974, which, at s.57(2) sets out the very broad nature of the arrangements that a solicitor may lawfully enter into with their clients in relation to non-contentious business ('Non-Contentious Business Agreements', of 'NCBA's), including what might be described as contingency, or outcome based arrangements, and specified the requirements for such arrangements, and s.59 which sets out the ability of solicitors to enter into Contentious Business Agreements ('CBA's) with clients.

It is important to note that both Contentious and Non-Contentious Business Agreements with clients are merely optional and that it is not necessary for a solicitor-client retainer in respect of contentious business to take the form of a CBA.

In contrast to s.57, s.59 expressly provides that nothing in that section shall give validity to (inter alia) any agreement by which the solicitor retained stipulates for payment only in the event of success (a 'conditional' fee).

This reflects the proposition that s.59 does not per se prohibit such arrangements but equally is not to be taken to permit them, in contrast to s.57 which does so expressly for non-contentious business.

The restriction on such arrangements comes not from the Solicitors Act   **10–04**
1974 therefore but from the common law prohibition on champertous arrangements. That prohibition has been relaxed by express statutory exception through in s.58 of the Courts & Legal Services Act 1990 (permitting Conditional Fee Agreements that comply with the requirements of ss.58 and 58A) and then more recently s.58AA of the same Act permitting Damages Based Agreements that comply with the requirements of that section.

It has been recognised judicially that such relaxation of the ability of solicitors to enter into such arrangements is a matter to be decided upon by Parliament and not a matter for incremental judicial expansion.[4]

Any conditional or contingency fee agreement relating to contentious business which does not comply with those requirements is unenforceable, either by operation of the express provisions of those sections or the common law.

Both s.58 and s.58AA contain provisions (s.58(5) and s.58AA(9) making clear that the statute does not limit the right to enter into a conditional or contingency fee agreement for non-contentious business—save in respect of employment matters). Accordingly, the position remains that as between solicitor and client the nature of arrangements that may be lawfully entered into, and the formality requirements that must be complied with in relation to those arrangements, are substantially more restrictive where the subject matter of the retainer relates to what may be classed as contentious business rather than non-contentious business.

If a solicitor enters into an unlawful and unenforceable retainer with his client, the likely effect is that the solicitor will not be entitled to payment of any fees for the work done, even if the solicitor's work was not done as the

---

[4] See Lord Neuberger MR (as he then was) in *Sibthorpe & Morris v LB Southwark* [2011] EWCA Civ 25; [2011] 1 WLR 2111 at 40–41.

conducting solicitor, but is still seen as the provision of litigation services (see, for example, *Rees v Gateley Wareing (a firm)*[5]).[6]

Entitlement to payment

10–05 The second category of provision relating to a solicitor's entitlement to payment from their client concerns the way in which a solicitor should bill that client in order to be able validly to claim fees from the client.

Again, the primary provisions are to be found in the Solicitors Act 1974 and again, the primary consequence is to impose a series of obligations and restrictions which differentiate the position from that of a normal contractual dispute.

Firstly, in relation to CBAs and NCBAs, the broad effect is that they determine the client's liability without right on the client's part to a full assessment, but that they are subject to an ability on the court's part to set aside the agreements if they are considered to be unfair or unreasonable. Where such agreements provide for remuneration by hourly rate, then the time spent on the case is capable of assessment.

The Act also provides the basic requirements for the form of a solicitor's bill of costs for both contentious and non-contentious business (s.69). A bill complying with s.69 (known as a 'statute' bill) is a fundamental requirement before a solicitor can bring an action to recover his costs and errors in the form of a bill are not infrequently a flaw in such actions. The statutory requirements have been amplified in case law such that it is now well established that a statute bill must be reasonably complete, must have a sufficient narrative[7] (though what is sufficient may be fact dependent) and should contain a satisfactory breakdown of the fees claimed.

10–06 An exception to the latter exists in relation to contentious business where a solicitor may deliver a 'gross sum' statute bill (s.64), though if this option is chosen certain additional rights to request further detail and/or challenge the bill are conferred on the client.

The rendering of a statute bill, whether on an interim or final basis, is important because it is the delivery of the bill that triggers the client's right to assessment of the costs claimed in the bill. There are strict time limits which apply, whereby the client's right to such an assessment reduces from an absolute right (s.70(1)), to a discretion on the court's part, which may be subject of conditions (s.70(2)) to a situation where either the client may have to show 'special circumstances' to obtain an assessment or the court's power to order an assessment may be removed completely (s.70(3)).

However, it is important to note that where the fees are unpaid and the solicitor sues the client for the unpaid fees the client is likely to have a common law right to dispute the quantum of the claimed fees, and therefore obtain an effective assessment, regardless of the time limits in s.70.[8]

---

[5] *Rees v Gateley Wareing (a firm)* [2014] EWCA Civ 1351.
[6] ss.57 & 61 respectively.
[7] See *Garry v Gwillim* [2002] EWCA Civ 1500 at 59–60.
[8] See *Turner & Co v O Palomo SA* [2000] 1 WLR 37.

The necessary form of a statute bill aside, perhaps the key issue which arises in solicitor client disputes is that in order to be able to render a statute bill on anything other than a final basis (that is to say other than when the work has been fully completed) there either must be an express or implied agreement allowing the solicitor to render 'interim' statute bills,[9] or the court must be able to identify a 'natural break'[10] in the matter at which it was appropriate to render a statute bill. If neither of these apply, then any interim bill will be merely an 'on account' bill, at best and will neither give the solicitor a right to sue for payment, nor trigger the time limits for the client's rights to assessment.

Solicitor-client assessment and disputes

The third set of provisions relate to the procedure for resolving solicitor-client disputes. As already noted, s.70 of the Solicitors Act 1974 sets out a set of time limits which apply to a client's right to assessment, such time limits generally being triggered by the delivery of a statute bill.   **10–07**

The basic principle is that a client may apply (usually by way of Part 8 claim or by defence to a claim by the solicitor) for an assessment of any bill or series of bills within these time limits and to satisfy any applicable test (such as special circumstances), though a solicitor is entitled to apply for an order for assessment of his own bill.

Where such an assessment is ordered, as a matter of discretion or right, prior to April 2013, CPR 48.8 applied. Until April 2013, CPR 48.8 confirmed that any assessment was to be on the indemnity basis. However, it also went further. In addition to the two key general indemnity basis principles (that is to say: (i) the fact that a test of proportionality does not apply; and (ii) that where a doubt persists as to whether an item was reasonably incurred or reasonably in amount the benefit of the doubt will be given to the receiving party[11]), CPR 48.8 confirmed:

(i) that where the costs were incurred with the express or implied approval of the client they shall be presumed to be reasonably incurred;

(ii) that where the amount of the costs was expressly or impliedly approved by the client, the amount shall be presumed to be reasonable; but that

(iii) where they are of an unusual nature or amount and the solicitor did not tell the client that as a result they might not be recovered in full between the parties, they are presumed to have been unreasonably incurred.

This latter point (CPR 48.8(2)) is an important point and may have a particular impact in the context of 'unusual' disbursements. It is a significant gloss on the general application of the indemnity basis.

Although CPR 48.8 did not strictly apply on a 'common law' assessment,   **10–08**

---

[9] There is substantial case law in this area. See *Re Romer & Haslam* [1893] 2 QB at 293 for the fundamental principle.
[10] For example, see *Re Hall & Barker* [1893] 9 Ch D 538.
[11] See, now, CPR 44.4(2) and (3).

the general practice of the courts appears to be to treat such an assessment in a very similar fashion to a statutory assessment.

CPR 48.10 (there was no CPR 48.9) and CPR 48 PD 54.1 provided a set of more practical guidance as to the mechanics of the conduct of a solicitor-client assessment (these provisions survived the reforms largely unchanged and the April 2013 amendments are considered below).

The key remaining statutory provision to note at this point is s.70(9) of the Solicitors Act 1974. This applies a very specific provision for determining liability for costs of the solicitor-client assessment, known as the '20 per cent rule'. Where the bill (or that part of the bill which has been referred for assessment—see s.70(5)) is reduced by one-fifth (20 per cent) or more, the solicitor pays the costs of the assessment.[12] Otherwise, the client pays the costs.

This is subject to the court being able to make a different order where it considers there are 'special circumstances', a situation which appears to have been open to greater argument in recent years, particularly where one or other party has made an effective offer.[13]

Accordingly, it can be seen that both in terms of the nature of the retainer, the ability of the solicitor to bill the client and sue for its costs and the mechanism that is used to determine any such dispute, the position as between solicitor and client is, and has long been, heavily modified from that which generally applies as between 'trader' and 'customer'.

In conclusion in this section, the availability of alternative remedies through the Legal Ombudsman should not be ignored. The ability of the Ombudsman to provide enforceable rulings in relation to fee disputes which are binding on the solicitor, provided the client agrees to the ruling,[14] in circumstances where the Ombudsman will take into account, but is not bound by the decisions a court might make in similar circumstances,[15] and to order the payment of compensation in addition where appropriate,[16] in what is usually a no costs environment,[17] and where the client's complaint, though subject to some basic time limits,[18] is subject to less complicated restrictions than under the Solicitors Act 1974, arguably provides a far more flexible and effective and, from a solicitor's perspective, potentially more dangerous source of redress for a client.

Effect of the Jackson reforms

10–09   This will be considered under a number of headings. Many of these headings relate to issues which have been considered in detail elsewhere and only their effect on the solicitor-client position will be considered here.

---

12   Save where the assessment was requested by the solicitor and the paying party did not attend the assessment.
13   See for example *Angel Airlines v Dean & Dean* [2008] EWHC 1513 (QB).
14   Scheme Rules 5.49.
15   Scheme Rules 5.37(a).
16   Scheme Rules 5.38(b).
17   Scheme Rules 5.39.
18   Scheme Rules 4.4 and 4.5.

Changes to the procedural rules in relation to solicitor-client assessments

CPR 48.8 and 48.10 no longer exist, but have been repeated in substantially **10–10** identical terms in CPR 46.9 and 46.10, including the important provision, now at CPR 46.9(3)(c) relating to the presumed unreasonableness of costs where they are of an unusual nature or amount and the client was not warned that they may not be recovered from the other party to litigation as a result.

For reasons which are not entirely clear, there has been a slight amendment to the wording such that where the rule used to provide that they were presumed to be unreasonable if the client was not warned that he might not recover 'all of them', the rule now merely provides that they are presumed unreasonable if the client was not warned that the costs 'might not be recovered'. This would appear to be merely a tidying up of the wording and is not thought to have been intended to introduce any substantive change.

Costs budgeting

Costs budgeting is addressed elsewhere.[19] From a solicitor-client perspective, **10–11** the most significant impact is likely to be that, where a costs management order is made reflecting either agreement between the parties or approval by the court after making revisions, there exists a clear restriction from that point onwards on the costs that the client is likely to be able to recover from the opponent if the litigation succeeds.

It is important that the client is made aware of that restriction and its effect. In particular, where, as will commonly, though not always, be the case, the retainer between solicitor and client provides that the client's liability is not limited to costs recovered between the parties, it will be extremely important, though perhaps difficult to achieve in practice, that the client is made aware of the likely shortfall in costs and is provided with an opportunity to provide an informed agreement to costs which fall outside the approved budget being incurred.

The practical approach to this is likely to differ from case to case (or at least type of case to type of case). However, as a minimum, it should be expected that at the outset the client will be told in clear, written, terms of the risk of a shortfall of costs even if the claim succeeds and costs are awarded, and of particular types of costs which will not or might not be recovered. The obvious example, post April 2013, is a success fee. Save for a limited class of cases, it is inexcusable not to tell the client, in clear terms, that where a success fee will be charged that success fee will not, in any circumstances, be recoverable from the opponent, even if costs are otherwise awarded and will be payable by the client alone. The same point applies to the costs of setting up a particular form of funding, or of considering After The Event insurance. More fact dependent examples might include the possibility of instruction of a QC, or of particular

---

[19] See Ch.4.

experts, or of particular types of costs being incurred (perhaps if an unusually large disclosure exercise is being contemplated).

Equally, the common warning in the past, that as a rule of thumb a between the parties recovery of two thirds (or 70 per cent) was likely is probably now both inaccurate and insufficient. What the client needs to be made aware of is the risk of a substantial shortfall generally, of particular items of costs that might be incurred and that those costs in particular might not be recovered, and that the client has a choice, which he should be given reasonable information in order to make, as to whether such costs are to be incurred (whilst, where appropriate, being informed whether, and if so why, the solicitor considers that those costs are appropriate, desirable or necessary).

10–12   Reference has already been made to the presumptions which apply under what is now CPR 46.9. A failure to make it clear to the client that a cost to be incurred is one which falls outside the budget (because, for example, it is not a recoverable cost or a cost disallowed on budgeting) may well result in that cost being seen as falling within CPR 46.9(3) or, in any event, may lead to the court being satisfied that it is unreasonable for the client to be held liable to pay that cost. By the same token, obtaining the client's express approval to the cost being incurred despite the probability of it being irrecoverable between the parties, because it is outside the approved budget, will give the solicitor the benefit of the s.46.(3)(a) and/or (b) presumptions.

It is, of course, in any event good practice (and possible essential) to provide the client with clear and accurate costs estimates, see for example Solicitors Code of Conduct 2011, IB 1.14–1.19.

Despite initial suggestions to the contrary (see, for example, HH Judge Simon Brown QC[20]), when CPR 3 Pt II was introduced, there was no requirement to obtain the client's signature or to record in any other way the client's approval or agreement that the costs in the Precedent H budget submitted to the court were reasonable or proportionate or in any other way were an appropriate sum to expend on the case. In addition, oddly, there is also no requirement that the terms of any costs management order are served on the client. The provision on the pilot scheme in the Commercial Courts under CPR 51 PD 51G para.6, which provided that the client should be notified with seven days of the budgeting hearing of the budget set by the court was also not carried through to the wider reforms.

However, it was clearly an intention of the costs budgeting reforms that effective between the parties costs management, whilst not fixing the price between the solicitor and client,[21] would be in the interests of the clients.[22] In the absence of express provision in the rules on costs management, it seems that in practice this might be achieved by the courts, on any subsequent solicitor-client assessment, placing a high burden on solicitors who charge

---

[20]   HH Judge Simon Brown QC, "Costs control Costs management & docketed judges: are you ready for the big bang next year?" (2012) April 6 & 13 NLJ 498–499.
[21]   See *Judiciary: Lord Justice Jackson's paper for the Civil Justice Council conference* (March 21, 2014), paras 5.2 and 5.7.
[22]   See Final Report, p.415, para.7.3 for example.

clients sums above the costs budget to show that the client received proper information in this regard and was given an informed choice as to whether to incur such costs, or at the very least was made aware when such costs were being incurred that they were unlikely to be recoverable between the parties.

Both caution and good practice suggest that where the costs budget which **10–13** is prepared shows costs potentially claimable between the parties which are materially less than those the client is liable to pay, the client should be given clear prior information and explanation in relation to this. The party/party costs budget filed under CPR 3.13 is the client's costs budget, not the solicitor's, and if the budget indicates any 'limitation' on the costs which might be claimed, let alone recovered or allowed, between the parties then the client should be informed of this.

One way to address this might be by producing a modified budget for the client, showing the additional sums the client may be liable to pay.

It is important to remember that between the parties costs are not generally intended to be a full indemnity for the client. There will almost invariably be an element of costs incurred which simply are not and never would be recoverable between the parties (a classic modern example being the costs of arranging or considering various forms of funding[23]). In addition, it will be rare that the costs awarded on a between the parties basis cover the full costs which might have been reasonably incurred on the clients instructions. The fact that the indemnity basis is the default basis for solicitor-client assessments expressly recognises this.

Equally, and perhaps even more importantly in light of the 'new' proportionality test, no test of proportionality applies on a solicitor client basis.

It is, therefore, unrealistic to expect that costs budgets, subject to rigorous review on the standard between the parties basis, applying a test of proportionality, should be expected also to set the proper level of costs on a solicitor-client basis, or that such budgets should simply be used by solicitors as their costs estimates on a solicitor-client basis unless those solicitors wish to restrict unduly the costs they might reasonably charge their clients.[24]

What the budgeting provisions do emphasise, however, is the fundamental importance of solicitors providing clients with clear and regular costs information both as to costs they may have to pay to their solicitor and costs they may recover from the other side if they are successful in their litigation (and which they may have to pay the other side if they lose) and, in particular, of explaining in clear terms how and why the costs the client may be liable to pay may differ from the costs to be allowed between the parties. A simple statement that 'if you are awarded costs against your opponent, the costs awarded are unlikely to cover our full costs' is no longer sufficient. A great deal

---

[23] See *Motto v Trafigura* [2011] EWCA Civ 1150; [2012] 1 WLR 657.
[24] Though the wording of the statement of truth for a costs budget (CPR 22 PD 2.2A) which refers to the costs being "a fair and accurate statement of incurred and estimated costs which it would be reasonable and proportionate for my client to incur" unhelpfully suggests that the budget could be seen as being a reflection of the costs chargeable (to the client), rather than reasonably recoverable between the parties.

more detail is now required—explanation of the test(s) of proportionality, of what costs budgeting means, of the various tests on assessment, the meaning of the retainer and so on. The standard retainer letter wording is unlikely to be enough. This needs to be tailored to the individual client and repeated at various intervals. With regard to the effect of costs budgeting, if the client is closely involved in the process and there is a process set up for what happens if the court does not allow costs, it may make for less argument later.

Proportionality

10–14 This has been touched on above. The new test of proportionality, introduced by CPR 44.3(5), was expressly intended to reverse the unsatisfactory test as clarified in *Lownds*[25] with a view to reducing the costs of litigation, at least where the assessment of costs is being carried out on a standard basis.

The precise effect of this new test remains to be seen and its impact is delayed as a result of the transitional provisions governing its introduction and the perceived need for higher judicial guidance as to its scope and effect. The fact that the new test applies in costs budgeting also does not seem to have produced any significant acceleration in understanding its likely impact.

However, if it is to serve its intended purpose, the ultimate outcome seems to be that there will be a reduction in between the parties costs. Further, that this will, by the very nature of the test and its intended use as a 'backstop' following the initial consideration of whether the costs are reasonable, be a somewhat arbitrary test, the precise effect of which will be difficult to predict in any given case.

Its impact seems likely to be greater in cases of relatively modest value, though again this remains to be seen.

All of this means that there is likely to be a greater shortfall between the costs recovered between the parties and those for which the client is prima facie liable on a solicitor-client basis and that this shortfall will potentially be proportionately all the greater in the very cases where the successful client's damages are lower. However, because of the uncertainty surrounding proportionality, the actual amount of reduction is hard to specify.

This serves to emphasise further the points in the preceding section as to the increased need for clear and regularly updated guidance to clients as to any potential shortfall. Even if this is just in broad terms and all that can be said is that there is likely to be a shortfall and no one can say for certain in what amount.

Whilst no test of proportionality applies on a solicitor-client assessment, a solicitor is obliged to discuss with a client, in a clear and accessible form, whether the potential outcome of a case is likely to justify the expense involved. Where a solicitor fails to provide clear information in this regard both at the start and during the case, and where the solicitor fails to warn the client, particularly in a low value claim, that there may be a substantial

---

[25] *Lownds v Home Office* [2002] 1 WLR 2450.

shortfall, it may reasonably be anticipated that the courts will take an increasingly hard line towards solicitor-client assessments of the shortfall costs.

The wider effect of 'Jackson'

The costs management reforms were intended to be part of a coherent package of reforms aimed at not merely reducing the cost of litigation, but improving the process. **10–15**

It is the express purpose of costs management that the court should manage not merely the costs to be 'incurred by the parties' (note, not merely 'recovered by' or 'allowed to' the parties), but also the steps to be taken.

In this regard, the reforms extend beyond the introduction of costs management and seek to give the courts more robust powers in relation to case management generally. These include explicit powers to restrict expert evidence by reference to specific issues (CPR 35.4), to limit the issues to be addressed by witnesses and the length and format of statements (CPR 32.2) and to take a more focused, and where appropriate, restricted approach to disclosure (CPR 31.5).

Although these matters do not necessarily directly impact on solicitor-client costs, they can arguably control spend. It is clearly an issue of vital importance that clients are made aware that, to the extent that there was before, there is no longer any guarantee of a system whereby the client can simply engage in 'chequebook' litigation. Clearly a client must be informed on occasions that, although it is open to the client to take a Rolls Royce approach to an aspect of litigation, the cost of doing so is unlikely to be recovered between the parties (for example, the instruction of a QC where the court considers it disproportionate).

Equally, there will increasingly be occasions where the client must be told that, however much it is prepared to spend, the cost will be to no benefit. This is not a question of recoverability but of restrictions on the client's options because of case management decisions There is little point in the client engaging a number of costly experts if it is likely that the court will direct evidence from a single expert on limited issues only and the client must be warned of this increased risk before the cost in incurred.

Case and costs management is looked at in more detail in **Chapter 4**.

Fixed costs claims

An element of fixed costs, whether in relation to certain aspects of the costs (such as trial costs in Fast Track claims) or the whole of the profit costs (for example in low value RTA claims) is an increasing part of the CPR and is a feature which is likely to expand in future. **10–16**

In principle, the ability of a solicitor to charge a client for work done is unaffected by the fact that the costs are fixed in whole or part on a between the parties basis. However, it is a clear and obvious point that, where the solicitor's retainer does not limit the costs payable by the client to those recovered between the parties, the client must be told in clear terms that the costs of the claim are, or might be, fixed and that, even if successful, there is likely to be a significant difference between the costs payable by the client and those recovered from the opponent. A failure to do so is likely to lead to an inability to recover any shortfall between the two.

It is important to remember that any arrangement whereby the costs to be charged to the client are limited to sums recovered between the parties is a species of Conditional Fee Agreement (a CFA 'lite'), on the basis that it is "an agreement . . . which provided for fees and expenses, or any part of them, to be payable only in specified circumstances",[26] even where it does not provide for a success fee, and therefore such an agreement must comply with s.58 of the Courts & Legal Services Act 1990 if it is to be enforceable.

Conversely, it should be remembered that between the parties cost are an entitlement of the client and are recovered in the client's name. In a fixed costs claim (and assuming that the indemnity principle is effectively disapplied,[27] where the costs recovered between the parties exceed the sums the client is liable to pay under the retainer, the balance belongs to the client, not the solicitor. Accordingly, where fixed costs are likely to apply, the retainer should usually provide that if fixed costs apply, the sum charged shall (as a minimum, whether or not also as a maximum) be set at the level of the applicable fixed costs.

Further details in relation to Fixed Costs generally may be found in **Chapter 7**.

Additional liabilities

10–17 Further details in relation to additional liabilities and funding options may be found in **Chapter 2**.

Save in limited circumstances addressed in other chapters, additional liabilities are no longer recoverable on a between the parties basis in relation to funding arrangements entered into on or after April 1, 2013.

In practice, particularly in the context of lower value personal injury litigation, prior to April 2013 it was rare for a client to be charged a success fee where that success fee was not recovered on a between the parties basis, save possibly where a small additional percentage was charged in respect of the delay in payment, as opposed to the risk of the claim winning or losing.

Whilst the charging of an unrecovered success fee to the client was more common in higher value and commercial litigation, it nevertheless remained relatively rare that such success fees ever became subject of a solicitor-client assessment.

The removal of between the parties recoverability is likely to see such success fees being challenged increasingly on a solicitor-client basis.

CPR 46.9 expressly includes a provision (CPR 46.9(4)) stating that in such circumstances the success fee is to be assessed by reference to all the relevant

---

[26] Courts & Legal Services Act 1990 s.58(2).
[27] See *Butt v Nizami* [2006] EWHC 159 (QB); [2006] 1 WLR 3307, as approved in *Kilby v Gawith* [2008] EWCA Civ 812; [2009] 1 WLR 853.

factors as they reasonably appeared to the solicitor (or counsel) at the time the CFA was entered into or varied (i.e. the same test that applies on a between the parties assessment) though, as noted, on a solicitor-client assessment, the benefit of any residual doubt goes to the benefit of the solicitor.

Accordingly, it will be at least as important as before that the solicitor keeps an accurate risk assessment in order to support any claimed success fee. Indeed, arguably the importance is increased since it is to be reasonably anticipated that the courts may take a harsher line towards the charging of success fees, particularly in lower value claims, where the success fee is being paid by a client or from a client's damages rather than by an opponent.

Of course, in personal injury claims, success fees are subject to maximum limits by reference to percentages of certain types of damages (essentially general damages and past loss) recovered. Nevertheless, it should not be assumed that this 'cap' on the maximum success fee chargeable will necessarily mean that the success fee cannot be challenged as long as it does not exceed that cap. **10–18**

For example, if the permitted classes of damages were £20,000 and the success fee, set at 100 per cent, amounted to £5,000 (which is precisely 25 per cent of the prescribed damages, and therefore the 'capped' maximum), it would still be open to the client to argue that the 100 per cent success fee was too high and should be reduced on assessment.

It will therefore be important to ensure that the success fee is set at a reasonable level, that the reasons for doing so are properly recorded, and that the client is made fully aware that the success fee will not be recoverable between the parties but will fall to be paid by the client.

A specific issue in this regard arose in relation to low value personal injury claims involving children (and possibly protected parties), where, pursuant to CPR 46.4, the general rule is that the court must order a detailed assessment of the costs payable by or out of any money belonging to a child or protected party.

In a number of cases it had been held on such assessments that it is 'unreasonable' to charge the child a success fee and to seek to deduct the same from the child's damages. The precise reasoning for this appears to be legally flawed—CFAs with success fees are a legitimate means of access to justice and the loss of recoverability between the parties was part of a package of reforms, including an increase in general damages, intended to offset (in part at least) the effect of lost recoverability.

It is perhaps notable that this is a repetition of an early problem following the original introduction of CFAs in 1995, when success fees were not recoverable, which was cured by a specific provision when the CPR was introduced in 1999 (CPR 48.9(5)), but which was removed in due course because it was thought unnecessary following the introduction of between the parties recoverability of success fees. The short point is that the court should be able to reduce the success fee because it was set at an unreasonable level, but otherwise should not disallow such fees. **10–19**

The position will be addressed with effect from April 1, 2015 by virtue of an amendment to CPR 21.12, introduced by clause 5 of the Civil Procedure (Amendment No.8) Rules 2014. Rather than the more simplified approach taken under the original 1999 regime, the amendment to CPR 21.12 will approach the matter by way of imposing limitations on the sums a Litigation Friend is entitled to out of any money recovered on behalf of a protected person.

A different approach is adopted depending on whether or not the damages awarded or agreed exceed £25,000. If they do not, the Litigation Friend's ability to recover costs will be limited to the (reasonable) success fee or sum payable under a Damages Based Agreement. If the sum awarded or agreed exceeds £25,000, a new CPR 21.12(7) will limit the Litigation Friend's ability to recover costs to a sum not exceeding 25 per cent of general damages and past pecuniary loss. Whether such restrictions are necessary given the ability of the court to scrutinize the reasonableness of costs and expenses and whether these restrictions will have an inhibiting effect on the willingness of individuals to act as Litigation Friends, or solicitors to act for protected persons, remains to be seen.

The introduction of Damages Based Agreements will bring a relatively new aspect to solicitor-client assessments. Although such arrangements have always been possible in non-contentious business, they have been rarely used.

In contrast with the position in employment cases, there are no specific regulatory requirements for advice to the client prior to the entering into of a DBA and accordingly, given the nature of DBAs, there is substantial scope for argument at the conclusion of the case as to whether the fee claimed was 'reasonable'. Cases will be heavily fact dependent, but where a DBA is used there is a clear requirement for very clear information to be given to the client as to the basis on which any DBA fee is set, for clear records to be kept of cogent reasons for setting the fee at the level chosen and, perhaps above all, for clear written information to be given to the client about the difference between the DBA payment being charged and the basis on which fees might be recovered between the parties if the case is won.

Reference has already been made to the Legal Ombudsman, which has already expressed its critical view as to the lack of clarity of CFAs and its concerns as to the risks of the same with DBAs.[28] Solicitors should not underestimate the need to make the key facts in relation to CFAs and DBAs clear in plain and, if necessary, repeated terms. The present reluctance to use DBAs in light of the poor drafting of the DBA Regulations 2013 should not obscure the fundamental need to ensure a consumer focused approach to the drafting of such agreements and related documentation where they are used.

The introduction of DBAs, the changes to CFAs and the loss of recoverability

---

[28]   See 'Complaints in focus: 'No win, no fee' agreements—*http://www.legalombudsman.org.uk/publications/no-win-no-fee/* [Accessed January 29, 2015].

between the parties of After The Event insurance premiums, together with the likely changes in between the parties costs recovery, mean that the range of funding options available to a client and the permutations in any given case are greater than ever. Whilst the risks have always been present, they are greater than ever and the obligation to give a client proper advice in order to allow the client to make an informed choice as to the appropriate funding option should not be ignored.[29]

Questions and answers

Q1. Have the 'Jackson' reforms changed the basis on which I, as a solicitor, can charge my client?

It was beyond the scope of the reforms to change the indemnity basis for   **10–20** assessment of solicitor client costs and that was neither their intention, nor is it their effect. The basic principle that such costs are to be assessed on the indemnity basis remains, and the core CPR provisions in relation to such an assessment, now at CPR 46.9, remain unchanged.

However, the anticipated reduction in between the parties costs, combined with the changes in funding methods, including the loss of recoverability of success fees, means that there is likely to be a greater number of cases, in particular in low value claims, where the solicitor seeks to charge a 'shortfall' to the client where, in the past, such a shortfall might not have been charged.

This is likely to bring a more regular and greater scrutiny to such claims, either by the courts or by the Legal Ombudsman.

Accordingly, whilst the basis on which such costs will be assessed has not changed, the practical effect may be that claims for 'shortfall' costs are more regularly disputed than before.

Q2. Can you advise the client of the full range of funding options but then say but we as a firm do not offer X, or Y or only offer X or Y on this basis?

Yes. This was a common situation with publicly funded cases (when public   **10–21** funding was more widely available).

A solicitor's duty is to consider, at the outset (i.e. at the time the client first seeks to instruct the firm) what forms of funding are reasonably available to the client and to advise the client accordingly. This includes advising the client that there may be other forms of funding available which the firm does not provide. This may include public funding or may, in certain circumstances, include other forms of funding such as CFAs or DBAs which the firm may not offer.

Section IB(1.16) of the Solicitors' Code of Conduct 2011 indicates that the solicitor should discuss with the client how the client will pay, including

---

[29] See *Truex v Kitchin* [2007] EWCA Civ 618 (solicitor's claims for costs disallowed for failure to advise as to the availability of legal aid) and *McDaniel & Co v Clarke* [2014] EWHC 3826 (QB) (solicitor's claim disallowed for failure to advice of availability of trade union funding) for two examples of the dangers.

whether public funding may be available, whether the client has insurance that might cover the fees and whether the fees may be paid by someone else, such as a trade union. This should not be treated as an exhaustive list, nor indeed as a list that applies full in every case. It is an indication only and, as with many examples in this context, is particularly suited to personal injury claims.

The ultimate requirement is to treat the client fairly and to ensure that the solicitor complies with the duty to act in their best interests, even if that might mean advising them of a form of funding which the firm does not offer which means that the client chooses to instruct a different firm.

Provided this is done, it is entirely proper to indicate that if the client wishes to instruct the firm the only terms which the firm is prepared to offer are the X or Y referred to.

Q3. My case is subject to costs management. Am I required to seek my client's approval to the budget and does the budget, if agreed or approved, limit the costs I can charge my client?

10–22   In answer to the first part of the question, no. There was some discussion of a requirement for the client to sign the budget, or the solicitor to confirm the client's agreement to the budget, but this did not make it into the final rules.

However, as a matter of practice, it is important that the client is aware of the likely costs of the claim and of how the costs which might be recovered from the opponent relate to the cost that the solicitor is likely to charge the client. It is also important that the client is made aware of how the likely costs of the claim might impact on the conduct of his claim. For example, if, as a result of the costs being seen to be disproportionate on a between the parties basis, the scope or extent of witness or expert evidence is likely to be restricted, the client needs to be made aware of the reasons for this and the options available to address it.

The client should be receiving regular costs estimates and updates on a solicitor-client basis anyway and differences between these and the between the parties budget should be highlighted so that the client has an informed choice as to whether or not to incur the additional costs.

As to the second part of the question, again the answer is 'no', unless the solicitor-client retainer is such that the costs chargeable to the client are limited to sums recovered between the parties. Even then, the final effect will not be known until the end of the case, when it is known whether the client has won, what costs order has been made, whether indemnity costs are awarded (CPR 3.18) and whether, if the budget applies, the budget is to be departed from for any 'good reason' (CPR 3.18). In any event, the budget only 'bites' on costs from the date of the budget (CPR 3 PD 3 E para.7.4).

Q4. Do the revised rules on Part 36 apply in a solicitor-client assessment?

10–23   There is a lack of clarity in this regard. There is a primary statutory provision dealing with the incidence of costs at the conclusion of a statutory assessment of solicitor-client costs, namely s.70(9) of the Solicitors Act 1974.

This provision cannot be, and has not been, displaced by CPR Pt 36 and continues to apply. However, that provision is subject to s.70(1), whereby the court can depart from the otherwise mandated outcome if there are 'special circumstances'. It seems to be increasingly accepted that the making of effective offers by the parties to the assessment is capable in principle, dependent upon the particular facts, of amounting to a special circumstances, and this would appear to fit with the ethos of both the CPR generally and the Jackson reforms in encouraging the making of offers to compromise disputes at an early and less costly stage.[30]

Accordingly, the making of a Part 36 offer may, on the facts of a case, be capable of amounting to a special circumstance, but the automatic provisions of CPR 36.10 and CPR 36.14 do not appear to apply because they conflict with s.70(9).

Whether a successful Part 36 offer therefore attracts any greater benefit than a Calderbank offer is open to argument. Given that the full rubric of Part 36 cannot apply, and Part 36 is intended to be a complete and self-contained code, it seems more likely that a successful Part 36 offer should be treated as an admissible offer under the court's general discretion under CPR 44.2(4)(c), assuming that the automatic consequences under s.70(9) do not apply.

Q5. Can I charge/recover for preparing the solicitor/client estimate?

10–24

It is assumed that this question refers to the costs of provision of costs information to the client rather than the costs of preparing a Precedent H for the purposes of between the parties costs management, which are limited by CPR 3 PD 3 E, para.7.2.

The (reasonable) costs of preparing such a between the parties Precedent H will, of course, form part of the costs payable by the client.

Time reasonably spent advising the client in relation to their own costs, whether by way of costs estimates, funding arrangements or the like should ordinarily form a part of the charges payable by the client. However, there will be a limit on the extent to which such time is recoverable. It is to be expected that solicitors have systems in place which allow them to properly record, monitor and analyse time spent and the cost of these is an overhead. The court will not expect that, save in exceptional cases, the solicitor will have to spend substantial time providing an initial estimate or updating that in due course.

---

[30] As an aside, similar principles developed under the CPR, such as penalising a party in costs for failing to negotiate also seem to be capable of being 'special circumstances'—see *Allen v Colman Coyle LLP* [2007] EWHC 90075 (Costs).

Index

Abuse of process
fixed costs, 7–14
Additional liability
solicitor and client costs, 10–17
After the event insurance
clinical negligence proceedings, 2–11
Coventry v Lawrence, 2–12
generally, 2–10–2–11
introduction, 2–01
qualified one-way costs shifting, and,
6–05
questions and answers
recoverability of policy premiums,
2–24–2–25
recoverability of policy premiums
change of solicitor post-LASPO,
2–24
staged premium policy incepted pre-
LASPO, 2–25
Allocation of business
costs management, 4–07
Allocation questionnaires
costs management, and, 4–06
Before the event insurance
qualified one-way costs shifting, 6–18
Calderbank letters
generally, 5–21
questions and answers, 5–34
Case management
see also **Costs management**
allocation of business, 4–07
assessment of costs, and, 4–20–4–21
case management conferences, 4–17
changes to CPR provisions, 4–02–4–21
compliance with orders, rules and
practice directions, 4–03–4–05
costs budgets
generally, 4–16–4–17
method, 4–18
variation, 4–19
costs management
cases covered, 4–15
effect on subsequent assessment,
4–20–4–21
introduction, 4–14
mediation, 4–17

method, 4–18
practical links to case management,
4–22
procedural requirements, 4–16–4–17
questions and answers, 4–23–4–59
variation of budgets, 4–19
directions questionnaires, 4–06
disclosure, 4–09
expert evidence
oral evidence, 4–12
provision of information, 4–11
introduction, 4–02
mediation, 4–17
overriding objective, and, 4–02
Part 36 offers, 4–13
practical links to costs management,
4–22
proportionality, 3–03
relief from sanctions, 4–05
settlement, 4–13
specific disclosure, 4–17
standard directions, 4–08
standard disclosure, 4–09
summary assessment, 9–05
witness statements, 4–10
Case management conferences
costs management, 4–17
Civil Justice Costs Review
costs management, 4–01
effect on solicitor-client costs,
10–01–10–24
establishment, 1–01
final report, 1–02
funding arrangements, 2–01
objective, 1–01
proportionality, 3–01
qualified one-way costs shifting,
6–01–6–02
recommendations, 1–03–1–04
terms of reference, 1–01
Clinical negligence
after the event insurance, 2–11
Compensation Recovery Unit
conditional fee agreements, 2–04
Conditional fee agreements
additional requirements, 2–04

calculation of success fee
  post-LASPO agreement, 2–28
capping of success fee
  status of agreement where total costs
    payable capped, 2–30
counsel's success fee
  post-LASPO agreement with solicitor,
    2–29
generally, 2–02
group claims
  recoverability of success fee where
    some claimants added post-LASPO,
    2–31
implementation issues,
  2–08–2–09
introduction, 2–01
long stop date
  issue of proceedings, for, 2–26
notification requirements, 2–07
percentage, 2–05
personal injury claims, 2–04–2–06
qualified one-way costs shifting, and,
  6–05
questions and answers
  calculation of success fee, 2–28
  capping of success fee and total costs
    payable, 2–30
  counsel's success fee, 2–29
  group claims, 2–31
  long stop date for issue of
    proceedings, 2–26
  recoverability of success fees,
    2–19–2–23
recoverability of success fees
  assignment of pre-LASPO agreement,
    2–19–2–20
  backdating agreement, 2–22
  counsel's success fee in post-LASPO
    agreement, 2–29
  death of client with pre-LASPO
    agreement, 2–23
  group claims, 2–31
  personal representatives, 2–23
  retrospective agreement, 2–22
  variation of pre-LASPO agreement,
    2–21
success fees
  calculation, 2–28–2–29
  capping, 2–30
  counsel, 2–29
  group claims, 2–31
  recoverability, 2–19–2–23
transitional provisions, 2–03

Costs assessments
  between the parties costs, and, 9–01
  costs management, 4–20–4–21
  court's powers, 8–05
  detailed assessment
    generally, 9–06
    questions and answers, 9–14–9–23
  indemnity basis, 7–07
  introduction, 9–01
  payments on account
    generally, 9–13
    questions and answers, 9–39
  proportionality, 3–03
  provisional assessment
    assessment, 9–09
    generally, 9–07
    oral hearings, 9–11
    post-assessment, 9–10
    pre-assessment, 9–08
    procedure, 9–07
    questions and answers, 9–24–9–38
  questions and answers
    detailed assessment, 9–14–9–23
    payments on account, 9–39
    provisional assessment, 9–24–9–38
    summary assessment, 9–14–9–23
  standard basis, 7–06
  summary assessment
    advance service of statement,
      9–04–9–05
    generally, 9–02
    N260, 9–03
    procedure, 9–02
    proportionality, 9–02
    questions and answers, 9–14–9–23
    statement of costs, 9–03–9–05
Costs budgets
  generally, 4–16–4–17
  method, 4–18
  proportionality, 3–03
  qualified one-way costs shifting, 6–17
  solicitor and client costs, 10–11–10–13
  variation, 4–19
Costs management
  cases covered, 4–15
  Civil Justice Costs Review, and, 4–01
  costs assessments, and
    generally, 4–20–4–21
    introduction, 9–01
  costs capping, and, 4–59
  detailed assessments, and, 4–56
  fixed costs, 7–16
  introduction, 4–14

mediation, 4–17
method, 4–18
overriding objective, and, 4–02
practical links to case management, 4–22
procedural requirements, 4–16–4–17
questions and answers
  additional claims, 4–26
  agreement between parties of proportionate directions and budgets, 4–33
  applications within CPR 3 PD E 7.9, 4–47
  basis of completion of Form H, 4–25
  breakdown between disbursements and fees, 4–41
  budget 'without prejudice' to assessment, 4–32
  budgeted sums exceeding sum provided under retainer, 4–40
  case management directions, 4–27
  case management hearings, 4–42
  client free to waste its own money, 4–39
  contingencies, 4–44, 4–47–4–48
  contractual right to indemnity costs, 4–50
  costs capping, 4–59
  'costs sanction' for unreasonable conduct, 4–35
  departures from budget, 4–36
  detail of assumptions on which budget based, 4–43
  detailed assessments, 4–56
  different hourly rate for budgeted and non-budgeted work, 4–31
  directions questionnaires not filed in time, 4–58
  disagreement as to allocation of claim, 4–46
  disbursement/fee breakdown, 4–41
  disposal stage of claim after default judgment, 4–45
  front loading of costs, 4–49
  global sums budgeting, 4–30
  'good reason', 4–36
  hourly rates, 4–28–4–31
  'incurred costs', 4–49
  incurring costs not allowed by court within budget, 4–39
  insertion of items in wrong phase of budget, 4–44

  interpretation of CPR 3.12(1) and (1A), 4–23–4–24
  'J-Codes', 4–37
  lower hourly rate retainers, 4–30
  multi-party disputes, 4–26
  nil-sum budgets, 4–49
  over-estimating costs, 4–53
  pre-trial checklists, 4–55
  prospective assessment of work required, 4–29
  recovery from client of more than budget, 4–38
  relief from sanctions, 4–57
  re-tracking Part 7 claims, 4–52
  role of court where parties agree budgets or phases, 4–33
  split trials, 4–25
  statements of truth, 4–38, 4–53
  sums to which percentages in CPR 3 PD E 7.2 apply, 4–54
  trial time requirement exceeds one day, 4–51
  under-estimating costs, 4–53
  unreasonable conduct, 4–35
  variation of budgets by agreement, 4–34
  'without prejudice' to subsequent assessment, 4–32
variation of budgets, 4–19

Counterclaims
Part 36 offers, 5–32

Damages-based agreements
between the parties costs recovery, 2–16
CFA 'lite', and, 2–17
employment proceedings, 2–14
future amendments, 2–18
generally, 2–13–2–15
hybrid DBAs, 2–17
introduction, 2–01
notice of funding, 2–27
percentage, 2–14
personal injury claims, 2–15
problem areas, 2–17
questions and answers
  notice of funding, 2–27
termination, 2–17
'ultimately recovered', 2–17

Delay
wasted costs orders, 8–03

Detailed assessment
costs management, and, 4–56
generally, 9–06
open offers

failure to make, 9–23
  Part 36 offers, and, 5–33
Part 36 offers
  generally, 5–22
  more advantageous result, 5–31
  open offers, 5–33
proportionality cross-check, 9–18
qualified one-way costs shifting, 9–22
questions and answers
  breakdown of time spent on
    documents, 9–17
  comparison of costs budget with N260
    or bill, 9–19–9–20
  late/no service of N260, 9–14–9–16
  open offers, 9–23
  proportionality cross-check, 9–18
  QOCS, 9–22
  status of *SB v MB (costs)* case, 9–21
Direct Access Scheme
  fixed costs, 7–18
Directions questionnaires
  costs management, 4–06
Disclosure
  costs management, 4–09
Discontinuance
  qualified one-way costs shifting, 6–22
Dishonesty
  qualified one-way costs shifting,
    6–10–6–11
Dispute resolution
  solicitor and client costs, 10–07–10–08
Employers' liability claims
  fixed costs, 7–03–7–05
  Part 36 offers, 5–18–5–20
Employment proceedings
  damages-based agreements, 2–14
Expert evidence
  costs management
    oral evidence, 4–12
    provision of information, 4–11
Fatal accident claims
  qualified one-way costs shifting, 6–08
Fixed costs
  abuse of process cases, 7–14
  background, 7–01
  barrister acting on own behalf, 7–17
  costs assessment
    indemnity basis, 7–07
    introduction, 9–01
    standard basis, 7–06
  costs management, 7–16
  Direct Access Scheme, 7–18
  employers' liability claims, 7–03–7–05

indemnity basis
  abuse of process cases, 7–14
  costs management, 7–16
  generally, 7–07
  litigation funders, 7–15
  questions and answers, 7–14–7–16
  unreasonable conduct cases, 7–14
litigants in person, 7–08–7–09
litigation funders, 7–15
low value personal injury claims
  EL/PL Protocol, 7–03–7–05
  RTA Protocol, 7–02
McKenzie friends, 7–10–7–11
public liability claims, 7–03–7–05
questions and answers
  abuse of process cases, 7–14
  barrister acting on own behalf,
    7–17
  costs management, 7–16
  Direct Access Scheme, 7–18
  fast track claims, 7–12
  indemnity basis, 7–14–7–16
  litigation funders, 7–15
  retainer arrangements, 7–13
  solicitor acting on own behalf, 7–17
  unreasonable conduct cases, 7–14
retainers, 7–13
RTA Protocol, 7–02
solicitor acting on own behalf, 7–17
solicitor and client costs, 10–16
standard basis, 7–06
unreasonable conduct cases, 7–14
Funding arrangements
  after the event insurance
    clinical negligence proceedings, 2–11
    Coventry v Lawrence, 2–12
    generally, 2–10–2–11
    introduction, 2–01
    questions and answers, 2–24–2–25
  Civil Justice Costs Review, and, 2–01
  clinical negligence proceedings, 2–11
  conditional fee agreements
    additional requirements, 2–04
    generally, 2–02
    implementation issues, 2–08–2–09
    introduction, 2–01
    notification requirements, 2–07
    percentage, 2–05
    personal injury claims, 2–04–2–06
    questions and answers, 2–19–2–23,
      2–28–2–31
    transitional provisions, 2–03
  damages-based agreements

between the parties costs recovery, 2–16
CFA 'lite', and, 2–17
employment proceedings, 2–14
future amendments, 2–18
generally, 2–13–2–15
hybrid DBAs, 2–17
introduction, 2–01
percentage, 2–14
personal injury claims, 2–15
problem areas, 2–17
questions and answers, 2–27
termination, 2–17
'ultimately recovered', 2–17
employment proceedings, 2–14
introduction, 2–01
personal injury claims
conditional fee agreements 2–04–2–06
damages-based agreements, 2–15
qualified one-way costs shifting, and
after the event insurance, 2–10
conditional fee agreements, 2–08
introduction, 2–01
questions and answers
after the event insurance, 2–24–2–25
conditional fee agreements, 2–19–2–23, 2–28–2–31
damages-based agreements, 2–27
pre-LASPO 2012 arrangements, 2–26
solicitor and client costs, 10–17–10–19

Indemnity basis
fixed costs
abuse of process cases, 7–14
costs management, 7–16
generally, 7–07
litigation funders, 7–15
questions and answers, 7–14–7–16
unreasonable conduct cases, 7–14
solicitor and client costs, 10–20

Inherent jurisdiction
wasted costs orders, 8–06

Intellectual Property Enterprise Court
Part 36 offers
application of cap on damages, 5–35

Jackson Review
establishment, 1–01
final report, 1–02
objective, 1–01
recommendations, 1–03–1–04
terms of reference, 1–01

Litigants in person
fixed costs, 7–08–7–09

Litigation funding
see **Funding arrangements**

Low value personal injury claims
fixed costs
EL/PL Protocol, 7–03–7–05
RTA Protocol, 7–02

McKenzie friends
fixed costs, 7–10–7–11

Mediation
costs management, 4–17
Part 36 offers, 5–29–5–30

Misconduct
wasted costs orders, 8–05

Non-party costs
generally, 8–07–8–08
questions and answers
'controlling', 8–12
disclosure of additional information, 8–13
examples of orders, 8–10
obtaining non-party order where costs order exists, 8–11
solicitors acting as litigation funders, 8–14

Offers
see **Part 36 offers**

Overriding objective
costs management, 4–02
summary assessment, 9–05

Part 36 offers
acceptance
costs budget not filed on time, where, 5–25
generally, 5–08–5–09
split trials, 5–23–5–24
time of withdrawal without notice, at, 5–26
background, 5–01
Calderbank offers
generally, 5–21
questions and answers, 5–34
change of terms, 5–06–5–07
costs management, and, 4–13
counterclaims, 5–32
detailed assessment
generally, 5–22
more advantageous result, 5–31
open offers, 5–33
EL/PL Protocol, 5–18–5–20
form and content, 5–05
generally, 5–04
Intellectual Property Enterprise Court
application of cap on damages, 5–35

mediation, 5–29–5–30
preliminary issues, 5–23
questions and answers
  acceptance of offer, 5–23–5–26
  cap on damages, 5–35
  costs budget not filed on time, 5–25
  counterclaims, 5–32
  detailed assessment, 5–31
  Hammersmith Properties, 5–28
  open offers, 5–33
  preliminary issues, 5–23
  refusal of offer, 5–27
  refusal to mediate, 5–29–5–30
  split trials, 5–23–5–24
  withdrawal without notice to
    claimant, 5–26
  without prejudice correspondence,
    5–36
reforms, 5–02
refusal to mediate, 5–29–5–30
refusal
  penalisation, 5–27
RTA Protocol, 5–18–5–20
split trials, 5–23–5–24
status of *Hammersmith Properties*, 5–28
transitional provisions, 5–03
unaccepted offers, 5–10–5–17
withdrawal
  generally, 5–06–5–07
  time of acceptance, at, 5–26
without prejudice correspondence, 5–36
Payments on account
generally, 9–13
questions and answers, 9–39
Personal injury claims
funding arrangements
  conditional fee agreements 2–04–2–06
  damages-based agreements, 2–15
qualified one-way costs shifting, 6–04
Pre-action disclosure
qualified one-way costs shifting, 6–04
Preliminary issues
Part 36 offers, 5–23
Proportionality
case management, and, 3–03
Civil Justice Costs Review, and, 3–01
conduct of paying party
  assessment stage, at, 3–14
  costs management stage, at, 3–13
  introduction, 3–12
costs assessments, and, 3–03
costs budgets, and, 3–03
determination criteria, 3–03–3–04

effect on litigation, 3–05
general concept, 3–02
introduction, 3–01
meaning, 3–03
questions and answers
  application of 'cross check', 3–09
  claims affected by requirement, 3–16
  conduct of paying party, 3–12–3–14
  costs exceeding sums in dispute, 3–18
  determinations of proportionate, 3–07
  distinction from reasonableness, 3–06
  'fixed sum' throughout life of claim,
    3–08
  'good reason' to depart from budget,
    3–09
  indemnity principle, 3–15
  overriding objective, 3–16
  purpose of assessment of what is
    reasonably incurred and reasonable
    in amount, 3–15
  relevance for indemnity costs order,
    3–17
  'sums in issue in the proceedings',
    3–11
  transitional provisions, 3–10
relief from sanctions, and, 3–03
solicitor and client costs, 10–14
Provisional assessment
assessment, 9–09
generally, 9–07
oral hearings, 9–11
post-assessment, 9–10
pre-assessment, 9–08
procedure, 9–07
questions and answers
  additional amount.9–27
  costs cap, 9–26–9–30
  costs only proceedings, 9–31–9–32
  interim applications, 9–28
  multiple awards of costs, 9–30
  oral hearings, 9–35–9–38
  proportionality, 9–29
  proportionality cross check,
    9–33–9–34
  service of replies to points of dispute,
    9–25
  success fees, 9–26
  VAT, 9–24
"Public liability claims"
fixed costs, 7–03–7–05
Part 36 offers, 5–18–5–20
Qualified one-way costs shifting
adverse costs orders, 6–08

application
  generally, 6–12–6–13
  questions and answers, 6–16
before the event insurance, 6–18
Civil Justice Costs Review, and,
  6–01–6–02
costs budgets, 6–17
defamation claims, 6–16
detailed assessment, 9–22
discontinuance of proceedings, 6–22
dishonest claims, 6–10–6–11
effect, 6–07–6–13
excepted proceedings, 6–04
fatal accident claims, 6–08
'fundamental dishonesty', 6–10–6–11
funding arrangements, and
  after the event insurance, 2–10
  conditional fee agreements, 2–08
  introduction, 2–01
generally, 6–04–6–06
introduction, 6–01–6–02
operation, 6–08
personal injury claims, 6–04
pre-action disclosure, and, 6–04
pre-commencement funding
  arrangements, 6–20
privacy claims, 6–16
purpose, 6–02
questions and answers
  before the event insurance, 6–18
  costs budgets, 6–17
  costs incurred pre-April 1, 2013, 6–19
  discontinuance of proceedings, 6–22
  personal injury and non-personal
    injury elements to claim, 6–15
  pre-commencement funding
    arrangements, 6–20
  relevant proceedings, 6–16
  unnecessary costs in unmeritorious
    claim, 6–21
relevant proceedings
  generally, 6–12–6–13
  questions and answers, 6–16
scope, 6–04–6–06
set off, 6–08–6–09
striking out, 6–08–6–09
transitional provision, 6–05
unnecessary costs in unmeritorious
  claim, 6–21
wider use, 6–14
Questions and answers
after the event insurance
  change of solicitor post-LASPO, 2–24

staged premium policy incepted pre-
  LASPO, 2–25
Calderbank offers, 5–34
conditional fee agreements
  calculation of success fee, 2–28
  capping of success fee and total costs
    payable, 2–30
  counsel's success fee, 2–29
  group claims, 2–31
  long stop date for issue of
    proceedings, 2–26
  recoverability of policy premiums,
    2–24–2–25
  recoverability of success fees,
    2–19–2–23
conduct of paying party
  assessment stage, at, 3–14
  costs management stage, at, 3–13
  introduction, 3–12
costs assessment
  detailed assessment, 9–14–9–23
  payments on account, 9–39
  provisional assessment, 9–24–9–38
  summary assessment, 9–14–9–23
costs management
  additional claims, 4–26
  agreement between parties of
    proportionate directions and
    budgets, 4–33
  applications within CPR 3 PD E 7.9,
    4–47
  basis of completion of Form H,
    4–25
  breakdown between disbursements
    and fees, 4–41
  budget 'without prejudice' to
    assessment, 4–32
  budgeted sums exceeding sum
    provided under retainer, 4–40
  case management directions, 4–27
  case management hearings, 4–42
  client free to waste its own money,
    4–39
  contingencies, 4–44, 4–47–4–48
  contractual right to indemnity costs,
    4–50
  costs capping, 4–59
  'costs sanction' for unreasonable
    conduct, 4–35
  departures from budget, 4–36
  detail of assumptions on which
    budget based, 4–43
  detailed assessments, 4–56

different hourly rate for budgeted and non-budgeted work, 4–31
directions questionnaires not filed in time, 4–58
disagreement as to allocation of claim, 4–46
disbursement/fee breakdown, 4–41
disposal stage of claim after default judgment, 4–45
front loading of costs, 4–49
global sums budgeting, 4–30
'good reason', 4–36
hourly rates, 4–28–4–31
'incurred costs', 4–49
incurring costs not allowed by court within budget, 4–39
insertion of items in wrong phase of budget, 4–44
interpretation of CPR 3.12(1) and (1A), 4–23–4–24
'J-Codes', 4–37
lower hourly rate retainers, 4–30
multi-party disputes, 4–26
nil-sum budgets, 4–49
over-estimating costs, 4–53
pre-trial checklists, 4–55
prospective assessment of work required, 4–29
recovery from client of more than budget, 4–38
relief from sanctions, 4–57
re-tracking Part 7 claims, 4–52
role of court where parties agree budgets or phases, 4–33
split trials, 4–25
statements of truth, 4–38, 4–53
sums to which percentages in CPR 3 PD E 7.2 apply, 4–54
trial time requirement exceeds one day, 4–51
under-estimating costs, 4–53
unreasonable conduct, 4–35
variation of budgets by agreement, 4–34
'without prejudice' to subsequent assessment, 4–32
damages-based agreements
notice of funding, 2–27
detailed assessment
breakdown of time spent on documents, 9–17
comparison of costs budget with N260 or bill, 9–19–9–20

late/no service of N260, 9–14–9–16
open offers, 9–23
proportionality cross-check, 9–18
QOCS, 9–22
status of *SB v MB (costs)* case, 9–21
fixed costs
abuse of process cases, 7–14
barrister acting on own behalf, 7–17
costs management, 7–16
Direct Access Scheme, 7–18
fast track claims, 7–12
indemnity basis, 7–14–7–16
litigation funders, 7–15
retainer arrangements, 7–13
solicitor acting on own behalf, 7–17
unreasonable conduct cases, 7–14
funding arrangements, and
after the event insurance, 2–24–2–25
conditional fee agreements, 2–19–2–23, 2–28–2–31
damages-based agreements, 2–27
pre-LASPO 2012 arrangements, 2–26
group claims
recoverability of success fee where some claimants added post-LASPO, 2–31
long stop date
issue of proceedings, for, 2–26
non-party costs
'controlling', 8–12
disclosure of additional information, 8–13
examples of orders, 8–10
obtaining non-party order where costs order exists, 8–11
solicitors acting as litigation funders, 8–14
notice of funding
damages-based agreements, 2–27
Part 36 offers
acceptance of offer, 5–23–5–26
cap on damages, 5–35
costs budget not filed on time, 5–25
counterclaims, 5–32
detailed assessment, 5–31
Hammersmith Properties, 5–28
open offers, 5–33
preliminary issues, 5–23
refusal of offer, 5–27
refusal to mediate, 5–29–5–30
split trials, 5–23–5–24
withdrawal without notice to claimant, 5–26

without prejudice correspondence,
5–36
payments on account, 9–39
proportionality
    application of 'cross check', 3–09
    claims affected by requirement, 3–16
    conduct of paying party, 3–12–3–14
    costs exceeding sums in dispute, 3–18
    determinations of proportionate,
        3–07
    distinction from reasonableness, 3–06
    'fixed sum' throughout life of claim,
        3–08
    'good reason' to depart from budget,
        3–09
    indemnity principle, 3–15
    overriding objective, 3–16
    purpose of assessment of what is
        reasonably incurred and reasonable
        in amount, 3–15
    relevance for indemnity costs order,
        3–17
    'sums in issue in the proceedings',
        3–11
    transitional provisions, 3–10
provisional assessment
    additional amount.9–27
    costs cap, 9–26–9–30
    costs only proceedings, 9–31–9–32
    interim applications, 9–28
    multiple awards of costs, 9–30
    oral hearings, 9–35–9–38
    proportionality, 9–29
    proportionality cross check,
        9–33–9–34
    service of replies to points of dispute,
        9–25
    success fees, 9–26
    VAT, 9–24
qualified one-way costs shifting
    before the event insurance, 6–18
    costs budgets, 6–17
    costs incurred pre-April 1, 2013, 6–19
    discontinuance of proceedings, 6–22
    personal injury and non-personal
        injury elements to claim, 6–15
    pre-commencement funding
        arrangements, 6–20
    relevant proceedings, 6–16
    unnecessary costs in unmeritorious
        claim, 6–21
recoverability of policy premiums
    change of solicitor post-LASPO, 2–24

staged premium policy incepted pre-
    LASPO, 2–25
recoverability of success fees
    assignment of pre-LASPO agreement,
        2–19–2–20
    backdating agreement, 2–22
    counsel's success fee in post-LASPO
        agreement, 2–29
    death of client with pre-LASPO
        agreement, 2–23
    group claims, 2–31
    personal representatives, 2–23
    retrospective agreement, 2–22
    variation of pre-LASPO agreement,
        2–21
recoverability, 2–19–2–23
solicitor and client costs
    agreement of client to costs budget,
        10–22
    effect of reforms on charging, 10–20
    notifying client of options available,
        10–21
    Part 36 offers, 10–23
    preparation of solicitor/client
        estimate, 10–24
success fees
    calculation, 2–28–2–29
    capping, 2–30
    counsel, 2–29
    group claims, 2–31
    recoverability, 2–19–2–23
summary assessment, 9–14–9–23
wasted costs orders
    extent of liability, 8–09
Relief from sanctions
    costs management
        generally, 4–05
        questions and answers, 4–57
    proportionality, 3–03
Retainers
    fixed costs, 7–13
    solicitor and client costs, 10–03–10–04
Road traffic accidents
    fixed costs, 7–02
    Part 36 offers, 5–18–5–20
Set-off
    qualified one-way costs shifting,
        6–08–6–09
Settlement
    Calderbank offers
        generally, 5–21
        questions and answers, 5–34
    costs management, 4–13

detailed assessment, 5–22
Part 36 offers
  acceptance, 5–08–5–09
  background, 5–01
  change of terms, 5–06–5–07
  detailed assessment, 5–22
  EL/PL Protocol, 5–18–5–20
  form and content, 5–05
  generally, 5–04
  questions and answers, 5–23–5–36
  reforms, 5–02
  RTA Protocol, 5–18–5–20
  transitional provisions, 5–03
  unaccepted offers, 5–10–5–17
  withdrawal, 5–06–5–07
questions and answers, 5–23–5–36
Solicitor and client costs
  additional liabilities, 10–17
  dispute resolution, 10–07–10–08
  effect of Jackson reforms
    assessment procedure, 10–10
    costs budgeting, 10–11–10–13
    introduction, 10–09
    overview, 10–15
    proportionality, 10–14
  entitlement to payment, 10–05–10–06
  fixed costs, 10–16
  funding arrangements, 10–17–10–19
  indemnity basis, 10–20
  introduction, 10–01
  overview, 10–02
  questions and answers
    agreement of client to costs budget,
      10–22
    effect of reforms on charging, 10–20
    notifying client of options available,
      10–21
    Part 36 offers, 10–23
    preparation of solicitor/client
      estimate, 10–24
  retainers, 10–03–10–04
Specific disclosure
  costs management, 4–17
Split trials
  Part 36 offers, 5–23–5–24

Standard basis
  fixed costs, 7–06
Standard directions
  costs management, 4–08
Standard disclosure
  costs management, 4–09
Striking out
  qualified one-way costs shifting,
    6–08–6–09
Summary assessment
  advance service of statement,
    9–04–9–05
  generally, 9–02
  N260, 9–03
  procedure, 9–02
  proportionality, 9–02
  questions and answers, 9–14–9–23
  statement of costs, 9–03–9–05
Variation
  costs management, 4–19
VAT
  provisional assessment, 9–24
Wasted costs orders
  appropriate court, 8–02
  court's powers on assessment, and, 8–05
  delay, 8–03
  evidence of costs incurred, 8–03
  extent of liability for conduct or advice,
    8–09
  guidance, 8–02
  inherent jurisdiction, 8–06
  introduction, 8–01–8–04
  misconduct, 8–05
  non-party costs
    generally, 8–07–8–08
    questions and answers, 8–10–8–13
  questions and answers
    extent of liability, 8–09
  solicitor/client relationship, 8–04
  statement of principle, 8–02
  three-stage test, 8–02
Without prejudice communications
  Part 36 offers, 5–36
Witness statements
  costs management, 4–10